Dreamweaver® MX
Weekend Crash Course™

Wendy Peck

Wiley Publishing, Inc.

Best-Selling Books • Digital Downloads • e-Books • Answer Networks • e-Newsletters • Branded Web Sites • e-Learning

Dreamweaver® MX Weekend Crash Course™

Published by
Wiley Publishing, Inc.
909 Third Avenue
New York, NY 10022
www.wiley.com

Copyright © 2002 by Wiley Publishing, Inc., Indianapolis, Indiana. All rights reserved.

LOC: 2002106042

ISBN: 0-7645-4930-8

Manufactured in the United States of America

10 9 8 7 6 5 4 3 2

1B/QT/QX/QS/IN

Published by Wiley Publishing, Inc., Indianapolis, Indiana
Published simultaneously in Canada

For general information on our other products and services or to obtain technical support, please contact our Customer Care Department within the U.S. at 800-762-2974, outside the U.S. at 317-572-3993 or fax 317-572-4002.

Wiley also publishes its books in a variety of electronic formats. Some content that appears in print may not be available in electronic books.

Wiley Publishing, Inc. is a trademark of Wiley Publishing, Inc.

About the Author

Wendy Peck jumped the fence from fashion design to professional graphic design in 1989. She began teaching computer graphics at the college level and for corporate clients in 1992. In 1997, after being on the Web for four years, she again changed her focus, turning her attention to Web design. Today, she divides her time between writing software books, including the popular *Web Menus with Beauty and Brains* (Hungry Minds, 2001) and articles on graphic design for WebReference.com (`www.productiongraphics.com`). She also writes for other publications, while reserving about half of her time for designing Web sites. Wendy lives with her rapidly shrinking family (kids leaving behind the teen years and moving out one by one) in Northwestern Ontario. She works from her home office, or increasingly, from the road, because she is an obsessive traveler. The middle-western and south-central United States is home to some of her favorite haunts.

The first edition of this book was dedicated to my kids.
Their influence on me has not changed.
This book is for Shawnda, Danille, and Brian.
My kids, my strength, my partners.

Credits

Acquisitions Editor
Carol Sheehan

Project Editor
Sara Shlaer

Technical Editor
Danilo Celic

Macintosh Technical Editor
Marc Garner

Copy Editor
Maarten Reilingh

Project Coordinator
Maridee Ennis

Graphics and Production Specialists
Sean Decker, Melanie DesJardins,
Laurie Petrone, Kristin McMullan,
Jackie Nicholas, Jeremy Unger

Quality Control Technicians
David Faust, Andy Hollandbeck, Angel Perez

Permissions Editor
Laura Moss

Media Development Specialist
Megan DeCraene

Proofreading and Indexing
TECHBOOKS Production Services

Preface

Welcome to *Dreamweaver MX Weekend Crash Course*. You can learn Dreamweaver in just one weekend. It may seem impossible to master a program as rich and powerful as Dreamweaver in such a short time, but you can. I have been using Dreamweaver for years and have discovered that most of Dreamweaver's power falls into several key areas. Once you understand the big picture, the details fall right into place.

With that in mind, I have designed this book with two levels. In the first section of the book, you create a simple Web site. This exercise allows you to learn the foundation techniques in a simple context. Then, when you are comfortable with the essential methods for creating reliable HTML code with Dreamweaver and have learned to avoid many of the pitfalls of Web design, you get to move forth and design a complex Web site. You'll find yourself drawing on your new knowledge from the early sessions and adding many of Dreamweaver's advanced features as you build a major site.

This is not a book on HTML, JavaScript, or CGI, but I have not ignored the fact that Web pages are built with HTML and other code. You learn how to work with the Design view, which allows you to see the code Dreamweaver creates as you build your pages. At the same time, you learn how to make sure that the code you produce will display on most browsers. However software, or even code alone, does not build effective Web sites. You also learn to organize a site plan, ensuring that your visitors can easily navigate your site, and how to place external scripts. Finally, I provide field-tested methods for creating great pages in an efficient manner. I earn my living using Dreamweaver, so I know time counts.

Dreamweaver MX includes features that were available only as part of Dreamweaver UltraDev in previous versions. However, there is much to learn in basic page and site preparation, so there is no space in a weekend course to include the dynamic data capabilities that are now part of Dreamweaver MX. But everything that you learn in this book will serve you well when you decide to move to producing dynamically generated pages.

Many enterprising graphic artists and programmers have built careers and businesses creating Web sites using Dreamweaver. Many employers now list Dreamweaver knowledge as a required skill. Some people use Dreamweaver to maintain their own business sites; others use it to build Web sites as a rewarding hobby. Whatever your goal, you are just one weekend away from mastering one of the most popular Web-site creation tools on the planet. Find an undisturbed space, put a "do not disturb" note on your door, and get ready to emerge Sunday evening with a valuable new skill.

Who Should Read This Book

This book is for beginner to intermediate Dreamweaver users. It is also perfect for those who understand the correct mouse moves to create a Web page in Dreamweaver, but do not feel that they understand the "why" behind much of what they do. In this book, you are never asked to blindly click — you always know why you are doing what you are doing. If you fall into any of the following categories, this book will help you reach your goals.

- **Beginners** who want to learn Web design.

- **Intermediate Web developers** who want to fully understand Dreamweaver and enhance their site building skills.

- **Individuals** who are working in the field, but wish to (or must) add Dreamweaver skills to their list of qualifications.

- **Back-end developers** who wish to (or must) add more page design skills to their list of qualifications.

- **Print designers** who want to add Web design to their list of qualifications.

How to Use This Book

This book is a trip right through the center of the most important and well-used features in Dreamweaver. It is designed to be a complete course, providing all the information you require to boost your Dreamweaver skills to a very high level. You'll get the most from this book if you complete every exercise. Some techniques may be very familiar to you, but there are so many tidbits of information, including the essential answer to why you would use a particular method, that the time spent completing any exercise will not be wasted. If you have experience with a technique, you can move very quickly through the steps. Each lesson builds on the exercises completed in the previous chapters, so skipping exercises may leave you without the prepared pages necessary to complete a later exercise.

Probably the most important reason for completing each exercise is for later reference. The topics in the book are clearly marked and will be easy to locate a few months from now. Reviewing a technique in the book later will be much more effective when you can also open the document, study the code, and compare the exercise you did then to the project you are currently completing.

Overview

The concept of this book is simple. You design a simple Web site with four pages to start the process. All graphics are provided on the accompanying CD-ROM, so you can work quickly through building the pages. In the second part of the book, you build a Web site using liquid table design, templates, Library items, and three different types of menus. The site is enhanced with a Flash movie. In other words, by Sunday evening, you will have created a site containing features that are found in the largest sites on the Web.

Friday Evening

In the first four sessions, I introduce the Dreamweaver interface, and how Dreamweaver sites work. You create a document that includes text and graphics by the end of this part.

Saturday Morning

During these sessions, you work through the basics of page layout, tables, and moving your site to the Web. By the end of this part, you'll have pages on the Web.

Saturday Afternoon

In this part you start to add interaction to your site. Links, image rollovers, and placing scripts are all part of these sessions. You also do some work with Dreamweaver's templates and Library items to start automating your work.

Saturday Evening

You definitely move past the beginner level as you start your second site at the beginning of this part. Here, you plan the site, create the templates and discover the Library items you will use, and move on to prepare those templates and Library items for compiling the site on Sunday.

Sunday Morning

This part moves you right into the topics that separate the true Web developers from the "wannabes." You'll be creating complex menus and JavaScript rollovers, controlling text with CSS (Cascading Style Sheets), and using automated site maintenance tools by the end of these sessions.

Sunday Afternoon

Don't think you'll be winding down slowly at the end of the book, because you certainly do not want to miss the fun features included in these sessions. Learn to work with layers and move objects around your pages with Dreamweaver's timelines. Create a page with frames. And see how you can apply your new knowledge in an efficient way as you focus on productivity at end the book.

Appendixes

These sections include the answers to your Part Review questions, a listing of what is on the CD-ROM, and information on using Dreamweaver with other software programs.

Layout and Features

The time symbols in the margin show you where you are in your lesson. You may wish to allow a few extra minutes for each session, rather than rushing past something you do not understand. I have also included "extra assignments" if you need or want more practice. Although I have carefully planned the time so that the work can be completed as promised, you should work at a pace that is best for you.

This is a cross-platform book. Instructions for both Windows and Mac users appear in the text. For clarity in the instructions, I have used the standard PC command of OK as the standard acceptance command. Mac users please translate any OK command to Open for OS9 and Choose for OSX.

Also scattered throughout the sessions are hints, tips, and relevant information about addendum topics and concerns. You'll find these items illustrated with the margin symbols shown below.

This symbol means that the accompanying information is important for broadening your awareness of Dreamweaver features, procedures, or perhaps Web development in general.

This symbol adds information to the material you are studying, provides an alternate method, or a time-saving suggestion.

This symbol is your warning of common errors that you might make while working with a technique.

This symbol indicates where you can find more information on the current subject elsewhere in the book.

You will require many files to complete the exercises in this book. This symbol advises you to copy certain files from the CD-ROM to your computer. Occasionally, this symbol refers you to more information on a subject contained in the Resources directory on the CD-ROM.

The symbol ⇨ indicates a menu path. For instance, if you see File ⇨ Save, it means select the File menu, and then select Save.

Ready, Set . . .

One little weekend — such a small amount of time to invest for so much knowledge. *Go* get it!

Acknowledgments

One amazing team of people made this book possible. I have never worked on a project this efficiently, with so many people delivering so many pieces of a puzzle right on time, every time. It's the only way it could have worked, but is still like watching a miracle.

My acquisitions editor, Carol Sheehan, prepared the course with efficiency and clarity. Great job. Sara Shlaer, my project editor, is a master of my weakest area — details. You let me worry about only what I did well, and it seemed so easy. Danilo Celic carried the huge job of technical editor. You helped me relax about keeping so many files, and references, and keystrokes perfect. I still can't believe some of the tiny, little discrepancies you caught. Marc Garner watched over the instructions and terminology for Mac users, and offered help above and beyond what was expected. Thanks so much. Maarten Reilingh, copy editor — how can you take my writing and make it sound just like me . . . but better? Amazing.

Micheal Roney and Andy King always deserve mention, as each recognized my ability to write, and challenged me to stretch further, faster.

My Mom, Isabel MacLean, in the vigilant style that only a teacher Mom can offer, forced my English knowledge, which gave me the tools I use today. My Dad, Jack MacLean, is not with us, but I know he would be tickled to see my name on the cover of a book. My sisters, Debbie and Heather form the rest of the family that has stood firm and fast through my entire life.

Val. My best friend and the person in the world most likely to make me stop working . . . which lets me continue. Marion, Elsie, Linda, you are always there for me, and your belief in me is never far from my mind. Jeff, you are so much a part of my life that I tend to forget to give you credit. I will never forget when you held my first book, after months of watching me work so hard, and said, "This is a *real* book!" I've always wondered what you thought I was doing.

Although they are nearly on their own now, my kids, Shawnda, Danille, and Brian, have had a dramatic influence on what I have been able to accomplish. The years that they stood firmly behind what I was doing, regardless of the cost to them, allowed me to build a wonderful career and a happy life. Kids who can have that effect on a parent's life are special, very, very special.

Contents at a Glance

Contents

Dreamweaver® MX
Weekend Crash Course™

☑ **Friday**

☐ Saturday

☐ Sunday

Part I — Friday Evening

PART

I

Friday Evening

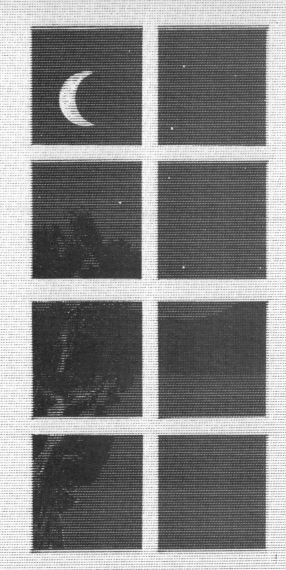

Introducing Dreamweaver MX

Session Checklist

✔ Previewing this crash course

✔ Understanding HTML

✔ Exploring HTML versus visual editing

✔ Understanding the limits of HTML

✔ Discovering what's new in Dreamweaver MX

✔ Understanding hosts and domain names

**30 Min.
To Go**

Before you start creating your first page, it is important to know where you are going and what you can and cannot expect from this course. Web development has no tidy beginning and end. Professional developers constantly struggle to concentrate their learning efforts, because it's impossible for one person to absorb all there is to learn about the field of Web development.

I am a working Web designer. I have carefully identified the Dreamweaver features that I use most regularly when creating client sites to determine what to include in this course. Some of the specialized features of this versatile program, such as working with dynamic data, are not covered, but you will learn what is necessary to create a full-featured site, containing unlimited pages with impressive visitor interaction. Most importantly, you'll learn how to use Dreamweaver to create sites offering full browser and platform consistency. Creating a page with Dreamweaver is a very small challenge, because the program automatically produces excellent HTML code. The real challenge is creating a page that will display consistently on the Web. That is the focus of this course.

Although Dreamweaver does create code automatically, do not allow yourself to be helpless when it comes to code. Your success will be directly related to the amount you learn about how the code you produce in Dreamweaver does its job. I will help direct you to the most important areas to study.

What This Crash Course Covers

First, this book is very much a hands-on exercise. I am not going to bombard you with page upon page of theory. You would most likely skip over those parts anyway, because you bought a software book to learn the software, right? The theory is included here, of course. How can you learn a program without understanding what concepts are being put to use? However, I mix hands-on exercises and theory so that you learn the concepts as you apply the commands in Dreamweaver.

Creating sites

You create two sites through the course. The first site is very simple, designed to teach you basic Dreamweaver functions such as how to place an image or create a table. I have deliberately kept this first site uncomplicated to allow you to focus on the basic operations.

The second site is not so simple. Armed with the knowledge to create basic layout and to insert graphic elements, you will create a full-featured site that can rival mid-range commercial sites on the Web. You'll create links, add forms, and create frames, plus add movies and sound. You'll also use Dreamweaver to create JavaScript code, Cascading Style Sheets (CSS), and Dynamic HTML (DHTML).

Creating cross-browser code

The pages you create in this book are constructed with HTML (Hypertext Markup Language), and I cover many HTML issues in depth. HTML is a pretty simple concept. However, each browser interprets the code in a different way, and browsers are inconsistent across PC and Mac platforms. This is the main reason Web developers pull out their hair. Please pay special attention to the tips and notes that apply to cross-browser and platform issues. I acknowledged earlier that you're really here to learn the software, but knowing where to find a feature in Dreamweaver's menu is not going to help you if your page goes upside down in Internet Explorer or displayed on a Mac.

Lest you think I am exaggerating on this point, my own Web site — www.wpeck.com — was perfect on all PC browsers, and it also passed with flying colors on a Mac with Netscape. On a Mac with a recent version of Internet Explorer, the first column, which was only 200 pixels wide, pushed the second column to the bottom of the first column. Result? Only a bulleted list of features was seen on the first screen. The text content was four screens below. Solution? One tag needed to be added. I cannot stress this enough: pay attention to the code!

Using automated features and optimizing your site

You'll learn how to manage your sites, automatically update changed pages, and check your site for problems. A small site can be managed manually, but you'll be amazed at how confusing and time-consuming it can be to maintain a site of even 10 to 20 pages. Dreamweaver offers many tools to make this job fast and accurate, and I cover that area in depth.

You'll learn to work with templates and library items, giving you the power to add editable elements to your site. Later, you can change the entire site by adjusting one file. You'll use both templates and library items on your second site. The Web is an ever-changing medium, and to keep interest in your site, visitors demand change. With a little forward planning, you can keep your content and style fresh with minimal effort.

Download speed is crucial. Many visitors will miss even the most carefully designed page if you do not ensure that they see results quickly when they visit your site. Web surfers are not patient people. You'll spend time learning to properly optimize code and graphics so that you do not sacrifice a fast-loading site for fancy layout or pretty pictures.

Some caveats

This book does not cover dynamic content, which means creating pages from databases. Although Dreamweaver MX has this capability, the scope of the subject is too deep for this book. I also leave aside graphic production. I assume that you have a source for images or that you can create your own images.

All images required for the exercises in this book can be found on the accompanying CD-ROM.

**20 Min.
To Go**

Understanding HTML

You can create Web sites without knowing how to view your code in Dreamweaver. However, if you want to create sites that are stable and reasonably consistent for every viewer, you have to understand how HTML works.

I was able to do quite well without viewing code when I first started with Dreamweaver. However, as I started to push to new levels and the issue of liquid pages emerged, I found I was often working in Code view. Had I not started with a solid understanding of how HTML worked, and the syntax and operation for each tag, I would have been held back from reaching my goals. Do not think of learning HTML as a problem; rather, think of it as an opportunity for more freedom in your design work.

See Session 8 for a full discussion on liquidity in Web design.

You should have at least one comprehensive HTML book in your library. I rec-ommend the *HTML 4.01 Weekend Crash Course* by Greg Perry, published by Hungry Minds, Inc.

What is HTML?

Design people like me tend to call HTML (Hypertext Markup Language) *programming*. Programmers will come up fighting and say it is not a programming language, but a markup language. My argument that HTML has funny little symbols and that you must type perfectly or it will not work, so it must be programming, holds no credibility. The programmers are right. HTML is a basic set of codes that tells a browser how to display text and images.

HTML is quite logical and, if you speak English, often self-explanatory. Each set of instructions is called a *tag*. Tags are placed around content to tell the browser how to display text and images on the page. Opening tags look like this <tag>, and ending tags look like this </tag>. As an example, the tag for boldface type is <b>. To make the word "Title" appear in boldface type, the tag would be <b>Title</b>, and the word would appear on the page as **Title**. If you wanted "Title" to be both bold and italic, the code would be <b><i>Title</i></b>, with the final appearance as ***Title***. See, quite logical. A little memorization and you will be well on your way to understanding HTML.

Hand Coding versus Visual Editing

Many Web developers believe that the only respectable way to create HTML code is to work in a text editor and to type your code by hand. Another group of developers has an equally strong conviction that you cannot create a nicely designed page unless you can view the final appearance as you work. This work is done in a visual editor such as Dreamweaver.

However, because of the strong coding tools in Dreamweaver, this debate is losing momentum. Dreamweaver is primarily a visual editor, but it is also a powerful hand-code editor. Most people naturally find their own working style somewhere between the two options.

I am a visual designer, a transplant from the print production world. I tend to design pages visually, and then spend more time working in Code view as the site develops. I know other designers who use the visual editor only for specific jobs, such as creating tables and JavaScript rollovers. Still other designers would not dream of using automated JavaScript, yet they rarely open the HTML window. The combinations are endless, and there is no single right way.

In this course, you work primarily in the Document window, which is the visual portion of the program. Figure 1-1 shows my normal working screen with Design view and the Properties Inspector active. You should check your HTML code as you go along. For specific tasks only, you'll type your code directly into the Code View window. This should give you enough experience with how each function works to carry on and find the combination that is perfect for you.

The important thing is to become comfortable with both visual and code work in Dreamweaver. If you restrict yourself to one or the other, you will not realize the full potential of the program.

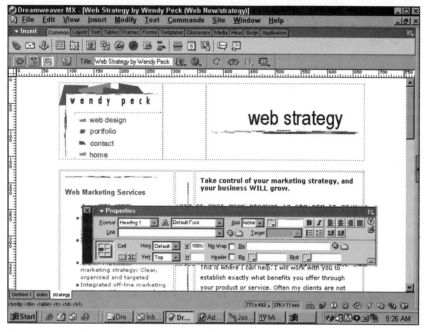

Figure 1-1 *The screen arrangement that I use most often is shown here. With the exception of the Properties panel, I prefer to keep my panels floating and collapsed (see the Files panel) to reserve as much screen area for the document as possible.*

Understanding the Limits of HTML

HTML was designed to present information in a legible way, not create pretty pages. Of course, give us humans a tool and we naturally push the limits. We have aggressively pushed the bounds for HTML.

However far innovation and changing standards have taken HTML, it is still a limited graphics-layout tool. Add to this that the same HTML page might be displayed on a monitor with low resolution and 256 colors, or on a supersharp, ultrahigh-resolution screen with millions of colors, and it's a wonder that any pages look good on the Web.

But wait — there is one more problem. Browser software does not offer any true standards. As designers have pushed the bounds of HTML, new tags have been added. New concepts such as Cascading Style Sheets (CSS) have been developed to control text and positioning. JavaScript has exploded in response to increasing demand for pages with interactivity and motion. Browser software has kept up with change, but each software developer has chosen different ways to respond to advances. In fact, browser-specific tags now in use have been added by software developers and adopted by Web developers. Unfortunately, these special tags may only be recognized by the browser that introduced them. Web design can be a minefield.

Dreamweaver smooths many of the bumps for you when dealing with HTML and related languages. Much of what I have described in the preceding paragraph is invisible in Dreamweaver, because the program automatically chooses the tried and tested route to deliver most design and layout requirements. For plain pages with text, tables, and a few images, you do not even have to think about the nonstandardized browser issues. However, start to stretch those bounds, even by a little, and you have to put some remedial action into place.

How do you know? Trial and error — and test, test, test. Dreamweaver includes excellent preview capabilities that reveal the most glaring differences between major browsers. As you design, you must make sure to check your page with Internet Explorer and Netscape Navigator, at a minimum. You will soon recognize how your design style works in each browser. Throughout this course, I highlight common problem areas in browser compatibility, and I present methods to create consistent results. Keep your eyes open for these tips and notes.

Although designers would not naturally choose to work within the limits of HTML, an element of pride results from taking a weak layout language and creating beautiful, functional pages.

If you are moving into the Web development world from a print background, begin this minute to forget everything you have ever known about creating a page. Keep your design principles in place; good design is still good design. But your success in this field depends on letting go of the control you have in print.

What's New in Dreamweaver MX

Dreamweaver has changed fundamentally with the release of the MX version. Dreamweaver MX is an updated version of Dreamweaver UltraDev, which was a separate product from Dreamweaver 4. Dreamweaver without the dynamic data capabilities of UltraDev no longer exists. Incorporating dynamic data involves a great deal of setup, too much for inclusion in this book.

***Dreamweaver MX Bible,* by Wiley Publishing, Inc., is an excellent source for information on the Dreamweaver MX dynamic data capabilities.**

The workspace has changed completely from Dreamweaver 4. Upgrading PC users have the option to maintain a Dreamweaver 4 style workspace, but I recommend leaving comfort behind to give the new interface a chance. It feels like a new program for a while, but I quickly came to love the new way of working.

Figure 1-2 shows the fully customizable interface. Notice the docked panels at the right. Any panel can be docked or float freely. I have the Properties panel floating on this screen (some habits aren't easy to give up). The Objects panel has been replaced by the Insert toolbar, shown near the top of the screen.

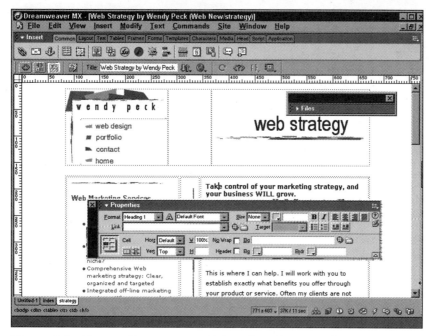

Figure 1-2 *The new Dreamweaver MX interface, featuring floating and docked panels, as well as the new Insert toolbar, which replaces the Object panel.*

The Site window from earlier versions has been replaced by the Site panel, which can be docked as shown here (PC only), or floating. One click brings the familiar split screen in a separate window maintaining the drag-and-drop convenience for moving files to the server. The Site panel also allows access to all files on your computer — no need to jump to your computer's file management system to locate a file outside your Dreamweaver site. Panels can be collapsed in both floating and docked mode. Note the collapsed panels at the lower right of the screen. It's hard to image anyone who won't be able to find a comfortable working environment with the options presented in Dreamweaver MX. Production speed appears to have been a focus for the Dreamweaver MX development team. There are professional templates available to kick-start your design project, and code snippets to quickly drop functions into your page. You can also create and store your own snippets in a handy panel. Template capability has been increased with the addition of optional regions and repeating regions, and you can now nest templates within templates, plus make tags editable. CSS support has been enhanced, and the new CSS panel displays your style sheet (as shown in Figure 1-3) and allows instant editing.

Many of the classic Dreamweaver functions have been enhanced. When you become comfortable with the new interface, you'll find that most of the new capability is right at your fingertips. This is an exciting upgrade.

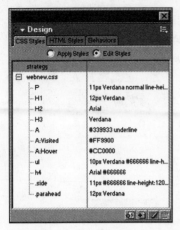

Figure 1-3   *Cascading Style Sheets can be displayed in the CSS panel for easy review and instant editing access.*

**10 Min.
To Go**

Is Your Host in Place?

Finally, I want to introduce an area you may need to work on before you create your first pages. Most of this book will cover work on your local computer, because you really do not work directly on the Web. Web designers create files and then upload the files to the Web, where they can be seen by anyone with an Internet connection.

Moving the files is a simple concept. You transfer files using FTP, much like you move a file from your hard drive to a floppy disk or other portable media. Dreamweaver MX has a built-in FTP function, so you need nothing else to move your files.

What is a host?

However, where do you put the files? A *host* is simply where you put your files. A host is a company (its location does not matter) that has set up a place to store your files and to make them available to the entire Internet. Most companies charge for this service — consider it rent for your site. Some free hosts exist, though you usually must tolerate ads on your pages, because the host must be earning revenue in some way to keep the service going.

The range of services that each host offers varies dramatically. For this course, you need a full service host, because you will be wandering into some advanced areas. I have included a list of free, low-cost, and full-service hosts on the CD-ROM included with this book, and I have made sure that any hosts listed offer the services required for this course.

A list of free, low-cost, and full-service hosts can be found in the file hosts.html in the resources folder.

If you prefer to find your own host, or already have one, you need to ensure that it offers full FTP and Common Gateway Interface (CGI) capability (preferably with direct access to a cgi-bin folder).

It's okay if you do not understand that last statement. By the end of the course, you will fully understand what FTP and CGI mean, but to get there, you need to have a host. If you are trying to find your own host, just copy the specifications from the preceding paragraph in an e-mail to your prospective hosting company. The hosting company should be able to tell you if it has the required capability.

You will need to have a host in place by the start of Session 5, Saturday Morning.

Domain names

Before you leave the topic of hosts, I want to cover one last detail. Many people confuse hosting with domain names, and I want to clear up any confusion.

You do not need to have a domain name to complete this course. All free servers provide you with an address that you can share with others so that they can access your files.

Here is my site as an example. My domain name is wpeck.com. It could also be wendypeck.com (which I also own), wpeck.net, wpeck.org, or wpeck.ca. These are all domain names.

I registered my domain name with networksolutions.com because, at the time, it was the only place to register a domain name. Currently, hundreds of domain registrars offer this service, most offering a one-year registration for under $20.

See a list of domain name registrars in the resources folder. The file is named registrars.html. (But remember, you don't need a domain name for this course.)

This is completely separate from your hosting company, though. Many beginners get quite turned around by this subject. To make things a little more complicated, you must provide information about your host when you register your domain. The registrar for your domain name must know where the files that go with the domain name will be stored. You must provide both a primary and a secondary Domain Name System (DNS) address for your host. DNS is the system that translates Internet Protocol (IP) addresses (which are numerical addresses) into easy-to-remember domain names. The help section of your host's Web site should have the DNS information you require to register a name. If not, contact the support staff for your host.

Done!

REVIEW

In this session, you learned what will be covered in this course, and you had an introduction to some of the basic ideas in Web design. It is important that you remember the following points:

- You will get the most from this course if you work through each exercise.
- You will create two sites as you work through this course.
- You should make a commitment to learn at least the basics of HTML.
- New features in Dreamweaver MX speed up your work and offer unlimited options to set up your workspace.
- You need a host to complete this course.
- A domain name is a separate issue from your host (although you need a host in order to create a site that can be reached through your domain name).
- You do not need to register a domain name to complete this course.

QUIZ YOURSELF

1. What is the main reason for learning HTML code, even though Dreamweaver produces it for you? (See the "Understanding HTML" section.)
2. What does HTML stands for? (See the "What is HTML?" sidebar.)
3. Designing pages that display consistently for every visitor is a challenge. What two factors most influence how the pages you create will display? (See "Understanding the Limits of HTML.")
4. What is the fundamental change that separates Dreamweaver MX from Dreamweaver 4? (See the "What's New in Dreamweaver MX" section.)
5. What is a host? (See the "Is Your Host in Place?" section.)
6. What is a domain name? (See the "Domain names" section.)

Getting Started

Session Checklist

✔ Understanding the Site panel and the Document area

✔ Working with panels in Dreamweaver

✔ Focusing on the Properties panel

✔ Using the menus

✔ Viewing your document

**30 Min.
To Go**

Although I could spend this entire book discussing HTML and Web design theory, let's roll up our sleeves and get started. This topic is never-ending and constantly changing. The best way to learn basic Web development is to leap in and get your hands dirty.

You must start by finding your way around in Dreamweaver. Dreamweaver's sole purpose is to create Web pages. Web pages are not useful unless . . . well, unless they are on the Web.

That statement is not as dumb as it may sound. Dreamweaver can be a little confusing in the beginning; half of its power comes from its ability to manage your site. To exercise the control it needs to keep the files on your site connected to one another, Dreamweaver creates its own organizational area for the files you have stored on your hard drive.

You create documents in Dreamweaver, but you create Web sites as well. Dreamweaver offers two separate areas that are very interrelated, but which are also very separate. One area is called the Site panel, where site information is stored and where the FTP capability that will transfer files to the Web resides. Individual documents are opened or created from the Site panel, and you can open as many documents as you desire at the same time. The second area is the Document window, where you add the content to your pages.

Just hold onto the idea that there are two separate — but connected — functions and you can move on.

The Site Panel and Document Area

Dreamweaver controls the site's files through the Site panel. Documents open in the main area of the screen. You'll learn how to work with the Site panel and the Documents area in the next two sessions, but I want to pause and give you a chance to become familiar with how sites and documents are managed.

Site panel

When you define a site, as you will do in Session 3, Dreamweaver scans the folder you specify and lists the folders it finds in the Site panel when Local View is selected. (See Figure 2-1.) You can move, rename, and delete files from this panel, and the changes will be made on your hard drive. If you make the changes to files when you are not working in the Dreamweaver screen, the Dreamweaver Site panel will reflect those changes as well. This window is simply an extra listing of what is on your hard drive in the specified folder. When you choose Remote View, the Site panel displays a list of the files on your remote server.

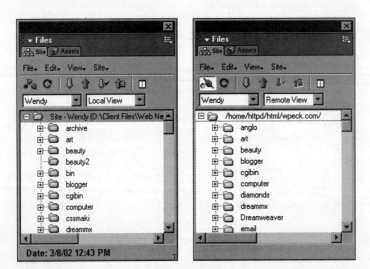

Figure 2-1   *The Dreamweaver PC MX Site panel with Local View active (left) and Remote View active at the right.*

You'll learn how to connect to the remote server in the next session, but I want you to understand the concept now. Dreamweaver MX offers a view of both your local and remote files at the same time. In Figure 2-2, I have connected to the remote server and clicked the Expand/Collapse icon in the top right corner.

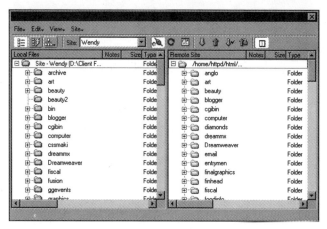

Figure 2-2 *When Dreamweaver is connected to a site, and the Site panel is expanded, both the local files (left) and the remote files (right) are displayed.*

Note that the Connection button is now depressed — the little plug icon is joined and the light is displayed. This indicates that you are connected to the site. The files listed on the left are the files stored in the root directory for the active site. The files listed in the right pane are those that are stored in the directory for the active site on your host's computer.

The Site panel is the control center for everything you will do in Dreamweaver. Experienced Dreamweaver users would never dream of moving or deleting an important Web site file in any other way but through the Site panel. Your hard drive is not smart enough to know when one file might be important to another. Dreamweaver is. If you change the location or name of any file within a Dreamweaver site, the program checks all links before the change is made and allows you to change your mind or update the files. It's like having a warning buzzer that prevents you from making a mistake with your files.

Document area

The active Document area of the screen resembles a word processing or desktop publishing window and is usually quite comfortable to use, even for new users. As you can see in Figure 2-3, it is easy to imagine what your page will look like while you work. This PC screen shows several panel groups active, but collapsed. The document is displayed on the left.

All changes to your document will take place in this window, and several documents can be open at one time. Note the tabs at the bottom left of the PC screen in Figure 2-1. You can toggle between open documents by clicking on the tabs. It is not unusual to be working on many documents at one time. Technically, there is no limit to the number of Dreamweaver documents you can have open at one time, but that statement is dependent on your system resources.

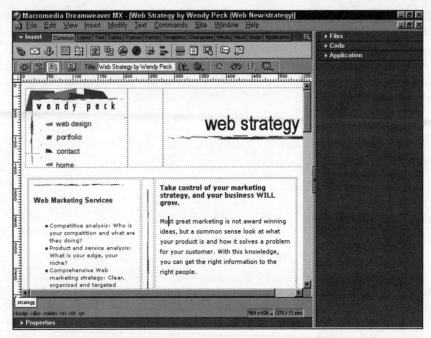

Figure 2-3   *The Document window with several panels active but collapsed.*

Touring the Document Area

Now that you have the functions of the Document area and the Site panel in your mind, take a closer look at the Document area of the screen. This is where you spend most of your time as you design your site.

The screen shown in Figure 2-4 is what you see when you create a new document in Dreamweaver. I have closed all panels for this sample. The principal elements of the Document area include

- **Menus:** Most functions in Dreamweaver can be accessed through the menus. I urge beginners to use the menus. Find out why in "Using the Menus," later in this session.
- **Rulers:** Rulers can be turned on for precise work.
- **Insert toolbar:** Replaces the Object panel and is used to add components to your document.
- **Toolbar:** The toolbar offers instant access to common actions as well as to the Code view.
- **Page title:** This is the title that appears when a visitor to your Web page bookmarks your site. Initially, Dreamweaver places Untitled Document in this field, but it should be changed on each page
- **File name:** Displays the path and name for your file.

- **Window size:** Dreamweaver offers simulations of various browser resolutions. Click the Window size drop-down list and choose the resolution you wish to duplicate to see how your page looks at smaller resolutions. This feature is valuable for liquid designs, which you create in Session 8.

- **File size/Download time:** This section displays the total size in kilobytes (K) of your page, and the approximate download time required. There are no excuses for slow-loading pages because you always have the size information available as you create your page.

- **Launcher bar:** One-click access to many panels and functions (must be turned on in the Panels preferences for Mac display).

- **Tag selector:** Lists the appropriate tags for the selected object. Clicking a tag in the Tag Selector automatically takes you to the location of that tag in Code view.

- **Open documents (PC):** Tabs represent currently open documents. The active document is shown by a white tab.

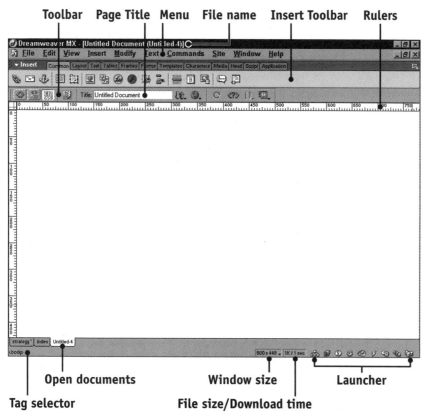

Figure 2-4   *The Dreamweaver MX document screen.*

You'll look at each of these features in greater depth as you move through the course. This is just the bare bones of the Dreamweaver tools. Next, you move to the rich array of panels, or small tool windows, that Dreamweaver offers.

Although you might be tempted to skip over the tool instructions, I urge you to resist. To help keep your workspace clean, many of the powerful tools are hidden — tools that can shave hours from your work and help you to produce better pages.

Working with Panels

**20 Min.
To Go**

The Dreamweaver developers must have known from the beginning that every user of Dreamweaver software would have different needs. The system of panels for storing many of the tools is perfect. If you are working on interactivity, you can work with the Behavior panel open. While you set up frames for your site, you can have the Frames panel open. When you move on to edit your text, close all your panels and work with a wide-open screen. This can be easily accomplished by selecting Window ➪ Hide Panels, or by pressing the F4 key on your keyboard. Restore the panels you had open by selecting Window ➪ Show Panels, or by pressing the F4 key again. I cover the functions and contents of individual panels as you proceed through building your pages, but there are some general methods that will help you get the most from the panels in Dreamweaver. You have some powerful customizing tools to work with, and you should always be on the watch for ways to streamline your panels.

I recommend that you don't customize your tools just yet. Let your work patterns develop a little and then make your changes.

Opening and closing panels

Obviously, to put a panel to work, you must open it. There are many ways to open panels. To open any panel, take the following steps:

1. Select Window from the main menu and a drop-down list appears.
2. Select the panel you wish to open. For this example, choose Behaviors.

Alternatively, you may click the symbol for the panel you wish to launch from the Launcher bar in the lower-right corner of your screen (not all panels are represented in the Launcher bar). For this example choose Behaviors ▧.

If you have not changed any default settings, the panel opens docked at the right side of the screen. To close a panel, simply click the menu icon ▤ at the top right of the panel window and select Close Panel Group from the drop-down menu that appears.

The panels in Dreamweaver MX are arranged in groups on a PC. To activate a panel in a group, simply click on the tab for the panel you desire. Figure 2-5 shows the Files group, with the Site panel active. If the Assets panel is active, the Assets tab will appear to be in front of the Site tab.

Figure 2-5   *Files panel group with the Site panel active.*

Collapsing and expanding panels

At times, you may find that you are using a panel too often to close it, but would like to get it out of the way for a few minutes. You can collapse a panel with a click, and expand it with the same action when needed.

To collapse a panel, click on the triangle icon to the left of the panel group name ▶ **Design**. The panel will collapse so that only the panel group name is visible. To expand the panel, simply click the triangle icon.

Floating and docking panels

One of the most powerful additions to Dreamweaver MX is the flexibility you have to arrange the panels. By default, panels are docked on opening. The Insert toolbar docks at the top of the screen. The Properties panel docks at the bottom of the screen, and all other panels open docked at the right.

To float any panel, drag the dot icon ▓ beside the panel group name away from the docking area. When you release the mouse button, the panel will be floating. To move the panel to a different location on the screen, drag the panel to the location you desire.

To dock the panel again, drag the panel to the edge of the screen. The Properties panel and Insert toolbar can be docked at the top or bottom of the screen. The remaining panels can be docked at the left or right of the screen.

Focusing on the Properties Panel

If I had to choose just one panel in Dreamweaver, my decision would be instantaneous. It would have to be the Properties panel, as shown in Figure 2-6. In fact, most users find that it is impossible to work without this tool. The Properties panel displays information about the selected object, and also provides easy access to editing for the object.

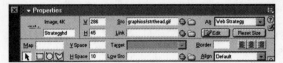

Figure 2-6   *The little power performer — the Properties panel.*

What does this little gem control? Text, and everything about text. You can specify any of the following items:

- fonts
- font attributes
- font color
- alignment
- ordered and unordered lists
- HTML styles like H1, H2, and Paragraph
- links

It also controls most table functions, including

- table columns
- number of columns and rows
- merge and split cells
- add or remove borders
- apply a background color to tables, rows, columns, and individual cells

And finally, the Properties panel provides the following controls for images:

- image source
- image dimensions
- creating links
- adding or removing borders
- alignment
- adding Alt tags
- naming images for JavaScript
- adding vertical or horizontal space
- creating image maps

It's not hard to see why you will find it hard to work without this tool. I like the shape of the panel, because it rarely seems to get in my way. I usually work with the Property panel expanded, but occasionally return to the smaller view with some properties hidden. You can toggle the two views by clicking the arrow in the lower-right corner of the panel.

Using the Menus

There is nothing especially surprising or difficult about the Dreamweaver menu system. However, I want to touch again on the subject of using menus.

Too often, people rush to memorize keyboard shortcuts by the dozen. They feel that if they know them all, they know the program. I have spent a lot of time teaching people to use a wide range of software, so I speak from classroom experience when I say that is not an efficient way to learn a program. When you learn a shortcut, what you have accomplished exactly is, well, you have learned a shortcut. Period. That's it. You have no concept of where that function fits within the whole scheme. You are not steadily mapping out the entire program.

However, when you learn keyboard shortcuts by using the program's menus, you end up in the same place as you would using shortcuts, but you also know the program intimately. Every menu item that has a keyboard shortcut will list that shortcut to the right of the menu listing. You can learn those shortcuts as you work.

Look at Figure 2-7. Notice how the Text ⇨ Indent entry shows Ctrl+Alt+] as the shortcut (Option+⌘+] for Mac). Yes, it takes a little longer to open the menu than to type a few keys, but look at what else you are learning without even concentrating. You work with text a lot as you create a Web page, and while you are setting your indent, you can also see how to create a list style, control the CSS for your site, and so on. When you need that information, you will know where to find it.

When you use a menu item often, eventually you switch to the shortcut naturally. You don't have to memorize it, because you have seen it many times. And don't forget, you have unconsciously noted everything that the menu contains.

You may rarely use the item above or below the menu item you use so often, and you will unconsciously skip the shortcuts on those items. I still do not know the frames shortcuts because I rarely use them. For the occasional page that I create with frames, the menu options will do just fine.

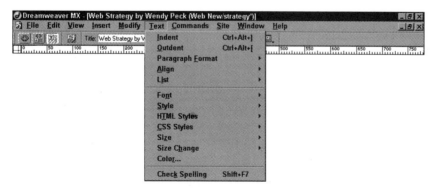

Figure 2-7   *Indenting text. Note that the shortcut is listed to the right of the menu item.*

Viewing Your Document

**10 Min.
To Go**

When you create a document in Dreamweaver, what you see on the monitor is only an approximation of how it will look displayed in a browser. To truly see how your page is progressing, you must know how your page looks on the Web. As you will see in the next session, however, uploading your page — while not complicated — is time-consuming if you have to upload the page to check it each time you make a change.

Luckily, Dreamweaver offers a quick, easy, and surprisingly reliable preview method right on your computer. Your document does not have to be saved before you preview it. All features, such as JavaScript or media, will function properly as long as your browser has that capability enabled or it has the necessary plug-in installed.

Defining your browser list

You have to tell Dreamweaver which browser you want to test. The first browser you install is set as the default browser. You can define up to 20 browsers to use for the preview, as long as those browsers are installed on your computer. As a bare minimum, you should have the current version of Internet Explorer and Netscape installed on your computer and defined as preview browsers in Dreamweaver. I also recommend that you have at least one Netscape 4.x version.

 You'll need to have current versions of Netscape and Internet Explorer installed for this course. You can download Netscape at http://netscape.com (select Downloads), and Internet Explorer from http://micosoft.com (select Downloads ⇨ Download Center).

To define a browser in Dreamweaver, take the following steps:

1. Select File ⇨ Preview in Browser ⇨ Edit Browser list.
2. Ensure that Preview in Browser is selected in the left portion of the window.
3. Click the + (plus sign) to open the Add Browser window.
4. Type in a name for the browser in the Name section.
5. Click Browse to indicate where the browser is stored on your computer, and then select the browser file.
6. Choose Primary or Secondary browser. You can preview your documents in your primary browser by pressing the F12 key. Pressing the Shift+F12 keys (PC) or the Shift+F12 keys (Mac) activates a preview in your secondary browser. You must use the menu to preview with any other browsers.
7. Repeat these steps to add another browser, if desired.
8. Click OK. Your defined browsers are now ready for previews.

Previewing your document in a browser

Figure 2-8 is a preview of a document in Netscape 6. To preview your document, take the following steps:

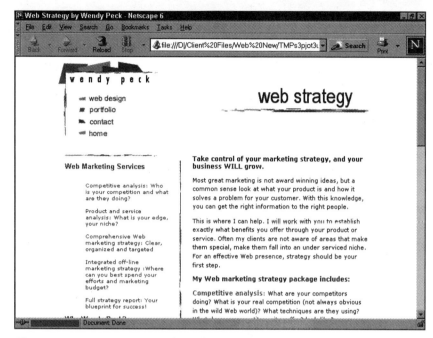

Figure 2-8 *A Document previewed in Netscape 6.*

1. Choose File ⇨ Preview in Browser and choose the desired browser from the list. A new window pops up in front of your document with your browser displaying your file.
2. Close the browser window to return to Dreamweaver.

You're almost at the action point. In Session 3, you define a site, and then you start making pages.

Done!

REVIEW

In this session, you learned how to find your way around Dreamweaver documents and the panels, as well as how to set up a browser to preview your document. Just to recap:

- The Site panel controls the files for your site.
- All work on documents is completed in the Document area of Dreamweaver.
- Dreamweaver creates and maintains its own listing of files on your hard drive when you define a site.
- When a site is connected through Dreamweaver FTP and the Site panel is expanded, both local files and files stored on the server are displayed.
- The Site panel controls all automated features for maintaining your site.
- You can have many documents open at one time, and access the desired document through the tabs at the bottom left of your screen.

- Dreamweaver panels allow you to choose which tools are on your screen, and can be docked or floating.
- The Properties panel offers controls for almost all of the elements in your document.
- Pages created in Dreamweaver must be previewed in a browser to know exactly how they will appear on the Web.
- You can add up to 20 browsers to the Dreamweaver preview list. Two of those browsers can be assigned as primary and secondary browsers and can be launched with keyboard shortcuts.

QUIZ YOURSELF

1. How many documents can you have open at one time? (See the "Document area" section.)

2. Where will a page title be displayed when a page is on the Web? (See the "Touring the Document Area" section.)

3. What is a Dreamweaver panel? (See the "Working with Panels" section.)

4. How do you dock or float a panel on your screen? (See the "Floating and docking panels" section.)

5. How do you expand or collapse a panel? (See the "Collapsing and expanding panels" section.)

6. Name four actions that can be done through the Properties panel. (See the "Focusing on the Properties Panel" section.)

7. What is the total number of browsers you can have available to preview your document? (See the "Viewing Your Document " section.)

Understanding Dreamweaver Site Structure

Session Checklist

✔ Understanding the Site panel

✔ Touring the Site panel

✔ Creating a root folder

✔ Defining a new site

✔ Defining a Dreamweaver site from existing files

✔ Understanding folder structure and links

✔ Changing a filename

✔ Viewing dependent files with a site map

**30 Min.
To Go**

N ow that you have learned some general Dreamweaver principles, it's time to move to hands-on work. In this session, you take a closer look at the Site panel, and then move on to defining a root folder. Finally, you define a site using existing files, and you create a site map.

Understanding the Site Panel

The Site panel is not complicated. In fact, it resembles most of the file management–type listings you will see. There's a lot of power hiding in this simple window, though, and you'll find that as you build more and more pages, or multiple sites, that this is where Dreamweaver has so much to offer.

Touring the Site panel

What better place to start than with a guided tour of what the Site panel offers? The Site panel includes a few strange names that are worthy of a short introduction — it always helps to know the terminology used in a new program.

You have already looked at the file listing in the Site panel. Take a closer look at this panel as you prepare to create your first site. Figure 3-1 shows the Site panel that has been expanded and is connected to the server.

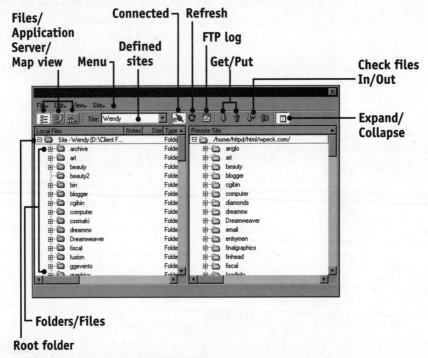

Figure 3-1   *The Site panel, expanded and connected to the server.*

The following list steps through each feature in the Site panel:

- **Menu:** As in most programs, nearly every command available in Dreamweaver can be accomplished through the menu system.

With each new version, Dreamweaver's site and document operations become more integrated. This is for user convenience, though, and not meant to blur the important distinction between document creation and site management. Make sure you always keep the two functions separate in your mind.

- **Files/Application Server/Map view:** The default — and most common — view is the Files view, as shown earlier in Figure 3-1. Dreamweaver also offers a Map view, which offers a graphic representation of the files shown in the Files view. The

Application Server view is used when working with dynamic data on a site, and is not used in this book.

- **Defined sites:** When you have several defined sites, they all appear in this drop-down window to provide you with fast access to any site.
- **Connected/Disconnected:** This screen shows a connected view.
- **Refresh:** When you need to refresh the view of your files, one click will do it.
- **FTP log:** Records the action as you use Dreamweaver's FTP function.
- **Get/Put files:** Terms for retrieving files from, and sending files to, the server. The terms are from the local perspective. When you Get files, you are retrieving them from the server to your local folders. When you Put files, you are sending them from your local folder to the server.
- **Check files in/out:** When more than one person works on a site, it is very easy to overwrite updates of another person's files. Checking files in and out prevents errors like this.
- **Expand/Collapse (PC only):** Toggles between the expanded Site panel view shown in Figure 3-1 and a single pane view, which shows only the Local or Remote files at one time.
- **Folders/Files:** Folders that are on your hard drive are in the Local pane; files on your server are in the Remote pane. Dreamweaver records the files it finds in order to maintain your site. Files created in any manner will appear in the Site panel when they are stored in the root folder or on the server.
- **Root folder:** The root folder is the path to where your site is stored on your hard drive; it is specified when you define your site.

This ends your basic tour of the Site window. It is simple and quite logical. Next, you take a quick look at some of the most important menu items, and then you define a root folder for your first exercise.

Learning the Site panel menus

It is boring to step through each individual menu item, and I hit all important menu commands in the upcoming sessions. Therefore, I won't take you on a full tour at this time. This is just an orientation to the menu structure as you begin to explore Dreamweaver.

The File menu for the Site panel can be a confusing place; it offers a mix of site and document commands. For example, you can rename a folder, which is very much a site command. You can also create a new document, which causes the Document window to open. In fact, most of the commands in the File menu are document commands, such as open, view, or check commands.

The Site panel is command central for working with Dreamweaver. When I am working on a site, although I can open a file through the main menu, I usually click back to the Site panel. Double-clicking a file listing opens the selected file (a shortcut for File ⇨ Open), and I find it invaluable to see the entire site structure repeatedly as I work.

The rest of the Site panel menus, however, contain only site-related commands. For example, the Edit menu concentrates on finding files through various methods, and the View menu lets you tell Dreamweaver how to display your site listings.

Files are moved — and most of the site management is done — in the Site panel menu. This is the powerhouse menu for the Site panel, containing the features you must get to know intimately.

Defining a Site

20 Min. To Go

You've arrived. Time to start creating that site I've been promising. However, hold on to those ideas for a few more minutes. You're not quite ready to start making pages yet. To create a successful Web project, you must work through an organizational phase.

Although it is natural instinct for many to just jump in and organize later — especially for us creative souls — you just cannot do that in Dreamweaver. In fact, that is an exceptionally bad idea for Web design in general. Pages in a Web site are always connected through links, and they often include menu items that must be created in a separate program. Failing to plan properly always results in more work, or worse: fragmented navigation.

The payoff for a little organization, however, is creative freedom. Do your homework, set up properly, and let Dreamweaver automatically look after all the irritating little details that can bog down your creative process. You'll be paid back in hours for the minutes you spend now.

Creating a root folder

The first step is to create a folder for your site. The folder can be located anywhere on your hard drive. For the sessions in this book, create your folder in the root folder of your hard drive. You only need to follow this suggestion to provide consistency between what your screen shows and the illustrations that I include in the book. If you can remember to adjust my instructions to include a different file path, feel free to create your root folder anywhere on your hard drive.

Using your normal folder creation method, create a folder named "holiday."

Defining a new site

Now that you have created your folder, tell Dreamweaver where the folder is located, and then create your site. (You are building a site from scratch in this example. The next section covers finding an existing site with Dreamweaver.)

To define a site with your holiday folder as the root folder

1. Open the Site panel. Set the panel to Local View.
2. Select Site ➪ New Site. The Site Definition window opens. The Local Info selection should be highlighted in the left portion of the screen.
3. Type **Holiday** into the Site Name area.

4. Click the folder icon at the end of the Local Root Folder option. Locate and select the holiday folder that you created. The Local Root Folder will now read C:\holiday\.

5. Make sure that the Enable Cache option is selected.

6. Click OK. Your site has been created. (See Figure 3-2.)

Figure 3-2   *Holiday site defined.*

Dreamweaver's Site panel now lists Holiday in the Site drop-down list box. The holiday folder is listed in Local View as the root folder. This is your working site for the next few sessions. You will return to it later. Now, it's time to build a Dreamweaver site from an existing set of files.

Defining a Dreamweaver site from existing files

You may have been building Web sites long before you decided to use Dreamweaver. No matter how you created existing Web sites, you can build a Dreamweaver site from your existing files, and put the power of site management and document editing to work for you now. In fact, the method used is identical to the steps you took in the previous section, but the results are different because Dreamweaver finds your existing files.

Locate the Session 3 folder on the CD-ROM and copy the folder named crash-course to your hard drive. It does not matter where you place this folder, as long as you can find it.

Follow the instructions from the previous exercise to define a new site called Crash Course. Use the Session 3 folder you just copied from the CD-ROM to your computer as the root folder. Your Crash Course site should contain two documents called firstpage.html and secondpage.html. There should also be a folder labeled art, containing a file named weekend.gif. Your screen should closely resemble Figure 3-3.

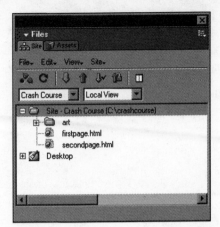

Figure 3-3 *The Site window with the Crash Course site active. Note how Dreamweaver lists all files in the directory. The art directory is expanded here. Simply click any + (plus sign) to expand the folder view. Click the – (minus sign) to collapse the folder view.*

If you want to create a new site from your existing files, follow the instructions to define a new site, but specify the location for your root folder. The root folder normally contains the start page (index.html) for your site.

10 Min.
To Go

Understanding Folder Structure and Links

As your final preparation to creating documents, you should study the way in which Dreamweaver works with folders and links documents. See how much of the responsibility for keeping track of changes falls to Dreamweaver, rather than on your shoulders. You are working with a site that has only two pages and one graphic file. As you work through making changes, remember that the action and result would be the same if you were making changes that affected 50 pages or 500 pages.

HTML supports only one page per document. You direct visitors to your site by linking one page to another. In almost all Web sites, each page links to many other pages, even if those links are only through the menu system. Once you add one link to a page, it is no longer independent. Make any change to the location of the file or name of the linked page outside of Dreamweaver, and you have a broken link in your site.

Changing a filename

Suppose you realize that you have made errors in your filenames, but you have pages linked to those pages with the incorrect names. Changing a filename is easy anywhere, but change just one character and your linked pages will no longer be able to find that file.

As one who has created and maintained sites without any automatic control, Dreamweaver's ability to quietly keep track of every single link is still magic to me. Enough talk! Here it is in action.

To change a filename, follow these steps:

1. Open the Site panel and select the Crash Course site from the drop-down menu to activate the site.

2. Click the file secondpage.html to select it.

3. Select File ⇨ Rename. The highlight changes to include only the filename.

4. Type **page2.html**.

5. Click away from the listing, or press the Enter key to accept the filename. The Update Files window opens, as shown in Figure 3-4. This window lists any files that are linked to the file you are changing, and asks if you want to update the files. Choose Update. Any reference to secondpage.html will be changed to page2.html in the listed documents.

6. Repeat Steps 2 through 5, renaming firstpage.html to **index.html.**

Figure 3-4   *Choosing Update automatically changes the link references in all of the listed files.*

Viewing dependent files with a site map

Look again at Figure 3-3. You now know that index.html and page2.html are linked, because Dreamweaver had to update the files when you renamed the files from firstpage.html and secondpage.html. But there is nothing that indicates that link. You can easily see links in documents, but there is no indicator in the Site window.

You can see all dependent files, as well as the entire structure of a site, by changing the view. In Figure 3-5, you can see index.html linking to both the image, weekend.gif, and the file page2.html.

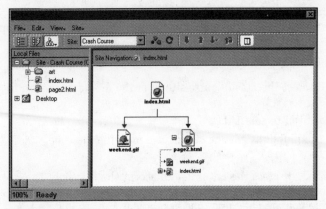

Figure 3-5 *Site map for the Crash Course site. Note how the index.html page is linked to both an image and another page. The page2.html file is also linked to an image, as well as back to the index.html page.*

To create a Map view of your site, you must first define a homepage for Dreamweaver:

1. In the Site panel, select Site ⇨ Edit Sites. In the Edit Sites window, highlight Crash Course and click Edit. The Site Definition window opens.

2. Select Site Map Layout from the list at the left of the window. Click the folder at the end of the Home Page field and browse to select the index.html file from the previous exercise.

3. Select Display Dependent Files and click OK and then Done to return to the Site panel.

4. Expand the Site panel.

5. Click and hold the Site Map icon to expose a drop-down menu. Select Map and Files.

Your screen should closely resemble the screen shown in Figure 3-5. The + (plus sign) indicates that there are more levels of linked files. In this case, however, the links will go on forever because the two files are linked to each other. You can collapse levels using the – (minus sign) beside the folder.

Note that the image file, weekend.gif, has no lower levels. However, it is linked to both index.html and page2.html. (Look for the image file in the page2.html list of dependent files.) It does not take a lot of imagination to see how the Map view can help you organize your site. The site map can be saved as a graphic file.

To restore the file view, click the Site Files icon.

You should now have a very good understanding of how Dreamweaver goes about managing your site. The solid foundation that you have built here will pay off over the next couple of days as you delve deep into Dreamweaver's capabilities.

In the next session, you build your first page. At long last.

Done!

REVIEW

You have just learned how to find your way through the Site panel and understand how files are linked. Remember the following items:

- All file management tasks are handled in the Site panel.
- The Site window controls the entire site.
- Every Dreamweaver site must have a root folder, and the root folder can be located anywhere on your hard drive.
- You can set up a Dreamweaver site from your existing files.
- Always make changes to site files from within Dreamweaver, not with your system file management.
- A site map provides an instant overview of your site.

QUIZ YOURSELF

1. When would you use Check files in/out? (See the "Touring the Site panel" section)
2. What happens when you Get a file? What happens when you Put a file? (See the "Touring the Site panel" section.)
3. What is a root folder? (See the "Touring the Site panel" section.)
4. What do you need before you define a new site? (See the "Defining a new site" section.)
5. Why must you make all changes to files in the Dreamweaver Site window? (See the "Understanding Folder Structure and Links" section.)
6. How can you create a site map that displays dependent files? (See the "Viewing dependent files with a site map" section.)

Creating a Document

Session Checklist

✔ Creating and opening a new document

✔ Viewing HTML

✔ Entering and editing text

✔ Adding images

**30 Min.
To Go**

Now that you have successfully defined a site, it is time to add pages and begin to build your Web site. In this session, you create a blank document and add basic elements, like images and text, to the page. You also continue to work within Dreamweaver's Site window, which is vital to preparing a good foundation for your site.

Creating HTML Documents

Each page on a Web site is an individual document (because HTML does not offer multiple-page capability). There is no limit to the length of a single HTML page, although experienced designers rarely create pages that will fill more than two or three screens in the published document. Later in this course, you learn to create links that connect your pages — much like pages in a book.

Publishing to the Web bears little resemblance to printing a page from your printer or sending a file to a professional print shop. Many experienced computer users have difficulty with the transition from print to Web pages. To avoid confusion and frustration, I strongly recommend that you think of working with Dreamweaver as an entirely new concept, rather than trying to translate your former knowledge to Web publishing.

If you have HTML coding experience, I recommend that you resist the natural tendency to do most of your work within the HTML editor. Dreamweaver will save you time once you have mastered the basic techniques. Check and tweak the code once it has been produced, but writing standard code by hand defeats the purpose of the program, and will delay your progress.

Creating a blank document

In the last session, you defined a site called Holiday. If this is the only site you have defined, Dreamweaver opens with Holiday as the default site. If you have defined other sites, select the Holiday site from the drop-down list at the top of the screen. There are several ways to create documents in Dreamweaver, but in the beginning, you should use the menu system.

Follow these steps to create a new document from the Dreamweaver Site panel:

1. If it is not already open, open your Files panel (Window ⇨ Site). The title on this panel is Files. The Site tab should be active.

2. Select File ⇨ New File from the Files panel menu (Mac: Site ⇨ Site Files View ⇨ New File). An entry appears with the label untitled.html. Make sure the name is highlighted and type **session4.html**. Click away from the filename to save the new name. You have created a blank document in the Holiday site. Make sure that your Site panel is close to the example shown in Figure 4-1. This will be important later.

3. Double-click session4.html in your Site window. Your document opens.

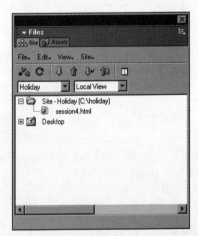

Figure 4-1 *A blank document is created in the Dreamweaver Site panel. This file is in the root directory for the site.*

Entering text and checking HTML

Technically, you can complete an entire Web site without seeing any HTML code. But, marketing claims notwithstanding, to create a Web page that displays properly in any browser and on any platform, you need to work with HTML code. I refer to HTML code throughout this course, highlighting the most common adjustments and providing troubleshooting hints.

Start right away to work back and forth between the visual display of your page and the HTML code window. When you created your document in the last step, it opened in a new window with a cursor in the upper-left corner. Although this looks like a blank page, Dreamweaver has already entered HTML code for you. Before you type anything on the page, look at the code that's already in place.

To view the HTML code and add text, follow these steps:

1. Locate the Code and Design View icons at the upper-left portion of your screen, as shown in Figure 4-2. The third icon, which is the Show Design View icon, should be depressed.

Show Design View icon

Figure 4-2 *The Design View icon is active, meaning that no code view is showing.*

2. Click the Show Code and Design Views, which is the middle Design View icon. Your window splits and the top portion of the screen displays the HTML code for your document. It should resemble the screen shown in Figure 4-3.

3. Return to Design View. Start your document with a simple text entry.

4. Type **If this is so easy, why does everyone make such a fuss about HTML?** Take another look at the HTML code. Note how the text you typed now appears with the code.

5. Return to Design View. Place your cursor at the end of the sentence you typed and press Enter to move the cursor to the next line.

6. View the HTML code again. Whoa! Where did all that code come from? HTML does not read the Enter key action like a word processor. You must have a <p> tag to indicate that there is a paragraph. Dreamweaver automatically sets that up. And the ? That is simply the code for a non-breaking space, meaning a space that does not start a new line. HTML demands that content be placed in a tag. Dreamweaver uses this code as a placeholder until more content is added.

7. Type **OK, so maybe it is a little more complicated than it looked at first**.

Check your code and you see that the placeholder code is now gone. There is a lot going on behind the screen in Dreamweaver. Keep checking as you move through the rest of the session. Not only will you gain understanding of the way HTML works, but you also gain an appreciation for the work that Dreamweaver saves.

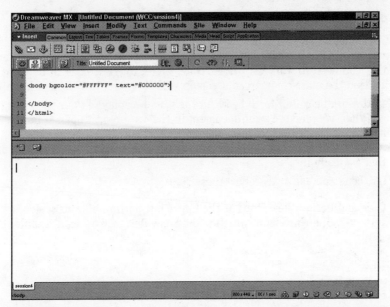

Figure 4-3   *HTML code for a "blank" page in Dreamweaver. Note that the cursor is not at the upper portion of the HTML screen, but at the end of the <body bgcolor="#FFFFFF" text="000000"> tag. All code above this point creates the document (Head), sets the background color to white instead of the default gray, and the text to black.*

You also have the option to view your HTML in a separate window, which some people prefer. You can open and close the HTML window with the F10 key, or by selecting Window ⇨ Others ⇨ Code Inspector in the main menu (see Figure 4-4).

I cannot stress enough the importance of making a commitment to become HTML-literate. You can learn a lot about how HTML code works by following the code as you create your document. Dreamweaver has an excellent reputation for creating "clean" code, which generally means that it does not produce a lot of extra code to accomplish a specific task. As you work through the exercises, peek at the code that is produced as you add an image, create a link, or complete any other action. Before you know it, you'll have the skill to enter your own code for the few areas where Dreamweaver does not offer every option.

To learn how to edit HTML in Dreamweaver, see Session 11.

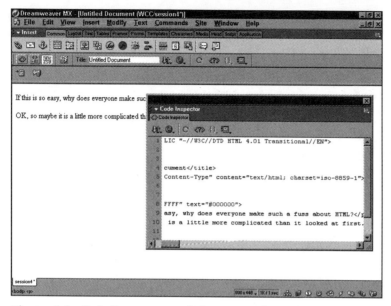

Figure 4-4   *Code Inspector panel shown over the Design view.*

Editing Text

**20 Min.
To Go**

HTML fonts are one of the main reasons I suggested that you leave any print experience behind. Because a page you create for the Web is read on your visitor's computer, you have very little control over the final appearance of text. Your page is displayed using fonts that are available to your visitor's computer, which means that the font you use must be installed on all the computers that might display the page. So your practical choices are limited to those fonts that are likely to be on most computers.

You will learn about CSS (Cascading Style Sheets) in Session 23. CSS handles text much more efficiently and provides tighter control.

Choosing your fonts

Dreamweaver has done much of the work for you in choosing fonts that will work on your page. Dreamweaver lists only the fonts that are typically available on every computer.

Follow these steps to choose a font in Dreamweaver:

1. If it is not already visible, open the Properties palette by choosing Window ➪ Properties.

   The second drop-down window from the left contains preset font choices. Note that there are several fonts listed with each choice. When a browser loads a page, it checks the user's system for the first font in the list, and then checks for the second, and so on, until it finds a font that it can display. The final entry in each of Dreamweaver's preset styles offers either sans-serif or serif as a choice. If the browser cannot find one of the named fonts, it uses the computer's default serif or sans-serif font to display the page.

2. Highlight the first sentence you typed.

3. Choose Verdana, Arial, Helvetica, and sans-serif from the drop-down menu options. The font changes.

Changing font color and attributes

The Properties panel is also used to change font color and attributes for your text.

Follow these steps to change color or attributes:

1. Highlight a word in the first sentence.

2. In the Properties palette, click the Bold icon to change the text to bold.

3. Click the Text Color well, and choose a color from the fly-out color palette, as shown in Figure 4-5. The color fly-out features only Web-safe color choices.

4. Check the code again to see the HTML code behind the text's appearance onscreen.

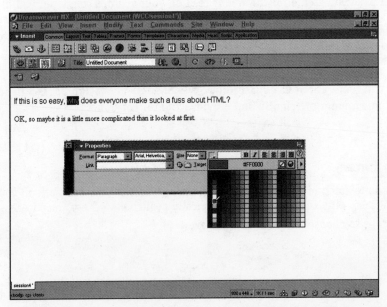

Figure 4-5 *The Properties panel is used to change text attributes. Note that the text is highlighted — a necessary step for any text editing.*

Changing font size

HTML offers only relative text sizing — not text sizing by specific size, which is common in the computer world. This simply means that each text size is set in relation to the other text in the document. Standards for relative font sizing vary across browsers and platforms, and you want your Web page to be readable by all visitors. Dreamweaver makes setting the chosen relative size easy.

Follow these steps to set a relative size font:

1. Highlight the second sentence and choose the value 2 from the drop-down Size option in the Properties panel. Because the default font setting is 3, the text becomes smaller.
2. Check your code again in the HTML window to see the code that Dreamweaver has entered while you worked in the document.

Applying an HTML style

You can also assign an HTML style to your text. H1 is the largest headline style, and H6 the smallest. The styles are designed to be used in a hierarchical way, with H1 forming main headlines, H2 forming a second-level heading, H3 forming a third-level heading, and so on. Although the styles continue up to H6, H4 through H6 are rarely used. The Paragraph style is meant to be the normal body text. See Figure 4-6 for samples of the HTML styles.

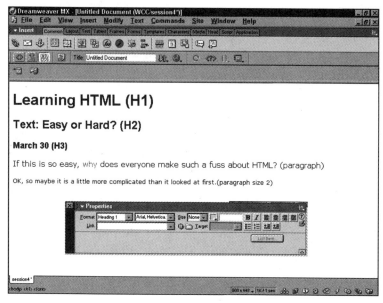

Figure 4-6 *A selection of the most commonly used HTML styles. The font has been changed to Arial, Helvetica, sans-serif for the headlines and Verdana, Arial, Helvetica, sans-serif for the paragraph text. Note how the Properties panel reflects the settings of the paragraph containing the cursor.*

HTML styles automatically add a break, so no line-break is needed. They can only be applied to full paragraphs. You do not need to highlight all the text you wish to change. Simply place your cursor anywhere in the paragraph and then choose a style from the Properties panel Format list.

Adding Images

**10 Min.
To Go**

You've learned to insert text into your page, but the Web has gone far beyond simple words. You want images — lots of them. Fortunately, Dreamweaver makes it very easy to insert images. However, you must return to the Site panel to organize where you store the images.

Creating a new folder

Images are best kept in a separate folder from the HTML documents. With graphic menu bars and rollover images, it is not unusual to create sites that contain several hundred images. Without organization at the start of the project, many hours are wasted locating files. Dreamweaver also needs to know where the images are stored, and it is much better to establish the location for all files first, before you place them in your document.

Follow these steps to create a new folder:

1. Open your Site panel. You will now create a folder for your images.
2. Highlight the holiday folder at the top of the Site panel. New folders are placed as a child of the active folder. Because you want your graphics folder to be on the first level, you must start from the original folder.
3. Select File ⇨ New Folder from the Site panel menu (Mac: Site ⇨ Site Files View ⇨ New Folder). Dreamweaver places a new folder under the starting folder with the default name Untitled. Type the word **art** to replace Untitled. Click away from the name to save.

File size is always a concern with HTML documents because size determines the download speed for the final page. I cover optimizing your graphic images later, but you can also keep your file sizes smaller by choosing small names for common directories. For example, using the word "art" instead of the more common "graphics" saves 5 bytes for every image. Five bytes may not be worth mentioning, but what if you have hundreds of images, many of which appear on every page of a 30-page site? For a large site, the savings are significant.

Inserting an image

Locate the file 4insert.gif in the Session 4 folder on the CD-ROM. Copy the file to your new holiday/art folder.

Start adding the artistic elements to your page. Take these steps to insert an image:

1. Activate your document. Like text, an image is placed at the cursor location.
2. Click at the end of the last sentence in your document and press Enter to advance the cursor to the next line.
3. Select Insert ⇨ Image from the main menu. Locate the image 4insert.gif in the holiday\art folder. Highlight the file to select it. Note that the image size and file size information is listed below the preview on the right side of the window (see the Select Image Source window in Figure 4-7).
4. Click OK to accept the choice and return to the document.

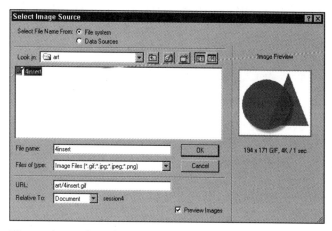

Figure 4-7 *The Select Image Source window. Dreamweaver only lists image files that can be viewed on the Web. PNG format files can be viewed by some browsers, but they are not in common use yet. GIF and JPG files are the only formats commonly used today for the Web.*

Save your document (File ⇨ Save) at the end of every exercise. Dreamweaver does not have an automatic backup feature, so frequent saves are wise.

Click the image in your document, and you see selection handles around the border of the image. Note that the Property palette reports the image size, as well as the path leading to the image.

You can drag an image to a new location, or delete it with the Delete key. You can also resize an image by dragging the selection handles, but that is absolutely not recommended.

Although you can resize an image in Dreamweaver, it is the worst possible way to accomplish a size change. Browsers take longer to load images that have been reduced in Dreamweaver, and the quality is usually very poor. You can resize the image in Dreamweaver to determine the desired size, but you always should return to an image-editing program to resize the image.

Done!

REVIEW

In this session, you learned how to create a document in Dreamweaver. Here are some important points to remember:

- File management should always be done in Dreamweaver's Site panel.
- Dreamweaver places text or images at the cursor's current position.
- A basic understanding of HTML code is important, even when using Dreamweaver. Make it a habit to check your code in the HTML Source window.
- You have very little control over text when publishing pages to the Web. Dreamweaver offers only the fonts that are commonly found on most computers.
- Text must be highlighted to change font attributes. However, an HTML style is applied to an entire paragraph, so highlighting the entire paragraph is not required.
- Create a separate folder to contain the images for your site. Organization is the key to effectively using Dreamweaver.
- Do not resize images in Dreamweaver.

QUIZ YOURSELF

1. How many pages can an HTML document contain? (See the "Creating HTML Documents" section.)
2. Where should you create a new document if you are a beginner? (See the "Creating a blank document" section.)
3. Why does Dreamweaver offer such a small selection of fonts to use? (See the "Editing Text" section.)
4. HTML offers only "relative font size." What does this mean? (See the "Changing font size" section.)
5. How do you move an existing image in a Dreamweaver document? (See the "Inserting an image" section.)

PART

I

Friday Evening Part Review

1. Dreamweaver is a visual editor, which means you can produce Web pages without understanding HTML code. Why is it important to learn HTML code?
2. HTML code is not necessarily displayed in the same way in different browsers. Why?
3. Why can you not have total control of text in a Web page?
4. What does it mean when a Dreamweaver panel is docked or floating?
5. What is the primary purpose for the Site panel in Dreamweaver?
6. Why is it a good idea for beginners to use the menu system as they learn Dreamweaver?
7. What is a context menu?
8. What is a Dreamweaver panel?
9. What must you do before you can preview a document in a browser?
10. Before previewing a page in your browser, is it necessary to save the document?
11. What is the difference between *Getting* and *Putting* files in Dreamweaver?
12. Can a Dreamweaver site be created with existing files, and how?
13. When you define a site, what is the role of the root folder?
14. How many pages can an HTML document hold?
15. What is a Dreamweaver site map?
16. What is the shortcut to open the Code Inspector in Dreamweaver?
17. Why does Dreamweaver offer such a small selection of font choices in the Properties panel?
18. Where do you adjust font size and color directly on a page in Dreamweaver?
19. Why should you create a new folder for the graphics and images on your site?
20. What graphic-file types can be used for display on the Web?

☑ Friday

☑ **Saturday**

☐ Sunday

PART

II

Saturday Morning

Defining a Dreamweaver Site

Session Checklist

✔ Understanding FTP

✔ Using Dreamweaver FTP

✔ Setting up FTP for your site

✔ Creating a folder on your remote site

✔ Transferring files to your remote site

✔ Transferring an entire site to remote server

✔ Editing files and folders on your remote site

So far, you have defined a site and created a document. There is just one remaining piece to pull it all together: getting your files onto the Web. I explained how hosting works in Session 1, and I am assuming that you have a host in place to receive your files. If you do not, please pause and complete this step.

**30 Min.
To Go**

You will find a list of low- and no-cost hosts on the CD-ROM, in the file hosts.html in the resources folder.

What Is FTP?

FTP is an acronym for File Transfer Protocol. FTP is the vehicle that Web designers use to publish their work. Instead of sending a file to a printer, Web designers send it to their servers using FTP. As a concept, it is really that simple. FTP is simply the tool that is used to transfer files from a hard drive to a server, and it makes the work accessible from a Web address.

Dreamweaver offers built-in FTP capability. When you have your FTP settings correctly specified, transferring files is no different than copying files from your hard drive to a disk. Invisibly, Dreamweaver keeps track of all your files and links, as you learned in the last session.

You are not required to use Dreamweaver to place your files on a server. FTP has been around for a long time, and you can find many excellent programs that can be used to transfer files from your computer to a server. However, when you use a separate program, you lose many of the automated site management tools that make Dreamweaver so powerful. For any of the work you will complete during this course, I strongly recommend that you use Dreamweaver's FTP.

Dreamweaver FTP

Dreamweaver's Site panel *is* the FTP screen. When you transfer a file from a local folder to the server, you are using FTP. Dreamweaver checks the file to see if there are any dependent files and then asks you if you would like to transfer those files along with the file or files you have specified. Dreamweaver also checks to make sure that you have saved the file you are transferring and gives you the opportunity to save the latest version if you have omitted that step. Other FTP programs can get your file to the server, but they cannot offer the extra safety features.

The following applies to you only if your host has full FTP capability: Many free hosts allow pages to be added only through the page-building tools offered on the site. In these cases, you will have to prepare your pages in Dreamweaver and copy your code to the appropriate template. If you are serious about Web design, I advise that you make the commitment to a site that allows full FTP access. Many of the low-cost hosts charge under $10 per month.

Gathering information for FTP setup

The first time you set up FTP, it may seem difficult. However, as long as you fill in accurate information, it will work. The secret is to collect the correct information.

Take a quick look at where you enter the information so that you know where you are going. Figure 5-1 shows the Remote Info screen on the Site Definition window for the Holiday site you set up in Session 3. You'll go there to enter your information in a few minutes. For now, I just want to move through each section to help you gather the correct information. You need all the following information to move on:

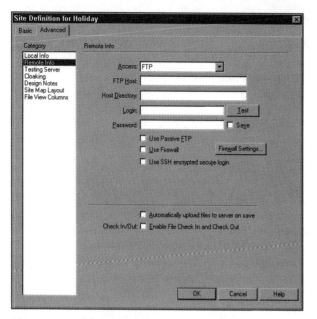

Figure 5-1 *The Site Definition window for the Holiday site, with the Remote Info section active and FTP chosen for Access.*

- **FTP Host:** This is the address for your host. It may be a simple address like `foresite. net`, or it may be DNS (Domain Name System) numbers such as 209.43.2.115. If you are uncertain, check the host's Web site, or ask your host for the correct entry. Unless this entry is correct, you will be unable to connect to your host.

- **Host Directory:** This directory is different for each host, and it states the path required to find your files on the remote server. Often, there is a long path to specify where your files will be stored. Check your host's Web site for this information, or ask your host for the correct path. Without the correct path specified, you may be able to connect to the host and you may be able to place your files, but nobody will be able to find them from the Web.

- **Login:** This is the user name you chose (or were assigned) when you signed up with your host. Unless this is correct — and it is usually case-sensitive — you will not be able to connect to your host.

- **Password:** When you signed up with the host, you chose — or were assigned — a password; passwords are nearly always case-sensitive. Without the correct password, you will not be able to connect to your host. You can have Dreamweaver save your password so you do not have to type it in every time by checking the Save option next to your password.

Dreamweaver hides the actual characters of your password and will not allow this entry to be copied. For safety, you should write down the password for your account and store it in a very safe place.

**20 Min.
To Go**

Setting up FTP for your site

Now that you have all the correct information at hand, you can activate the FTP function for your Holiday site. You must provide FTP information for each site you define.

Take the following steps to define your FTP settings:

1. Open Dreamweaver's Site panel.
2. Select Site ⇨ Edit Sites. The Edit Sites window opens.
3. Select the Holiday site from the list and choose Edit. The Site Definition window opens.
4. Select Remote Info from the Category list.
5. Select FTP from the Access drop-down list box. Several blank fields appear.
6. Type the address for your FTP Host as previously described.
7. Type the correct path for your Host Directory as previously described.

If you are planning to place your files in a remote folder that is not the root folder for your server, you must create the folder on the server before you specify it as the Host Directory for your site. For example, I have the Holiday site in a folder called holiday on my wpeck.com **site. Before I was able to specify the whole path, including the holiday folder, I had to connect to the root directory and create the holiday folder in my remote root directory. I then changed the Host Directory for the Holiday site to the holiday folder in my root site.**

8. Type your user name (log-in) and password as previously described. Click the test button to ensure that your information is correct.
9. Click Save to save your password for future sessions.
10. Leave all other options unchecked and click OK. Click Done in the Define Sites window to complete the process. If the information you gathered is correct, and if you entered it all perfectly, you should be ready to connect to your server.
11. Click the Expand/Collapse icon to expand the Site panel. Make sure you are online (however you connect to the Internet must be active). Select Site ⇨ Connect, or click the Connect button. An alert window opens informing you that Dreamweaver is attempting to connect to your server address.

If all the information you entered is correct, you quickly see a listing in the right column that reflects the path you entered as your Host Directory. Figure 5-2 shows that there is a long path to the directory. In fact, the final directory, holiday, does not have room to display correctly.

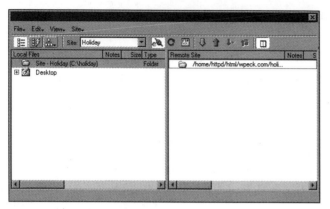

Figure 5-2 *The Holiday site is connected to the server when you see the root folder for the remote site.*

If your Internet connection is behind a firewall, see your technical advisor for instructions on setting up your FTP.

Congratulations! You are now ready to start publishing to the Web. Be sure to test that all systems are go while you become more familiar with files and folders in Dreamweaver.

On the other hand, you may not be celebrating right now. If your FTP connection did not work, step through the process again, right from the start. If that does not solve the problem, get in touch with the technical support people for your hosting company. Make sure you include all the entries you made while attempting to make the connection. Use the titles that you find listed near the beginning of this section, and retype the settings that you used in your unsuccessful attempt. Most likely, the support staff will instantly spot your error and quickly get you up and running.

Dreamweaver creates a log of FTP activity during a session. If you select View ⇨ Site FTP log in the Site panel menu, you see everything that happened during the current FTP session. Read through to see if you can identify the problem. It may not make sense to you, but it could help your technical support representative solve your problem for you. Simply select the text in the file and paste it into an e-mail to transfer the report. This lets your technical support person know exactly where you are having trouble.

Creating a Folder on Your Remote Site

In Session 4, you created a document with the highly creative name of session4.html. You also created a folder called art, into which you placed 4insert.gif, an image from the CD-ROM. Now you want to transfer these files to the Web.

It is vital that you keep the same structure for your remote files as you have for your local files. To that end, I actually make you work a little harder for this exercise than is required. I don't make you do that forever — just for this one little exercise. And I won't keep you in the dark.

Although Dreamweaver does the work for you, it's important for you to know how to create a folder on a remote site yourself. You might occasionally want to make a few manual changes. On rare occasions, the automatic transfer and folder creation does not work correctly.

In this exercise, you create a new folder in your Holiday site to reflect the structure of your local site.

Take the following steps to create a folder on the remote site:

1. Make sure that the Holiday site is active and connected to the remote server. Expand the Site panel to show both local and remote files.

2. Highlight the folder in which you would like to place the new folder, in this case, the root directory on the remote site.

3. Select File ⇨ New Folder from the Site panel Menu (Mac: Site ⇨ Site Files View ⇨ New Folder). A new folder appears with its name, Untitled, highlighted. Type **art** to name the new folder.

The remote and local folder structures are now identical.

Remember that Dreamweaver keeps track of all files and folders, which files are linked to other files, and so on. To transfer everything you have in the Holiday folder, simply tell Dreamweaver to transfer the HTML file to the remote server. Dreamweaver asks if you want to include all the dependent files. When you say yes, all files are transferred, creating folders as necessary to place dependent files.

Transferring files to your remote site

It's time to transfer your files. Take the following steps to transfer the files:

**10 Min.
To Go**

1. Make sure your Holiday site is open and that you are connected to the remote server. If your Site panel view is collapsed, expand it to show both local and remote files.

2. Highlight session4.html in the local window. Drag the file to the root folder in the remote site.

3. An alert window appears asking if you would like to include the dependent files. Select Yes. An alert window opens providing transfer details, such as which file is currently transferring to the remote site.

With all folders expanded in both the remote and local sites, your screen should closely resemble the screen shown in Figure 5-3. Note that while you only specified that the file session4.html should be transferred, the file 4insert.gif was also transferred, because the session4.html requires this image to display properly.

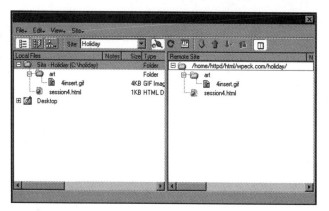

Figure 5-3 *The remote and local sites are identical.*

You should be able to see this page on the Web now. Open your favorite browser and type in the correct URL for your site in your address bar, for example, `www.youraddress.com`. You will also need to tell the browser which file to view, because you have not yet created an index.html page. (index.html is the common name for the start page on any Web site, and all other pages link from there.) In this case, though, you are going to tell the browser to go to your address and find the specific file. To carry on the example, the full address is `www.yourname.com/session4.html`.You may have set up the Holiday folder as part of another site, as I have done on my own site.

Transferring an entire site to the remote server

You can create a Dreamweaver site from files you created before you started using Dreamweaver by simply defining a site as you did in Session 3. Now you need to get that site onto the Web, but you don't want to do it one file at a time.

In Session 3, you created a second site called Crash Course. Now you are going to create a new folder in the Holiday remote site to place the Crash Course site online. Although this may seem a little confusing to start, it is another idea I want to present to you while you have examples with only a few files that are not critically important. In effect, you are going to create a site within a site.

Take the following steps to prepare to transport the Crash Course site to the remote host:

1. With the Holiday site active, follow the instructions in the previous section and create a folder in the Holiday remote site called **crashcourse**. Make sure that the Holiday site root folder is selected when you create the new directory.

2. Activate the Crash Course site. Following the directions for creating FTP settings, create FTP settings for the Crash Course site. Use the same values as you did for the Holiday site, but add crashcourse/ to the Host Directory path. This sets the path to the Holiday root folder and points to the crashcourse folder.

3. Connect the Crash Course site to the server. Note how the root folder for the site is the path to the Holiday site with the addition of crashcourse. (Hold your cursor over the root folder to see the full path, as shown in Figure 5-4.) Although the Crash Course site is located in a folder on the Holiday site, as far as Dreamweaver is concerned, the Crash Course remote site starts with the crashcourse folder.

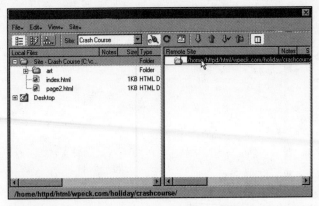

Figure 5-4 *Although you know that the crashcourse folder is part of the Holiday site, Dreamweaver ignores anything in a site listing that is above the root folder. Your remote files may be on the left, depending on your settings.*

You are now ready to move the Crash Course site to the server. You will do this with one action. Although you only have a few files and one folder in this site, the exact same operation would transfer a site with many folders and hundreds of files.

Take the following steps to move the Crash Course site:

1. Make sure that the Crash Course site is active and connected to the server.
2. Highlight the root folder on the local site, which will be C:\crashcourse (PC) or Macintosh HD:crashcourse (Mac) if you have created the folders exactly as I have.
3. Drag the root folder on the local site to the root folder of the remote site.
4. An alert window will pop up asking if you wish to put (transfer to the server) the entire site. Click OK. The entire site will be transferred to the remote server.
5. Click the Refresh button beside the site listing in the upper part of the screen. This will rearrange the files and folders to display exactly as the local site is delayed. The order of appearance makes no difference. I simply want to avoid confusion at this point.

The remote site and local site are now identical.

Because you are transferring the entire site, you are not asked whether you wish to have the dependent links transferred with the files. All files in that site will be transferred, which naturally includes all dependent files.

To see the connection between the Holiday and the Crash Course site, activate the Holiday site again, and connect to the server. As you can see in Figure 5-5 (all folders have been expanded), crashcourse is a folder in the Holiday site. Because crashcourse is a level below the Holiday site on the remote server, it will show in the Holiday remote site. It is not, however, part of the Holiday local site, because Crash Course has a completely different root folder.

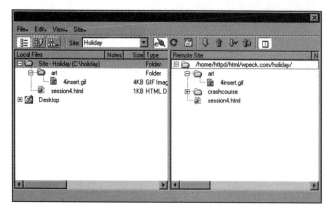

Figure 5-5 *The Holiday site shows the crashcourse folder. When the Crash Course site is active, however, there is no indication of the Holiday site, because the Holiday root folder is one level higher than the Crash Course root folder.*

Finally, activate the Crash Course site again and you will see that there is no indication of the Holiday site, except in the path to the Crash Course root folder.

The path to view your Crash Course site on the Web will be http://your-site.com/holiday/crashcourse/. **Because you do have an index.html page on this site, you do not need to specify a filename.**

I know this is a little complicated, but it is vitally important for you to understand the relation between root and local sites, as well as root folders on the local and remote sites. It is not unusual to have small sites within larger sites, and this is the best way to see how the local and remote sites relate to one another. Once you have fully mastered the concepts, you will have a lot of freedom to create your own sites.

If you have only a tentative grasp of the last exercise, make it a point to come back a little later in the course and follow through again. Now that the seeds have been planted, you'll find that it will become clearer as you work through the rest of the course and become more familiar with the folder structures.

Editing Files and Folders on Your Remote Site

There is no difference in how you work with files on the remote or the local site. As long as you are connected to the Web, you can delete, move, or rename a file on the remote server exactly as you do on the local site. Simply choose a file from the remote directory and edit as desired.

Be careful here: Always consider that Dreamweaver must be aware of any changes. Most often, changes are best completed on the local site, with the files uploaded to the remote site to update the site.

I delve deeper into site and file management in Sessions 10, 12, and 26.

In the next session, you build pages with more definition, including new pages that form your first small site.

Done!

REVIEW

Remember these points from this session:

- File Transfer Protocol is used to transfer files from your hard drive to the Web.
- You should always use Dreamweaver's FTP to move your files.
- Every host has different settings for FTP.
- You can edit files and folders on the remote server, but it is best in most cases to make changes on your local copy and upload them to the remote server.
- You can drag and drop local files to your remote server.
- Dreamweaver can transfer an entire site to the Web.

QUIZ YOURSELF

1. Why should you always use Dreamweaver to transfer files for your site? (See the "Dreamweaver FTP" section.)
2. If your FTP connection to a host is not working, what information should you send to the technical support division of your hosting company? (See the "Setting up FTP for your site" section.)
3. How can you make sure that your password is saved for future FTP sessions? (See the "Gathering information for FTP setup" section.)
4. Where can you find the FTP Site log, and how can it help technical support assist you? (See the "Setting up FTP for your site" section.)
5. The remote and root folders can be different. How can this be, and why might it be a good idea? (See the "Transferring an entire site to the remote server" section.)

Building a Dreamweaver Site

Session Checklist

✔ Understanding tables versus CSS positioning

✔ Creating a paper mock-up

✔ Creating and editing a table in Dreamweaver

✔ Aligning a table

✔ Inserting an image

✔ Inserting text

✔ Aligning elements in a table

**30 Min.
To Go**

In this session, you start to build a working site. All of the images and text you require are provided for you so that you can concentrate on learning the techniques. This is the first of two sites you create in this Crash Course. The first site includes all of the basic techniques you require for every site you will build. The second site, starting with Session 17, provides the opportunity to work with Dreamweaver's advanced features.

You start this project by learning about tables. Although tables were never meant to provide page layout in the original HTML specifications, designers looking for more page layout control quickly put them to use. The Web has never been the same.

Tables versus CSS Positioning

There are three methods for producing a layout for Web pages. The first is using nothing but HTML markup, which offers very little control. With monitors reaching well over 1000 pixels wide as a standard resolution, HTML alone will not display text with line lengths that are easily read.

The second method, Cascading Style Sheets (CSS), offers the power to position your content with great flexibility, relatively simple code, and exceptional control over the appearance of your page. However, and this is a huge however, there are still major compatibility issues with many browsers. Using CSS for positioning, Dreamweaver has the capability to produce pages created in layers (see Session 27). It is easy, but only CSS experts can do the troubleshooting that ensures pages can be viewed by older browsers. This is not the place for beginners to be working if their pages will be seen by the general public.

Please do not ignore CSS positioning. Set up a personal site and learn how to troubleshoot for the various browsers. I guarantee you that your effort will not be wasted. CSS is the future of page development for the Web.

Currently, however, tables still offer the best option to create pages that are well organized and compatible with all browsers. Used properly, tables are the most dependable tools to control your layout. Using them properly means planning your layout and tables carefully before you start to build your page. I cannot stress this point enough. Some people plot their table structure out on paper before they start designing. I generally start with a test page, planning my tables and layout in Dreamweaver. I rarely use my test page, preferring instead to use it as a testing ground, and then I recreate the table structure on a clean document.

Whether you test tables on paper or on the computer, make sure that you make this stage a regular part of your creation process. It is very difficult to change your table structure on a page with all the content in place. Successful tables and clean code work hand in hand. It is much faster to work cleanly than to clean up the mess later.

Tables are often badly used — more so when a program like Dreamweaver is used as the creation tool. Tables are so easy to build in Dreamweaver, it is quite common to get carried away by the impulse to control every single inch of the screen. Placing one table inside another table — known as *nesting* — can be a very effective way to create your layout. However, moderation is the key.

Never nest many tables to create your layout. Tables must be used intelligently. If you find you are creating tables within tables within tables, you are heading for trouble. Not only will your page load very slowly, but many browsers do not handle nested tables well (see Figure 6-1). A little creative thinking will usually present a much better option than nesting many tables.

Keep my warnings in mind as you move on to creating tables. I don't want to make you nervous, but if I'm going to overemphasize just one point, this is a good place to pick. Clean, working tables will make your design life a pleasure. Many nested tables and code that has been edited many times, leaving behind spaces and assorted disorder, will lead to self-destructive behavior that can leave you bald.

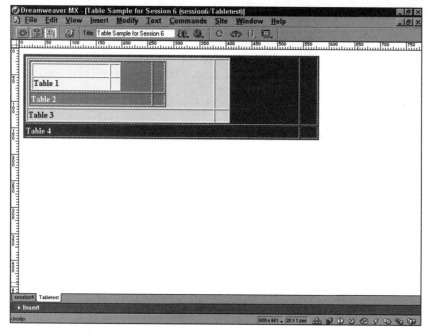

Figure 6-1   *Four nested tables — exactly how tables should NOT be used for Web design. Although it is an easy way to control layout, the increased load time and unpredictable results in some browsers make the cost too high.*

Creating a Table in Dreamweaver

I know die-hard hand-coders who use Dreamweaver for one task only — creating tables. The following code is an example of a two-row, two-column, empty table:

```
<table width="75%" border="1" cellpadding="10">
  <tr>
    <td> </td>
    <td> </td>
  </tr>
  <tr>
    <td> </td>
    <td> </td>
  </tr>
</table>
```

Now imagine that you require four columns and four rows, and you can see why you might be reluctant to do the typing, not to mention the confusion factor once the cells are filled with content.

Dreamweaver provides the tools to create and edit tables easily. Make sure you understand the basics of this section before you move on to the next session, which stretches
your table beyond the basics.

To simulate the production method I recommend, you start here with a test page. I guide
you step-by-step through the table creation, of course. Finally, you create a new page with
a fresh table into which you place images and text.

Creating a paper mock-up

As I mentioned earlier, many designers prefer to plot their direction on paper before they
open Dreamweaver. Figure 6-2 is the hand-drawn layout of the table you will build in this
session. Notice how I have drawn the cells of the table and then worked the content over
several cells. You must have a general idea of how tables work before you can create a drawing like this for your project.

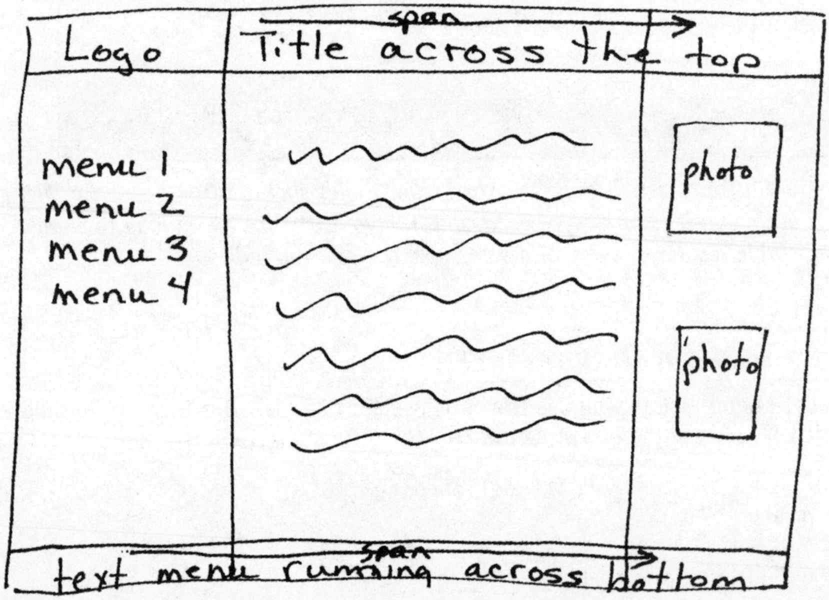

Figure 6-2 *A hand-drawn table layout provides a quick way to design your table.*

> **Drawings and test tables can be a little like the chicken and egg question.
> Which really comes first? If you are new to tables, you may have better luck
> experimenting with a few test tables in Dreamweaver before you attempt to
> draw a mock-up diagram. But why bother if you have already figured it out
> in the test file? A drawing will help you to see the structure of your tables
> and can help keep you on track as you insert your content. This is especially
> true if you are using nested tables.**

Creating a table

Now that you know where you are going, start building your table. You work from a blank document created from the menu in your Holiday site. This method of creating a table is interchangeable with creating a menu from the Site panel that you learned in Session 4.

1. Make sure that the Holiday site is active.
2. Create a new document from the menu. Save your file. Select File ⇨ Save As **tabletest.html** in the root folder of the Holiday site, C:\holiday\ if you have used my examples.
3. Working in Show Design View, select Insert ⇨ Table. The Insert Table window opens.

   Take a look at the mock-up drawing shown earlier in Figure 6-2. You can see that you need three columns and three rows for this table. Type **3** for the Row value and type **3** for the Column value. Do not leave the Insert Table window yet.
4. Set the Cell Padding (margin between content and cell border) to **10** and the Cell Spacing (distance between cells) to **0**.
5. Set the width to **570**, and then choose Pixels from the drop-down menu. This means that your table will be 570 pixels wide. You will use percentages for widths when you build your second site.
6. Make sure the border is set to **1**. This will place a 1-pixel border around the table and between each cell. For no borders, the setting should be 0.

 Although you do not want a border on your finished table, it is a good idea for beginners to lay out their tables with the borders turned on. It is much easier to see where the table cells are located with the border visible. The border can be turned on and off at any time.

7. Click OK, and your table appears on the page as shown in Figure 6-3.

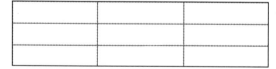

Figure 6-3   *Empty table with borders turned on for easy editing.*

Aligning a table

Usually, the first task you want to do with a table is align it on the page. If the table is to be aligned to the left of the page, do nothing; left alignment is the default table alignment. This exercise is to align the entire table to the right, center, or left of the page. (Content is not affected by this command. Soon you will look at aligning content within the cells.)

Take the following steps to align a table on the page:

1. First, select the table. Place your cursor somewhere in the table, and then select Modify ➪ Table ➪ Select Table OR click the `<table>` tag in the Tag Selector area at the bottom left of the screen.

You can also select a table by clicking the border. When selected, the table border will be darker and the sizing handles will appear.

When the table is selected, the properties for the table are listed in the Properties panel, as shown in Figure 6-4.

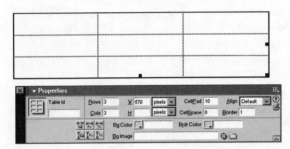

Figure 6-4 *Selection handles indicate that the table is selected. The Properties panel lists properties for the selected table.*

2. With the table selected, choose Center from the Align drop-down menu in the Properties panel. Your table is now located in the center of your document.

This is a perfect time to take a peek at the HTML code that you have produced. Click either the Show Code View button or the Show Code and Design View buttons. Trace through the main table properties `<table>` and through the series of table rows `<tr>` and cells `<td>` to understand the structure of your table.

Editing a table

**20 Min.
To Go**

Even with the best preplanning, you often need to adjust a parameter or two for your table. With the Properties panel, adjusting a table is a breeze. Your table must be selected to make changes, but any properties, including the number of rows or columns, can be adjusted in the Properties panel. You are going to remove the border from this table. I usually work with my table borders set to 0, because Dreamweaver does show an outline for the table cells, but this is a good adjustment to keep in mind. Once your table is filled with content, borders and structure may become hidden in tightly placed graphics. Setting your borders to 1px will often show a problem that is invisible when the border is set to 0.

Take the following steps to edit table borders:

1. Select your table as you did in the previous example.

2. Change the Border value to 0 in the Properties panel. Click away from the entry to save the change. As shown in Figure 6-5, note that Dreamweaver marks the table and cell position with dotted lines when the border value is set to 0.

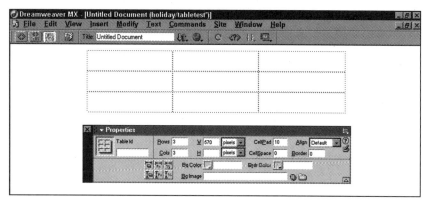

Figure 6-5   *The same table as the one shown in Figure 6-4, but with the borders set to 0.*

For accurate proofing, you can make even the dotted table borders disappear. Select View ⇨ Visual Aids ⇨ Table Borders to toggle table borders on and off.

Merging table cells

Your table is starting to look like the diagram shown in Figure 6-2, but you have a little work to do yet. Refer back to the diagram and note that there are two areas with "span" notations. The top row has only two columns, and the bottom row of the table has one column. You must join the column cells to create this layout.

Take the following steps to merge columns for your layout:

1. Click inside the top-center cell and drag across the center and right column of the top row. Both cells will be selected, as indicated by darker borders.

2. Click the Merge icon near the lower portion of the Properties panel in the Cell section. (Notice the position of the cursor in the Properties panel in Figure 6-6.) The selected cells will be merged.

3. To merge the bottom row, click in the lower-left cell and drag across all three columns to select them.

4. Click the Merge icon to merge the cells. Figure 6-6 shows the completed merge from Steps 1 and 2, with the lowest row of cells selected and ready to be merged.

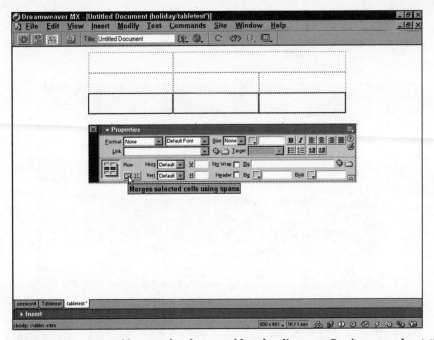

Figure 6-6 *Your table now closely resembles the diagram. Don't worry about the difference in the row heights; the content will force the height as it is inserted into the cells.*

I recommend that you go back to the beginning, create a new document, and work through this entire exercise again. Even better, try to do it without following the text step-by-step. It is very important that you thoroughly understand and remember the methods described here. Work through the exact same steps, but name the file you create in the first step index.html.

If you are already familiar with Dreamweaver tables, or if you feel quite confident that you know how to create a table and merge cells, simply save the file you created as index.html.

Inserting Content into Tables

**10 Min.
To Go**

Now that the table is constructed, you can start to add your content. You have already inserted one image, but now you want to place an image into a table cell. There is a lot more to consider when inserting images into tables. I am going to have you start from scratch. First, you must copy the content files from the CD-ROM that accompanies this book.

Files for this exercise are in the Session 6 folder on the CD-ROM. Locate and copy the contents of the art folder into the c:\holiday\art folder (or into the art folder in the root directory for your Holiday site). Make sure that you do not end up with two levels of art folders.

Copy worddoc6.doc and textdoc6.txt to c:\holiday (or into the root folder for your Holiday site). Check your Site panel, with Holiday active, to ensure that they are in the right location (see Figure 6-7).

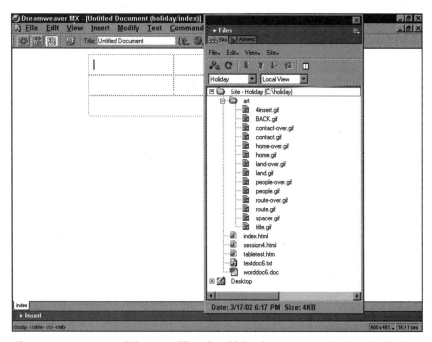

Figure 6-7 *Your Holiday site files should be the same as this list if all files have been saved to the correct location.*

Inserting images

Place the logo in the upper-left cell of your table to start.

1. Place your cursor in the upper-left cell of the table. Your image is inserted at the cursor's location.

2. Select Insert ⇨ Image. The Select Image Source window opens. Select title.gif from the art folder. A preview of the logo appears in the right side of the window. Click OK (PC) or Open or Choose (Mac). Don't worry that your cells seem to be moving at this point. You will get your content into the appropriate places and work on the layout in a few minutes.

For clarity in the instructions, I have used the PC command of OK as the standard acceptance command. Mac users please translate any OK command to Open for OS9 and Choose for OSX.

3. Insert your cursor into the left column of the second row. Repeat Step 2 to insert the file route.gif.

 When you place an image, the image is selected when you return to your document. You are going to place four images for the menu directly beneath another in the same cell. To accomplish this, you must get your cursor back and place a line break to place the next image. With the image selected, press your right-arrow key. This will remove the image selection and place the cursor line that contains the image.

4. With your Shift key held down, click Enter. This inserts a break (<br>) tag, which moves the cursor to the next line without the extra space that a paragraph tag (<p>) inserts.

5. Insert the image file people.gif. This is a good time to look at your HTML code to see how your table looks with content, as well as the <br> tag.

6. Repeat Steps 4 and 5 to insert the land.gif and contact.gif image files.

7. Repeat Steps 3–5 to insert both photo6a.gif and photo6b.gif into the middle row of the right column. Refer to the hand-drawn diagram in Figure 6-2, shown earlier, if you need a guide to place the photos.

Inserting text

Now that you have the images in the table, you are going to add the text. Don't worry if everything looks out of balance. It is important to get the content into place before worrying about fine-tuning the layout. In this example, you enter text manually as well as paste text in from a file.

Take the following steps to create the headline:

1. Place your cursor into the second column of the top row. Type **A tour through our country**.

2. Highlight the text you just typed. In the Properties panel, change the font to Arial, Helvetica, sans-serif. Change the font size to 4. Click the B icon to add the bold attribute to the text.

Take the following steps to insert the body text:

1. Open the file worddoc6.doc (Microsoft Word) or textdoc6.txt (plain text). Select all the text and select Edit ⇨ Copy to copy it.

2. Insert your cursor into the middle cell of the second row and choose Edit ⇨ Paste.

Now that the images and content text are all in the table, it's time to fine-tune the layout. You can specify widths for columns to hold the content in place.

Specifying column width

Although the columns and rows are correctly set up, you must instruct the browser as to how wide to display each column. Different browsers display information — especially tables — in many forms. You can add some control with specified widths.

I delve much deeper into controlling column layout in Session 7, which moves into liquid design.

This sample is a very simple fixed-width table. You must keep a few basic table principles in mind. First, no matter what width you specify for a column, it will never be smaller than the largest graphic it contains. You could specify that every cell in a column should be 75 pixels wide, but if you have a graphic in any cell that is 100 pixels wide, all cells in that column will expand to 100 pixels. The column can be larger than the largest image, but it cannot be smaller.

Never use Dreamweaver's click-and-drag sizing for columns and rows. It is tempting to drag a cell border and place it where you want it; it works very well in Dreamweaver. But browsers do not always — or even often — follow. Also, table height is automatically set when you resize columns or rows, a setting that is rarely required.

Place your widths in the second row. You cannot specify the width of a merged cell, and row two has no combined cells. Placing a width command in one cell controls the width for the entire column.

Take the following steps to correct the layout of your table:

1. Click inside the left column of the second row. Make sure that you can see the cursor and that you do not have an image selected. Your image is 163 pixels wide, so you want your column to be 163 pixels. Enter **163** as the W value, near the center of the lower section of the Properties panel.

2. Click inside the right column of the second row. Specify **100** for the width of the column.

   The left column and the right columns in this table require the space for the images. Because the table width is fixed at 570, a little math will give you the correct size for the center column. Subtract the two column widths from the total table size to determine the width for the center column (570 – 163 – 100 = 307).

3. Click inside the center column of the second row and specify **307** pixels for the width of the column.

   Your table should now closely resemble the sample shown in Figure 6-8. (Note: The bottom row of the table is not visible.)

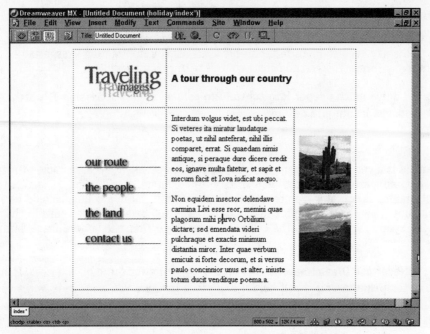

Figure 6-8 *The corrected layout after specifying column width.*

Aligning content in tables

You can align each table cell independently, both horizontally and vertically. Left alignment is the default setting.

 Never specify left justification when it is not needed. HTML naturally defaults to left alignment, and specifying left does nothing but add code, which adds to download time.

Take the following steps to change the alignment for a cell:

1. Place your cursor in the upper-right cell containing the headline.
2. Select Center from the Horz (Horizontal) drop-down menu in the Cell area of the Properties panel (see Figure 6-9).

   The rest of the cells in your table are fine with the default alignment.

You also can select an entire column or row and specify justification. Simply move your cursor over the upper border of the column or over the left border of a row until the cursor changes to a solid arrow. Click, and the entire row or column will be selected.

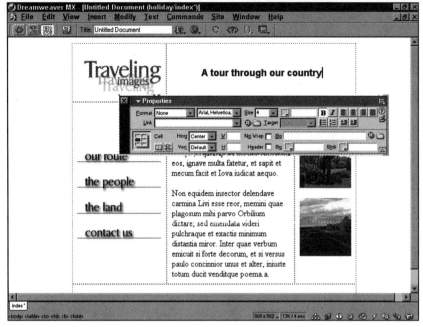

Figure 6-9 *Setting the horizontal alignment (Horz) for the cell changes the head-line text alignment to center.*

Done!

REVIEW

- Tables are used for dependable, cross-browser–compatible Web page designs.
- Properly designed tables can help you control layout.
- Nesting tables can increase download time and cause problems for some browsers.
- Most table editing is accomplished with the Properties panel.
- Merging table cells can help you create a more exciting page layout.
- It is important to watch your code as you are building tables; much of the trouble-shooting work you do involves tables.
- Text can be added by typing directly into Dreamweaver, or by cutting and pasting from a word processing program or a text editor.
- Setting column widths can help to control your layout, but column heights rarely need to be adjusted and setting them should be avoided.

QUIZ YOURSELF

1. What advantage do tables have over using CSS positioning for page layout? (See the "Tables versus CSS Positioning" section.)

2. Why should you not nest tables? (See the "Tables versus CSS Positioning" section.)

3. Why should you view a table with a border of 1 pixel when your design does not call for borders? (See the "Creating a Table in Dreamweaver" section.)

4. How do you enter a non-paragraph line break
? (See the "Inserting images" section.)

5. Why should you never use Dreamweaver's click-and-drag function to move column or row borders? (See the "Specifying column width" section.)

6. What is the default justification for any element in Dreamweaver? (See the "Aligning content in tables" section.)

Using Tables for Liquid Design

Session Checklist

✔ Understanding monitor resolution

✔ Designing for varied resolutions

✔ Understanding liquidity

✔ Creating liquid design in Dreamweaver

✔ Creating a table using percentage values

✔ Inserting a clear GIF placeholder

*30 Min.
To Go*

When you are designing your page, the hardest thing you face is not where to place your graphics or text, or even what colors you should use. The hardest part of designing for the Web is that you have no idea what monitor, what platform (Mac or PC), and what browser will be used to display your page.

This chapter is devoted entirely to overcoming the differences in monitor resolution that affect the display of your pages. You build a page that will grow and shrink as the monitor resolution changes, preventing horizontal scrolling at low resolutions, and yet filling the screen for high-resolution monitors. The term *liquid design* is a popular way to describe this design principle. More than almost any other design technique, adding liquidity to your design gives your work a professional look and feel. Any designer can make a page that looks good at one resolution on one platform and in one browser. The skill comes in being able to say, "Bring them all on — my page is ready."

Understanding Monitor Resolution

Resolution is, quite simply, the number of pixels that your monitor uses to fill your screen. It is expressed in a pixel value, with the width first. If your monitor is set to 800 × 600 pixels, your monitor is using 800 pixels across and 600 pixels down to show everything onscreen. If you are viewing a document that is 850 pixels wide, you must scroll to the right to see all the information. Likewise, if the monitor has more than 600 pixels of information to display, a scroll bar will be provided to allow you to see the information on the lower edge of the document.

Computer users of some experience can change the resolution settings for their monitors, but most do not. The vast majority of monitors are never changed from the factory-set resolution, which means that as a designer, you are building pages that will be seen on monitors ranging from 640 pixels wide to over 1500 pixels wide, and that value is increasing as each new generation of monitor is introduced.

Although monitor size and resolution have some degree of association, you must not make the mistaken assumption that the two are directly related. There is no reason why a 15-inch monitor cannot be set to either 640 or 800 pixels wide. Likewise, a 17-inch monitor is most likely set to 800 or 1024 pixels wide, but it also can be set to 640 pixels and — if your eyes are very good — even into the 1200+ pixel range.

What does resolution mean for design?

In Web design, try to keep any scrolling to a minimum. Web designers turn themselves inside out to prevent horizontal scrolling, because scrolling in two directions is frustrating and confusing for visitors.

I have included an optional exercise for you. If you are entirely comfortable with how content and monitor resolution work together, this exercise will waste your time. If, however, you have only a tentative grasp of this concept, you should take a few minutes and watch as a graphic creates a scroll.

Locate the Session 7 folder on the CD-ROM. Copy the file linetest.html to your Holiday site root folder. Copy the files redline400.gif and redline1200.gif to the art folder of your Holiday site root folder.

Take the following steps to see a horizontal scroll caused by a graphic:

1. Copy the files to your Holiday site as described in the preceding CD-ROM note.
2. Open the linetest.html document. Note how you must scroll a long way to the right to see the end of the red line. This line is 1200 pixels wide.

If your monitor is set for a very high resolution, you will not see a scroll. Reset your monitor resolution to a width less than 1200 to see the effect described here.

3. Now replace the 1200-pixel line with a line that will fit. Double-click the red line to open the Image Source window. Select redline400.gif and click OK. The scroll disappears. Even if you use a smaller view for your window, the line still fits without a scroll as long as the window size is greater than the length of the line (plus a few pixels for the window borders).

4. Note how the text wraps to the window, no matter what the size. This session addresses keeping text in place later in the session. For now, it is only important that you understand that graphics can create a horizontal scroll, and that you should work hard to prevent this from happening in your design work.

5. You can delete the files used for this exercise because you will not need them again.

Now that you have seen the result of content forcing a scroll, you should see a little more clearly why monitor resolution is so important to us as Web designers. When you are designing for print, you can do nothing unless you know the size of the paper for your project. But in Web design, you simply do not know the size of your paper.

Designing for varied resolutions

You must choose a main resolution for your design work. I have always worked with the lowest common resolution for my design work. When I first started with design, that meant 640 × 480 pixels. As the older monitors and video cards dropped out of service, and the number of people using 800 × 600 pixel resolutions increased to over 50 percent, I switched. Even though monitor widths such as 1024 pixels are now quite common, I still do my work with my monitor set to 800 pixels wide.

I design for scroll-free display at an 800-pixel width. If I can create a scroll-free display for 640-pixel-width monitors without affecting the design, I will work hard to create that effect. However, the number of low-resolution monitors in use is declining every day, and it is very difficult to create pages that display without a scroll at low resolution and still fill a 1024-pixel-wide screen.

There is a compromise, even when you choose to allow a scroll at 640 pixel widths. It is a good idea to place the most important information in the left and center portions of the screen. Place the least critical information in the area that can only be accessed by scrolling when seen on a low-resolution monitor.

It is always the best practice to have all the most important information available on a page without scrolling either vertically or horizontally. The area of the screen that is presented when a visitor first lands is known as "above the fold," a term borrowed from the print world, and is the prime real estate for any page. You can simulate lower-resolution displays in Dreamweaver by clicking on the Window Size setting in the status bar at the bottom of the document screen.

**20 Min.
To Go**

Understanding Liquidity

Once you understand the resolution "problem" and have enough information to make your personal or professional choice as to which resolutions to use as your targets, you are only a short distance along the road to creating liquid design. The major work comes when you try to create liquid pages or, as one of my students paraphrased, "stretchy" pages. However, I have never lost my delight at how Dreamweaver makes such short work of complicated tables — the backbone of liquid design.

The terms *liquid, ice,* and *jelly* have become a popular way to explain the different types of pages commonly in use on the Web. Liquid implies that the content will stretch and shrink as the window resizes. Ice pages contain content at a fixed size; the pages look exactly the same no matter what the monitor resolution or window size may be. Ice pages are anchored to the upper-left corner of the screen. Jelly pages, like ice pages, have content with a fixed width. However, jelly pages are centered on the page so that the extra space around the content in a higher-resolution monitor will be divided equally on either side of the content.

Liquidity works through variable-width tables, using the principle that text line length will naturally expand and shrink as its container becomes larger or smaller.

In the last session, you placed a table. You made that table 570 pixels wide. Whether you view that table with a 640-pixel-wide monitor or at the highest resolution, cutting-edge monitor, that table will still only cover 570 pixels. However, you have a powerful tool in another HTML table command — `<table width="x%">`, where *x* is the percentage of the screen you wish your table to fill.

Compare the sets of tables in Figures 7-1 and 7-2. In Figure 7-1, two tables are shown. The upper table has a table width of 95%, while the lower table has a fixed width of 760 pixels. On an 800-pixel-wide display, the two tables are nearly identical.

Skipping down to Figure 7-2, you see quite a difference from the previous figure. This view is in a reduced window. See how the upper table is still displaying all the content with a slight margin on either side of the table — 95 percent of the screen is still filled. The right portion of the lower table is not even visible though, because the table is fixed and the window is now smaller than that fixed size.

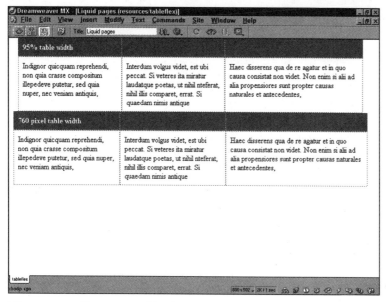

Figure 7-1   *The upper table is set to 95% width, with the lower table set to 760 pixels. With an 800-pixel-wide display, the tables are nearly identical. Figure 7-2 shows how they differ.*

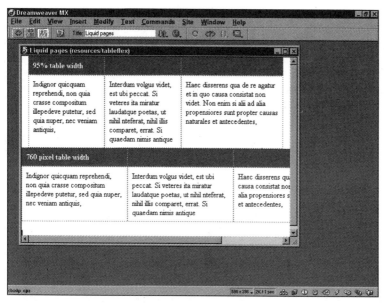

Figure 7-2   *When the window size is reduced, the upper table set to 95% simply shuffles all the content into a smaller space. The fixed-width table, however, cannot adjust, and the right portion of the content is hidden. Note the scroll bars have appeared.*

Liquid Design Basics in Dreamweaver

Although it takes a little more work in the planning stages, the rewards for using liquid design include better use of screen space (often called *screen real estate*) at higher resolutions, and a more professional appearance for your pages. Designers may hate to see horizontal scroll bars on their work, but it can be equally disturbing to see your carefully balanced page tucked up in one tiny little corner of a huge screen.

I am not so sure how dedicated I would be to liquid design if I had to hand-code my designs, however. Liquid design depends heavily on carefully planned tables with specified cell widths, and often with a nested table or two. If you do your planning right, Dreamweaver gives you the tools to quickly deliver dynamic liquid design.

Creating a table using percentage values

Start with a table that has borders and no content. You create this table in exactly the same way as you created the fixed-width table in Session 6, but here you specify different values.

1. Activate the Holiday site and create a new document. Name this document route.html.

2. Select Insert Table. The Insert Table window will open. Create a 3-column, 3-row table with a Cell Padding value of **10** and a Cell Spacing value of **0**. Specify the width as **95%** and the border as **1**.

3. Before going any further, stop and reduce the size of your Dreamweaver document window. Increase it again. Note how the table becomes smaller as the window gets smaller. This is the basic principle behind liquidity.

4. Just to make sure you have the difference down solidly, edit your table to have a width that is approximately 100 pixels less than your own monitor resolution. For example, if you are using an 800-pixel(wide display, select the table and change the width in your Properties panel to be 800 pixels – 100 pixels = 700 pixels. Make sure there are no docked panels open, and reduce the size of your document window. Notice how a scroll appears as soon as you make your window smaller than the set table size.

 You will have to change the % to pixels value in the drop-down box beside the Width entry field.

5. Reduce your window size and you will see that the table stays the same size but creates a horizontal scroll: *non*liquid design.

6. Return the table width to 95%.

Adjusting cell size with percentage values

That's pretty cool, but what if you don't want equally sized columns? No problem . . . well, maybe a few problems, but nothing that can't be solved. You have to find the problems first, though.

Take the following steps to specify the size of your columns:

1. Insert your cursor into the left cell in the second row of the column (you edit the first row later in this session). In the Properties panel, specify the cell width (W) as **20%** (make sure you type the % sign; without the % sign, the 20 means 20 pixels).

2. Insert your cursor into the center cell in the second row of the column. In the Properties panel, specify the cell width (W) as **50%**.

3. Insert your cursor into the right cell in the second row of the column. In the Properties panel, specify the cell width (W) as **30%**.

How's your math? Add the cell percentage widths of 20% + 50% + 30% and you get 100%. But wait! Isn't your table 95% wide? Yes, it is, but the two numbers are NOT related. The table is taking up 95% of the available window. The cell widths must add up to 100% of the table width (for this example).

With a table set up as this one is, the table width ranges from approximately 570 pixels wide for a 640-pixel-wide resolution (95% of approximately 600; don't forget there are a few pixels needed for window borders, scroll bars, and so on), to over 1000 pixels for a 1200-pixel-wide resolution. The cell widths adjust according to the size of the table. For example, the left column, which is set for 20% of the table width, ranges from approximately 114 pixels to over 200 pixels wide for the same resolutions previously described.

But what if you need more control than that for your design? Read on.

Combining percentage and fixed-column widths

10 Min. To Go

First, let me offer a caution. You can exhibit a reasonable amount of control over how your page displays, even with liquid design. However, when you are using percentage widths, you have to accept that, rather than designing exactly how your page will look, you are designing for a range of appearance. A page designed to be perfect at 800 pixels wide will look a little squished at 640 pixels. It is also likely to be a little more spread out than you would like at 1200 pixels wide. You are working to provide a great page to the majority of browsers, and an acceptable page that is easy to use for all who fall outside of your defined range.

What you can do is control at least part of the page so that menu columns and graphics display as they should. This is most often accomplished by combining fixed- and percentage-column widths in one table. A common and reliable setup is to have the left columns fixed and to have the columns at the right expanding and contracting.

In other words, you need to change the values of the column widths in the table you just created.

You may wish to open the file index.html in the Holiday site, because you will be following this layout closely as you build the next page.

Creating a fixed-width column

To begin, make the left column a fixed width. Insert the first menu item before you adjust the width, as you take the width value from the graphic.

Before starting the next exercise, locate the Session 7 folder on the CD-ROM. Copy the files photo7a.jpg, photo7b.jpg, and spacer.gif to the art folder of your Holiday site.

1. Open the Holiday site and the document route.html (it may still be open).
2. Turn off your borders by selecting the table and specifying Border **0** in the Properties panel.
3. Insert your cursor inside the left cell of the top column. You are going to add the logo file to this cell. Select Insert ⇨ Image. The Insert Image window will open. Locate the file title.gif in the art folder. Select the file, and then click OK to return to the document. You will not see much change in the table.
4. Make sure that the graphic you just placed is selected (selection handles and a border will appear around the image). You need to know what width to set your left column, and you will use the graphic width to tell you. You want this column to be consistent no matter what resolution the viewer is using.

   Look at the W and H values in the Properties panel. These list the width and height of the selected graphic. Your width is 163. Make a note of this value.
5. Press your right-arrow key once to deselect the graphic. The cursor will move to the right of the graphic but remain in the same cell. You need to position your cursor here in order to specify the width of the cell. Replace the 20% value listed in the W field with **163** (make sure the % sign is removed). This sets your cell width to 163 pixels.
6. You also want to place the photos into the right column. Insert your cursor into the right column of the middle row. Then, insert photo7a.jpg and photo7b.jpg with a <p> tag (Enter for PC; Return for Mac) between them.

See Session 6 for detailed instructions on inserting two images into a column.

What do you have now? You have a graphic inserted that will prevent the left-hand column from ever shrinking smaller than the image, plus the cell padding, or 163 pixels + 10 + 10 (cell padding on both sides of the cell). In addition, you have told Dreamweaver to make that cell 163 pixels wide, which means that it will not be larger than it is now.

There are exceptions to the last sentence that I cover in the next session, but for our purposes here, this is a true statement.

Controlling percentage and fixed-width column layouts

You have a decision to make at this point. The left column is fixed. But what are you going to do with the other two columns? There are two choices for a liquid design. You can set the columns so that both columns flex with the number of available pixels. The result would be that your text would have longer and shorter lines, depending on the page size. In addition, the column containing your images would expand and contract. Because the images are a fixed size, the only thing that can happen is that the white space will increase or decrease. With larger images, this might be a good choice, but you risk having very small images floating far away from the text, which would likely look disjointed.

Isn't it too bad that you can't set the outer column to be fixed, and just let the text expand and contract to fill the window? The good news is that you can do that. The bad news is (you knew that was coming, didn't you?) that you do have to watch how far you ask your text to stretch. Good communication calls for short paragraphs, especially on the Web. When you are asking your text to do all the stretching to make a page liquid, you risk having one-line paragraphs at high resolutions, which look hideous and are very hard to read.

The answer? Add a little extra space to the photo column. That will give you very short lines of text on a 640-pixel-wide screen. Remember, though, that you are more concerned about your mid-range resolutions. Your photos are 100 pixels wide. If you set the right column to 150 pixels, you can help the text a little. But you must do more than just set the width of a column to add white space.

Using a transparent GIF to control layout

Most browsers will not observe your 150-pixel cell measurement. They do not respect white space and will push your text right over to the photos anyway. You have to convince the browser that you really want that space, and you use a neat little trick to do that. You insert a 1px × 1px image that has been created as a transparent graphic, meaning that it is completely invisible.

Follow these steps to place this graphic at the end of the cell:

1. Position your cursor to the right of the second image and press Enter to move the cursor to follow the images. Press Enter one more time to allow some separation between the photos and the transparent GIF you will place. This image is invisible, so you want it away from your content for easier editing. Insert the image spacer.gif from the art folder in your Holiday site. Do not proceed until you have read the next step; you need the image to remain selected.

2. Check your Properties panel and you will see the size listed as 1px × 1px. Change the width (W) value to **150**. This forces the graphic to 150 pixels and holds the column at that width.

3. Use your right-arrow key to deselect the graphic and position the cursor in the cell. Specify **150** for the cell width (W) value.

4. With your cursor still in the cell, set the cell alignment to Center in the Horz drop-down menu in the Properties panel.

Centering the photos in this column allows you to play with a few more pixels toward a liquid design. You could align to the left and have the photos close to the text, but a wide white space would occur at the right because the 95% table-width setting allows ever larger margins as the resolution is increased. Setting the alignment to the right would align your photos nicely along the edge, reducing that white space, but the photos would then appear too far from the text for solid unity. By using center alignment, you cheat both problems a little. Liquid design is a series of compromises. You do get very good at spotting the opportunities before too long.

Adjust a transparent GIF to the size you require using the W and H fields in the Properties panel, but never resize a graphic in Dreamweaver. The capability is there, but that does not mean you should use it. Graphic programs have better controls for retaining image quality as the size of the image is reduced. Often, I will resize an image in Dreamweaver just to determine the required size, but I *always* take the image back into a graphics program to properly resize it.

Using 100% width for a column

The final step in setting the parameters for your table is to specify what your center column width should be. So far, you have a 163-pixel column containing the 163-pixel title graphic. You have a 150-pixel column held open by a 150-pixel GIF file and containing images that are 100-pixels wide. Your table is 95 percent of the screen width. What are you going to do with the center column?

If you specify a fixed width for the text column, you no longer have a flexible table. But how can you tell what percentage of the table remains available? Good point; you have fixed widths in a flexible table. I was not bad in math, but that is way past what I can calculate.

Luckily, the solution has nothing to do with calculated numbers. In fact, you can use 100% as a message to the browser to "use whatever is left for this column." It seems a bit strange, but think about it for a minute. You have a left column that cannot be less than 163 pixels because the graphic will not collapse. You have the same setting for the right column because you inserted a 150-pixel graphic — the transparent GIF. The table is going to cover 95% of the screen no matter what, as long as graphics do not override that width. By telling the center column that it is to take up 100% of the space, you are telling it to cover what is left.

Remember that browsers do not always respect the widths you specify. You have the two outer columns set so that they can be no smaller than the specified width. The 100%

command tells the browser that you do not want it to decide that the left or right column deserves more space.

Finishing this page

Follow Figure 7-3 to finish the page. Refer back to Session 6 as you put the page together if you need guidance to place the menu images. Add home.gif at the top of the menu items, but delete the route.gif image. You are creating the page that matches that menu item; you do not want it to appear in your menu list, because that is very confusing.

Don't worry at this point if the page is not perfect. You will make a few changes as you move through the techniques in later sessions, and you need to do a final check before you can call this complete.

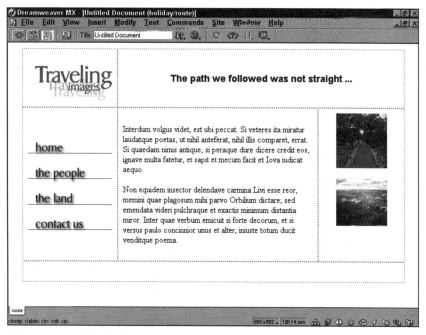

Figure 7-3 *The final appearance for the route.html page at this point. You will make changes as you learn new techniques.*

Done!

REVIEW

Keep these points in mind:

- You must be aware of monitor resolution at all times when you are designing for the Web.
- The most common monitor resolution widths today are 800 pixels and 1024 pixels.

- It's a good idea to place the least important information on a page at the right if you are designing a page that will have a scroll at 640-pixel-width display.
- Tables with percentage values are an efficient way to create liquid design because they collapse and expand with varied monitor resolutions and window sizes.
- You can use a combination of fixed- and percentage-width columns in a column with a percentage width.
- Although you can control the appearance of a liquid page to some extent, you cannot completely control it.
- Browsers will ignore even fixed-width cell sizes if there is no graphic content to keep the cell at that size. You use a transparent, or invisible, GIF file to force cell widths when there is no content.
- Never resize a photo or image in Dreamweaver. It is better to take the image into a graphic program to resize it.

QUIZ YOURSELF

1. What does it mean when a monitor is 800px × 600px? (See the "Understanding Monitor Resolution" section.)
2. What is the result when a graphic is larger than the screen width? (See the "What does resolution mean for design?" section.)
3. What do the terms *liquid, ice,* and *jelly* mean? (See the "Understanding Liquidity" section.)
4. When you set a Dreamweaver table to a width of 95%, what is it 95 percent of? (See the "Creating a table using percentage values" section.)
5. When the number 100, with no value such as pixel or %, is entered into the Properties panel of Dreamweaver, what size will be applied to that value? (See the "Creating a fixed-width column" section.)
6. When a column is specified to be 200 pixels, and a graphic is inserted that measures 250 pixels, what will the resulting size of that column be? (See the "What does resolution mean for design?" section.)
7. Why should you never use Dreamweaver to reduce the size of a photo? (See the "Using a transparent GIF to control layout" section.)
8. Why does a transparent GIF image keep a column at the same size as the GIF file's width? (See the "Using a transparent GIF to control layout" section.)

Enhancing Tables with Background Color and Images

Session Checklist

✔ Adding a table background color

✔ Adding a table background image

✔ Adding a table row background

✔ Adding a table cell background image

✔ Setting up a preview browser

✔ Previewing your page

✔ Troubleshooting table backgrounds

**30 Min.
To Go**

In the previous two sessions, you put basic pages together. You learned how to make your content fill the screen and how to plan your pages so that as many visitors as possible would see attractive, meaningful pages. With that base, you can move on to adding design touches that make your site more visually pleasing. You start by adding color and images to your page and table backgrounds.

Enhancing Tables

Tables are the basis for most layout on the Web. Table backgrounds are the perfect place in which to add color, because very little code is required to specify table or individual cell background color. You can fill a page with color without adding significantly to the download time for your page.

You can add background color to full tables, rows and columns, or individual cells. In addition, you can nest one table inside another. The range of possibilities is endless. One of the best ways to learn more about how to use tables creatively is to find sites on the Web that you like. You can view the source file for any Web page in your browser. Study how the designer has constructed tables and used backgrounds to create the look. All current browsers allow you to save individual pages to your hard drive and open them later in Dreamweaver. With Internet Explorer, you can also save entire Web sites — however, you must never use the code you save to produce your own pages without requesting and receiving permission from the creator, preferably in writing. To do so is illegal and unethical, and just not fair.

Start with the easiest of all table background enhancements: adding a table background. You are going to create a special page for the table background exercises, because no single page should ever have as much added to it as you are going to learn. (In this session, you're working on test documents, although you will apply what you learn here in future sessions.) Make sure that you save the test pages. They will be a valuable resource for the future.

 You should check your code with each step you take, especially when you are working with tables. When you start into complicated liquid layout, reading your table code becomes very important for troubleshooting.

Adding a table background color

Take the following steps to add a background to an entire table:

1. Open your Holiday site and create a new file named tablecolor.html. Open the new document.

2. Create a 3-column, 3-row table with the following parameters: CellPad **10**, CellSpace **10**, Width **95%**, and Border **1**.

3. Select the entire table. In the Properties panel, click the color well for Bg Color. Select a light color from the color palette; I used a light yellow (see Figure 8-1). The color number appears in the Bg Color field, and your table fills with that color.

Adding a cell background color

Often, you may only want to add color to one cell, or to a few cells. The process is similar to adding the color to the entire table, but your selection method is different.

1. Place your cursor in the left column of the top row. To change the color in one cell, you do not need to make a selection. As long as your cursor is in that cell, the color will be added.

2. Click the color well beside the lower Bg field near the lower portion of the Properties panel. Choose a dark color from the color palette and the cell fills with that color.

3. If you want to add color to more than one cell — but not to a full row or column — select only those cells. With Ctrl (PC) or ⌘ (Mac) depressed, select the first and third cells in the bottom row. Choose your background color as you did in Step 2, but choose a different color. The selected cells fill with the chosen color.

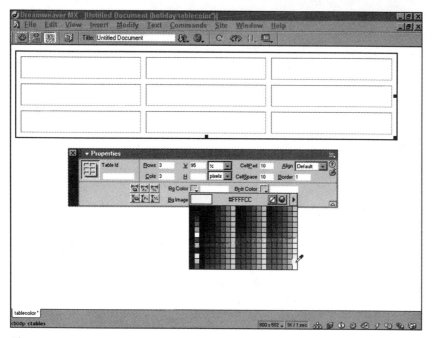

Figure 8-1 *Choosing a background color for an entire table.*

Adding background color to a row or column

Although you can add color to rows or columns cell by cell, there are more efficient ways to add color. In the case of table row backgrounds, working cell by cell creates extra code.

Row background color

Now take a minute or two to see this in action, because it is a very simple way to illustrate how you can create unnecessary code.

1. Click inside the first cell of the second row. Apply a black background to this cell. Repeat this action one at a time for the remaining two cells in the row. Your code for that row will look like this code:

```
<tr>
 <td bgcolor="#000000"> </td>
 <td bgcolor="#000000"> </td>
 <td bgcolor="#000000"> </td>
 </tr>
```

2. Select the entire row by placing your cursor anywhere in the row and choosing the appropriate <tr> tag from the lower-left portion of your screen. You can also choose the row with your mouse. Move your mouse pointer over the left border of the table, at the position of the row that you wish to select. When the cursor changes to a thick arrow, click, and the entire row will be selected.

3. In the Properties panel, select the full entry in the Bg field. Use Delete to remove the entry. The selected row now has no background color. Do *not* deselect the row.

4. Redo the background color, but apply it to the entire row. With the row selected, click the color well beside the Bg field. Choose black from the upper-left corner of the color palette. Again, deselect to confirm the change.

5. Check your code. It should be the same as the following code. You do not have to be a code expert to realize that this is a lot less code. To be exact, the difference is 34 characters — and 34 bytes — nearly 30 percent less.

```
<tr bgcolor="#000000">
<td> </td>
<td> </td>
<td> </td>
</tr>
```

Never think that a little extra code will do no harm. Although you are only saving a few bytes with this one example, sloppy work as you apply attributes can add significantly to the download time over many entries and many pages. It also makes the code much harder to troubleshoot when you encounter browser display problems.

Column background color

Although adding a background to a row and to a column is identical in method, the resulting code is different. The row background is controlled by the <tr> background command. However, HTML has no column background command, so backgrounds are applied on a cell-by-cell basis — it cannot be avoided. I wanted to make sure I stated that clearly so that you do not spend time trying to figure out why you have exactly the same code for this exercise that I was so adamant about preventing in the previous exercise.

Take the following steps to apply a background to a column:

1. Select a column by holding your mouse pointer over the top border, within the area of the column that you wish to select. When the cursor changes to a thick arrow, click to select the column. You can also select a column by clicking and dragging from the first cell to the last cell in the column.

2. Click the color well beside the Bg field and select a color. The cells in the column will fill with the chosen color.

Removing a background color

Take the following steps to remove a background color from a table, row, column, or cell:

1. Select the table, row, column, or cell from which you would like to remove the background color. Use the same selection methods that you used to add the color.

2. Highlight the color number in the Bg or Bg Color field of the Properties panel, and press Delete to delete.

Cell padding and spacing with background color

20 Min. To Go

Cell padding and spacing can be confusing. *Padding* refers to the amount of margin within each cell, while *spacing* refers to the distance between cells. For separating text and images, the two commands do not differ much. However, as soon as you add color to backgrounds, they become fundamentally different.

I would like you to see this in action. The table you created earlier has a Cell Padding value of 10 and Cell Spacing value of 10. You are going to add a bit of text to a few cells. You then copy the table and change the values.

1. Type **Test padding and spacing** into one light-colored cell and into two cells that are side by side, preferably with the same colored background. You will have to change the color of your font to a light color if you have used dark colors for your backgrounds. Note how the text does not spread right to the edge of the cell. This is cell padding at work. The distance between the dotted table borders is the cell spacing.

Don't worry if the text forces the table out of balance; it does not matter for this exercise. However, If you would like the practice, set the column widths to 33%, 34%, and 33% to bring it back into line.

2. Select the entire table. Then, select Edit ⇨ Copy HTML to copy the table.

3. Click at the right edge, behind the table, to place the cursor. Press Enter two times to move the cursor down.

4. Select Edit ⇨ Paste HTML to paste a copy of the table.

5. Select the new table and change the CellSpace to **0**. The cells are now right against one another with no spacing. See how the text still has a margin in the cell? This is because you did not change the CellPad value. Figure 8-2 shows the two versions.

Save the file that you have worked with for this exercise. It will make a good reference document for you in future exercises.

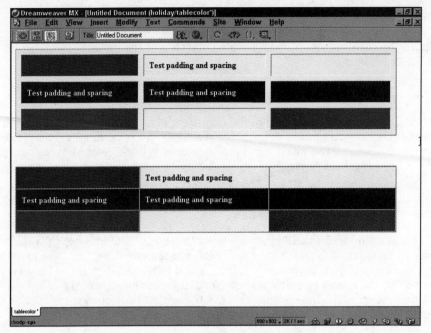

Figure 8-2   *The upper table has cell spacing and padding set to 10. The lower table has the cell spacing set to 0, and the cell padding remains at 10.*

Inserting Table Background Images

Color is fun to work with and adds very little to file size, but you can also add a lot to your pages by using images as backgrounds for your tables. Theoretically, any image can be used as a background, but there are some limitations. You could add a different background image to every cell in a table. However, each image would slow your page load. You must always walk a balance between appearance and load time.

But why would you use an image as a background rather than just placing an image? First, a table background will not affect the dimensions of your table. Remember when you placed an image and the image size forced your column and row size? A background will not do this. The cells will shrink and grow, showing more or less of the background as determined by other content.

If you want to place other content, such as another image or text over your image, you must use a background.

You are going to create another page that you can save for future reference. It can be valuable to have a simple, correct version of a technique to refer to when you are having trouble with that technique later on. Once you have added content, it can be tough to trace down exactly where everything should be. Comparing correct code to your troubled code is the fastest way to trace down a problem.

Locate the Session 8 folder on the CD-ROM. Copy the file back8.gif to the art folder of your Holiday site.

Inserting a table background

Now create a table and add a background.

1. Open your Holiday site and create a new file named tableback.html. Open the new document.

2. Create a 3-column, 3-row table with the following parameters: CellPad **10**, CellSpace **10**, Width **95%**, and Border **0**.

3. Select the entire table. In the Properties panel, click the Browse for file icon beside the Bg Image field. The Select Image Source window will open. Select the file back8.gif from the art folder.

Your table now has a background. Later in this session, you'll preview this table in both Internet Explorer and Netscape Navigator. First, move on to placing a row background and cell background.

Inserting a table row background

When you do not want a background to cover your entire table, you can specify that the background image appear only in a row. The background information is added to the <tr> tag. Create another table to add the row, and then add the cell background.

1. Place your cursor to the right of the table you created in the pervious exercise. Press Enter two times to move the cursor down.

2. Create a 3-column, 3-row table with the following parameters: CellPad **10**, CellSpace **10**, Width **95%**, and Border **0**.

3. If there are no dotted table borders showing when you return to the document, turn on your table borders. Select View ⇨ Visual Aids ⇨ Table Borders.

4. Select the top row. In the Properties panel, click the folder beside the upper Bg field. The Select Image Source window will open. Select the file back8.gif from the art folder. Your background appears in all three cells, but there are white spaces between the cells.

5. Select the table and change the cell spacing to **0** to remove the spacing between cells.

6. Type **This is the top row** in the first cell of this row. (The reason for this entry will become clear in a few minutes.)

Inserting a table cell background

Finally, add a background to a cell. The background information is added to the <td> tag.

1. In the same table, select the first cell of the second row. In the Properties panel, click the folder beside the top Bg field. The Select Image Source window will open. Select the file back8.gif from the art folder.

2. Repeat Step 1 for the second and third cells in the third row.

3. Type **Cell background** in each of the three cells with cell backgrounds. Your table should now resemble the sample shown in Figure 8-3. I have added percentage widths to both tables to control column size.

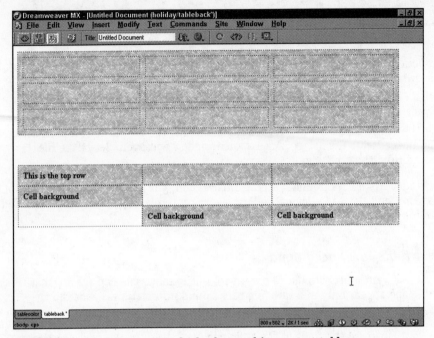

Figure 8-3 *Final appearance for background image test tables.*

   Leave the table backgrounds for a few minutes, and set up your preview browsers. Once you can preview the tables, I'll discuss what you can and cannot do with table background images.

10 Min.
To Go

Previewing a Dreamweaver Document

As you work, you should preview your page often, at least in the two most popular browsers: Internet Explorer and Netscape Navigator. In addition to letting you know that the browsers are interpreting the code to match the layout you created, a preview will also activate functions that do not display in Dreamweaver, such as JavaScript.

For a refresher on how to define a preview browser and preview your Dreamweaver document, review the "Viewing Your Document" section in Session 2.

You must have Internet Explorer and Netscape Navigator installed on your computer for this course. If you would like to add other browsers — for example, Opera — the steps you take are provided in Session 2.

Once you have your preview browsers set up in Dreamweaver, you are ready to see how the browsers are interpreting your pages. You are about to be introduced to one of the toughest elements of Web design. The code you have produced is correct — well, technically correct. However, each browser has its own way of handling that code.

It's a great idea to start a notebook or an electronic note file to keep track of all the browser oddities you discover. You'll save hours in the future if you take the time to make a few simple notes now.

Table Backgrounds and Browsers

If you have not already done so, preview the document that you created in the background images session in both Internet Explorer and Netscape Navigator. Leave both windows open and compare. Considering that these two previews came from the same document in Dreamweaver, the differences are rather astounding. Figure 8-4 shows the result, but you will be better able to see the subtle differences on your own monitor at full size.

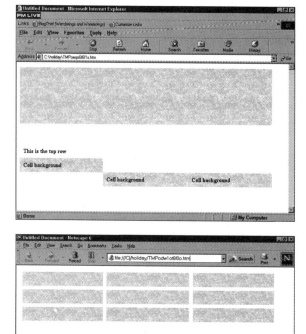

Figure 8-4 *One page and two displays. Notice how the Netscape Navigator 6 version places spaces between the table cells, and that Internet Explorer 6 does not display the row background.*

Assessing the browser interpretation of table backgrounds

Internet Explorer is doing a great job of displaying a unified background in the table and in the cells in the second example. But where is the table row background? Welcome to Web design.

I am going to add a disclaimer. You *may* see a table row background with your platform and Internet Explorer combination.

My disclaimer also tells a lot about this industry, because it is almost impossible to make an absolute statement about *every* browser on both platforms.

Now look at the Navigator preview. Netscape Navigator is not kind to table backgrounds, as you can see in the upper table. You can remove the gaps by specifying 0 cell spacing, but the pattern will start over with every cell. It is almost impossible to get a seamless table background in Navigator by using a background for the entire table.

But isn't that a table row background working perfectly? Yes, it is. Well . . . almost. Look closely at the row and you will be able to see a break in the pattern at each cell. The <tr> tag is recognized, but the background image starts over with each cell.

Working around browser interpretations of backgrounds

By comparing what Internet Explorer and Netscape Navigator can do to your table backgrounds, it becomes clear quickly that this is an area that takes great thought and planning. Often, the fix you apply to correct a problem in Navigator creates a new and different problem in Internet Explorer.

First, if there is another way to accomplish the effect you desire, I would recommend you use it. For example, one way around the problem with backgrounds is to use nested tables. You'll explore that process in Session 19. However, there is too much power in backgrounds — especially <td> backgrounds — when creating liquid design to dismiss them as too complicated or buggy.

You can create separate pages for reading by different browsers. You must create a JavaScript "sniffer," or code that determines what browser and platform your visitor is using. The code then calls for the appropriate page, which has been custom designed for that browser and platform. This is not a popular method, however, because you must create as many sites as the combinations of browsers and platforms you wish to serve.

Never design your page for just one browser and then place a notice on your site that the visitor should use only that browser. It does not take much extra studying to learn how to create code that can be used by all browsers. If you are — or you plan to become — a professional designer, you *must* learn to create cross-browser-compatible code. That is your job!

I have included this set of examples so that you can study what the effects are and make decisions based on what you have seen here. I never create a background for any table tag that has a horizontal repeat, and I usually use only the <td> tag to add a background image for liquid design. (Your second Web site for this course will incorporate this method.)

Each design situation is different. You may come up with a very creative solution to use a background in your table that will work for only one situation — the one you are working on. However, having the samples you created here to refer back to later as you are trying to work around some of the problems will be truly valuable.

Finally, once in a while, it is not a table background you require, but a page background. The next session discusses this.

Done!

REVIEW

Keep these points in mind:

- You can add background color to full tables, table rows, or table cells.
- To add a background color to a table column, you apply a background to all table cells in that column.
- You can select an entire row or column in a Dreamweaver table by clicking in the left or upper border for that row or column.
- You can remove a background color by deleting the entry in the Properties panel.
- Table background images can be applied to full tables, table rows, or table cells.
- Netscape Navigator and Internet Explorer interpret table backgrounds in very different ways.
- When using table backgrounds of any type, you must plan and test carefully.

QUIZ YOURSELF

1. Why is it important to not copy another designer's code directly? (See the "Enhancing Tables" section.)
2. What are the three different types of background color or images that can be added to a table? (See the "Enhancing Tables" section.)
3. There is no code for adding a background to an entire column. How do you add background color to a column? (See the "Adding background color to a row or column" section.)
4. What is the difference between cell padding and cell spacing? (See the "Cell padding and spacing with background color" section.)
5. How does Netscape Navigator interpret a table's background? (See the "Inserting Table Background Images" section.)
6. What is the benefit in specifying a primary and secondary browser in Dreamweaver? (See the "Previewing a Dreamweaver Document" section.)

SESSION

9

Adding Backgrounds, Meta Tags, and Links

Session Checklist

✔ Adding a page background image or color

✔ Setting page margins

✔ Adding meta tags

✔ Adding links to images

✔ Adding alt tags to images

✔ Adding links to text

✔ Creating a text menu

**30 Min.
To Go**

Over the last few sessions, you have been working with tables. In the overview of the Dreamweaver program, that might be seen as backwards, since you are just now moving on to setting basic attributes for pages. However, since tables control almost all layout, I prefer to have that knowledge as the first step.

In this session you focus on the overall appearance of your page. You learn to add page titles, keywords, page descriptions, and background color. Finally, you learn how to create links without text and images. By the time you finish this lesson, you will have all the tools needed to finish your first site.

Creating a New Page

Locate the Session 9 folder on the CD-ROM and copy all the files to the art folder of your Holiday site.

Before you move on to the exercises that follow, it is time to create the rest of the pages in your site. Create pages named people.html, land.html, and contact.html in the same way as you created the previous pages, referring back to Sessions 6 and 7 if you stumble. Place any two of the images you copied from the Session 9 folder on the CD-ROM on the new pages. Add a page headline for each page. Place the correct menu items to reflect the current page, i.e., make sure that the home menu item is in place and that there is no menu item for the current page.

 You may find unexpected gaps between your menu images. The fix is simple, but finding this particular glitch can be an all-day procedure if you do not know how to look for it. Check your code. There may be a space or two between the image tag and the <br> tag. That's the culprit. Remove those spaces and your menu will tighten right up. HTML is supposed to ignore spaces, but it does not always do so. Make a note of this tip somewhere, because it will occur again.

Setting Page Properties

Anything that affects the entire page is created through the Page Properties window (Modify ⇨ Page Properties). This includes page settings for text colors, margins, and background. I'll walk you through a step-by-step example for the most valuable page property features, starting by adding a background color to the page.

Adding a background image or color

You can use an image for a page background. It is best to use a background image that is designed to repeat in one direction only. Small, textured tile patterns are also perfect, because they are designed to repeat seamlessly over any background distance. The background you used for your table in the last session is a perfect example of a tiling background image. The background image for this exercise is already in your art folder.

To use an image as a page background, follow these steps:

1. Open one of your pages.
2. Select Modify ⇨ Page Properties to open the Page Properties window.
3. Click the Browse button beside the Background Image field and select the file BACK.gif from the art folder. Click Apply if you want to implement the effect without leaving the Page Properties dialog box, or click OK to accept the change and return to your document.

You now have a background for your page. Add the background to the other pages in the site if you like the look.

A background color is added in the same way, but you select a color from the Background Color well. When you select both a background color and a background image, the background color will display while the background image loads.

You may wish to try adding a white background to the main text cell. The background you added to the page does not interfere badly with the text legibility, but nothing is as clear as a white background with black text.

20 Min. To Go

Adding a page title

Your page title is important. This is the information that will display in the title bar of your visitors' browsers as they view your page. Your page title also becomes the bookmark name when someone bookmarks your page. In addition, the page title is used in search engine listings, and may have a bearing on the relevance of the page ranking your page receives. Try to make your page title meaningful.

To create a page title, do *one* of the following:

1. Type your title in the Title field in the Dreamweaver toolbar. Use **Traveling Images: The People** for the title of the people.html page, or create your own title. OR

2. Select Modify ⇨ Page Properties and type your page title in the Title field near the top of the Page Properties field.

Add a similar title to each of the pages in your site, modifying the entry to reflect the content on each page.

Adding Head Properties

Head content includes any information that falls between the <head> and </head> tags at the beginning of any HTML page. This is where you place meta tags, hidden information about the document. Some meta tags, including keywords for search engines and page descriptions, have been predefined in Dreamweaver and can be entered by selecting that option from the menu. The head also contains many specialized codes, such as JavaScript. For this exercise, you add a page description, keywords, and an author meta tag.

When you are adding head content, you should enable a small bar that displays an icon for each head tag. Select View ⇨ Head Content from the main menu. Keep this view open while you walk through the following exercises so that you will be able to see the new items added to the head content.

Adding a page description

The text you specify as a page description will appear in search engine listings. To add your page description, select Insert ⇨ Head Tags ⇨ Description, and then type **The story of a trip across this great country** (or feel free to create your own description). Click OK to accept the changes. Note that a new icon has been added to the head content display.

Inserting keywords

Many talented people are making a living exclusively by helping businesses achieve high listings in the search engines. Anything I can say on the subject in one paragraph would not even scratch the surface. Suffice it to say that choosing and using keywords is important.

To add keywords, select Insert ⇨ Head Tags ⇨ Keywords. Type in **trip, tour, family,** *place names* (add some state or province names here), or use your own keywords in the Insert Keywords window. Click OK to return to the document. Note that a new icon has been added to the head content display.

Adding other meta tags

You can enter any data you choose in a meta tag. Designers often use meta tags to add a creation date and author information. The tag consists of two separate entries. The name entry gives the tag a title, such as creation date, and the content entry contains the listing "July 17, 2002."

To add an author tag, select Insert ⇨ Head Tags ⇨ Meta and the Meta window will open. Make sure that Name is selected in the Attribute drop-down box and type **Author** in the Value field. Type your name in the Content area. Click OK to return to your document.

Editing head content

Once you have created a head tag, you can easily edit it. Make sure you have Dreamweaver set to display head content (View ⇨ Head Content). Click any tag in the head section and the Properties panel will display all the relevant information — which you can edit. Figure 9-1 shows the keywords tag.

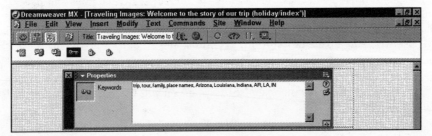

Figure 9-1   *Click any head tag and you can edit content in the Properties panel window.*

Creating Links

I promised you that you would have a site on the Web by noon today, and we are right on schedule. The one task left is to create links to allow visitors to visit all of your pages. You will create links to other pages, as well as to other sites on the Web. You will also create a special link to automatically open a visitor's e-mail program so they can send you a note.

Your site is still a little rough. But you'll need the room for improvement because you have more techniques to learn. Knowing how to retrieve and edit a file, and then get the file tucked safely back on your server, is extremely important. You will fine-tune the site and learn to perform the correct FTP transfers at the same time. For now, you must get those pages connected.

You will spend a lot of time on links, and different types of links, in Session 12.

Adding links to images

Images are often used for menu items. The menu you created for your first site is created from graphics. It takes a surprising amount of code to create a link, but Dreamweaver makes short work of this operation.

Take the following steps to create a link from an image:

1. Open index.html from the Holiday site.
2. Click the "our route" graphic menu item to select it.
3. In the Properties panel, click the folder next to the Link field. The Select File window will open. Choose route.html and click Select to return to the document. The graphic will not change appearance in any way, but when it is selected, you can see the link information in the Properties panel.
4. Make sure that the border value is set to 0 in the Properties panel.
5. Repeat Steps 1 through 4 with the next three menu items, choosing people.html, land.html, and contact.html, respectively, for the linked files.

That is all there is to creating a link with a graphic. You can now go through the rest of your pages and create links for all your menu items.

If you find an unexpected blue border on your image, setting the border value to 0 will remove it.

Adding Alt tags to images

Have you noticed the little information tags that pop out when you hold your cursor over a graphic? That is the Alt tag (or if you want to get technical, the Alt attribute of the IMG tag) in action (see Figure 9-2). People who browse with image display disabled will see a note telling them about the image that is supposed to appear in that location.

Visually impaired people depend on voice translators to tell them what is on a Web page, and Alt tags are read to tell the visitor about that image. You can also use Alt tags to provide the visitor a little more information about the link. In short, Alt tags are a very good idea. They are required for your page to be validated by any industry-standard rating systems, such as the W3C (World Wide Web Consortium) or Bobby, which many government agencies insist upon for their sites.

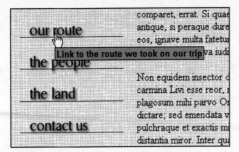

Figure 9-2 *Alt tags display as the cursor is held over a graphic. These tags help people who cannot display or see graphic displays.*

  W3C offers a code validation service with which you can test your pages for W3C validity (www.w3.org/). Bobby is a service provided by CAST (Center for Applied Special Technology) to test HTML pages for accessibility (www.cast.org/bobby/). It is an excellent idea, especially if you are a beginner, to visit both sites, study the issues around accessibility and valid code, and also to test your pages.

Dreamweaver makes it very easy to add Alt tags. Take the following steps to add Alt tags:

1. Open the index.html page from your Holiday site.
2. Select the "our route" graphic.
3. Type **Link to the route we took on our trip.** in the Alt field in the right side of the Properties panel. Figure 9-2 shows the result when previewed in Internet Explorer.
4. Repeat Steps 2 and 3 for each graphic on the page. For the menu items, create a sentence similar to the one you created in Step 3. For the photos and logo, you can type just what it contains, or you can type something similar to **Picture of _____.**

There isn't a lot of work involved to make a big difference to those who cannot use graphics to help them gain access to the information on the Web. It also adds a professional touch to your pages, and may help improve your ratings with search engines. For images that do not add content to your page, like spacer graphics, you can use * (asterisk) as the Alt tag value.

Adding links to text

10 Min.
To Go

In much the same way that you added a link to your images, you can change any text into a link. The difference is that the text you want to link must be highlighted. There is no limit to the number of words you can use to create a single link. Just select all the text you want to include, as described in the following steps:

1. Open the index.html file from the Holiday site.

2. Insert your cursor beneath the menu in the left column. Press your Enter key to create a space between the menu item and the cursor, if necessary. Type **Please make sure you visit our Route page**.

3. Double-click, or click and drag, to select the word Route. In the Properties panel, click the folder beside the Link field. Choose route.html from the Select File window. Click Select to return to the document.

Your text will now appear blue with an underline when the text is deselected (this is the default link appearance). You will learn how to adjust link colors in a later session. Figure 9-3 shows the link appearance with the linked file displaying in the Properties panel.

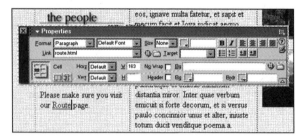

Figure 9-3   *Text with an added link. Note how the linked filename appears in the Properties Inspector.*

Special links

The links that you just created connect your visitors to other pages on your site. You can also create links that link to other sites, or that open your visitors' e-mail programs so they can send you a note. These links can be added to images or to text, each using a different type of link code.

You will learn about linking to a specific place on a page with Named Anchor links in Session 12.

Linking to other pages

To add a link to another Web address, select your image or text, and type in a full Web address.

1. In the index.html document, insert your cursor below the text you added in the last exercise. Type **You can buy books at Amazon.com**.

2. Highlight Amazon.com. In the links field in the Properties panel, type **http://www.amazon.com**. Your text changes to indicate that it is a link. When your visitor clicks this link, she is taken to the Amazon.com site. For links to other sites, it is important that you specify the full address for an external site, including the `http://` portion of the address.

Linking to e-mail

If you want your visitors to be able to send you a note directly from your site using their own e-mail program, you can choose to add a mailto link.

1. Below the text you entered in the previous exercise, type **Send an e-mail**. Select the word "e-mail."

2. In the links field in the Properties panel type **mailto:(your e-mail address)** with no parentheses; for example, **mailto:wpeck@wpeck.com**. Your text changes to indicate that it is a link. When your visitor clicks the link, his e-mail program opens, and a new message is started, ready for him to type his note.

3. Add a similar link to the main content area of the contact.html page. You learn to create a form in Session 14, and can create a form on the contact page for extra practice.

 Your content text is moving away from the top of the page as you add to the left column. Insert your cursor in the text column, and select Top in the Vert field of the Properties panel to correct.

Creating a Text Menu

Now that you know how to create a link from text, you can build a text menu. If you place a text menu at the bottom of each page, visitors will not have to scroll back to the top for the menu, and those without graphics enabled can use the text option.

I prefer to create my text menus in a table. I also tend to nest the menu table in the main table, although some designers disagree with this method. If you do not want to nest tables, you can place the text menu table below the main page table.

Take the following steps to create a text menu in a table:

1. Open the index.html document from the Holiday site.

2. Insert your cursor into the last row of the layout table. This row should have all of the cells merged to create one large cell from your work in Session 6. If the cells are not merged, select the cells and merge them.

3. Select Insert ⇨ Table, and then specify a table of one row and four columns. Set the cell padding to 10, and set the cell spacing to 0. Set the width to 100%, and set the borders to 0. Click OK to return to your document. The original table row now contains your new table.

4. Type **our route** into the first table cell. Type **the people** into the second table cell. Type **the land** into the third cell. Type **contact us** into the final cell.

5. Select the four cells of the menu table by clicking and dragging. Set the cell alignment to center by choosing Center from the drop-down Horz menu in the Properties panel.

6. Create a link for the first menu item by selecting the text and linking to route.html. Repeat this step for the next two menu items, choosing the appropriate file for the link.

7. Add a mailto link to the Contact Us menu item.

Your text menu for this page is complete (Figure 9-4). Create the same menu for each page. You can copy this table and paste it into each document. However, the text will need to be changed for each page, because you do not want the active page to be listed. You also want to add a home menu. Each page will have four menu items. For example, route.html will have home, the people, the land, and contact us as menu items.

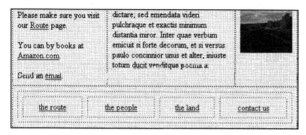

Figure 9-4　*The completed menu for index.html.*

This was a fast and furious lesson. It's time to leave document creation and focus on FTP issues for the next session.

Done!

REVIEW

You have covered important information in this session, although much of it was similar in nature. Here are the important things to remember:

- Settings that affect the entire page are adjusted in the Page Properties window.
- When you add page titles, descriptions, and keywords, you should choose your words with care, because these properties are used by the search engines.
- You can create your own meta tags to present information in the head of the document. Head content can only be seen in the document code.
- Alt tags are very important for many Web users.
- Links are added in much the same way for both text and images in Dreamweaver.
- Text menus provide an extra level of navigation for your visitors, and they can be very useful for those who cannot view images.

QUIZ YOURSELF

1. Where can you change the page background color or image in Dreamweaver? (See the "Setting Page Properties" section.)

2. Why is a title important for your page? (See the "Adding a page title" section.)

3. Where does a page description appear with a finished page? (See the "Adding a page description" section.)

4. Where do you specify link information for both text and images? (See the "Creating Links" section.)

5. Where do Alt tags appear on a final page, and what other purpose do they serve? (See the "Adding Alt tags to images" section.)

SESSION

10

Transferring Files

Session Checklist

✔ Moving files

✔ Using global replace

✔ Transferring multiple files

✔ Cloaking a folder

✔ Finding a file on the remote server

✔ Retrieving files from the server

✔ Updating files

**30 Min.
To Go**

Y ou have your rough site completed, and now it is time to transfer it to your server. When I am creating a new site, I do not use this exact workflow. I usually create the first page drafts, and then place them on the server to make sure everything is working right. I then bring the remaining pages to a near-finished state before transferring them to the server.

For this exercise, though, I want you to have working examples to learn Dreamweaver's site management tools, so you are placing files that you know need to be edited. You will transfer the files to the server, and you will then retrieve them to make your edits. Although I always try to minimize the number of trips back and forth, it is a rare page that does not make several journeys from remote to local and back again, despite my best efforts.

Now it's time to get those files to the server.

Preparing Your Site

Before we tap into the full power of Dreamweaver's site management tools, you are going to clean up your local folder. As you worked through the previous sessions, you created a few extra files that have no purpose for the site. Having local files that are not required for the remote site can create confusion.

I am going to keep things simple and have you create a new folder that holds all of your reference files and any working files you create. Not only will this clean up your site and provide a folder to Cloak (see below), but you will also see the Dreamweaver file tracking process in action.

Keeping your files neat and in logical order is vital for Web designers.

Transferring files within a Dreamweaver site

You need only five documents for the Holiday site. You've already created the following page files: index.html, land.html, people.html, route.html, and contact.html. However, you also created several reference files and imported text files. Move these to a new folder by following these steps:

1. Open the Holiday site panel, and create a new folder. Click on your root folder listing to highlight, and choose File ➪ New Folder.

   OR

   Right-click (PC) or Ctrl+click (Mac) and choose New Folder from the drop-down menu.

   However you get to New Folder, name your folder **resources**.

2. Now that you have a folder, move your extra files into the folder. Highlight all files in the root folder except the files you need for your site: index.html, land.html, people.html, and route.html.

3. Click and drag the selected files, moving your cursor over the resources folder. Release the mouse button and the Update files listing will appear.

   Dreamweaver searched through your site and checked for any links that would be affected by the move you requested. In this case, you should receive a list that reflects only the files you are moving, because these files are not linked to the remaining documents. However, each of these files must be updated, because their relation to any dependent files will change. Dreamweaver automatically makes the link changes if you choose to update the files.

4. Select Update.

If you moved these files to a new folder outside of Dreamweaver, the Site panel would reflect the changes, but the links within the files would not change. Your graphics files and any other connected file would be broken when you opened the document again, forcing you to manually change every link.

Cloaking a folder

Now that you have a folder containing the test files, you can tell Dreamweaver to ignore it in all site operations with Cloaking, a new feature in Dreamweaver MX. You can still work with the files normally, but when it comes to any automatic site functions, a cloaked folder is not considered. To cloak a file, do *one* of the following:

1. In the Site panel, highlight the resources folder. Select Site ⇨ Cloaking ⇨ Cloak from the Site panel menu. A red line will appear through the folder icon and through any file icon within that folder.

   OR

2. Right-click (PC) or Ctrl+click (Mac) the resources folder. Select Cloak from the fly-out menu.

You can uncloak a folder by repeating the same steps but selecting Uncloak instead of Cloak. That's all there is to it.

Using the Find and Replace command

20 Min.
To Go

It is not unusual to discover that you want to make a change to a word you have used on every page. Often, you find this in final checks when you are preparing to upload your site.

Dreamweaver has nearly unlimited find and replace capability. You can search and replace plain text, HTML source codes, and specific tags, or you can use the advanced text search to customize what you would like to find. You can perform your searches in the current document only, in the current site, in a specified folder, and in selected files. (Choose files in the Site window.)

You are going to change the contact menu item to read "contact" instead of "contact us." Because you are going to replace the menu item in all the files in a folder, you can perform the replace from any page. If you were performing a replace on only one page, you would need to have that page open. You must have the text menu completed for each of your documents before proceeding with this exercise. (See Session 9.)

1. Open index.html from the Holiday site. Select Edit ⇨ Find and Replace. The Find and Replace window will open.

2. To replace text or code through the entire root folder, choose Folder from the drop-down Find In menu. Click the folder icon to specify the root folder for your Holiday site.

3. Choose Text from the Search For drop-down menu. Type **contact us** in the field beside the Search For menu.

4. Type **contact** in the Replace With field.

5. Click Replace All. An alert will pop up, warning you that you cannot undo changes in documents that are not open. This is a warning to be heeded. When you are replacing text across an entire site or folder, make sure that you know exactly what you are doing. Click OK.

If I am doing a global search and replace, I usually test my replace on one page by selecting the Replace, rather than Replace All option, before I do the global search and replace. It is easy to neglect to include a space or similar tiny error. If you are making changes that cannot be undone across 50 documents, you want to make sure that you have it right.

6. Dreamweaver will go to work, open the Results panel, and list all the changes it
   makes. Figure 10-1 displays the listed changes in the Results panel. Close the
   Results panel.

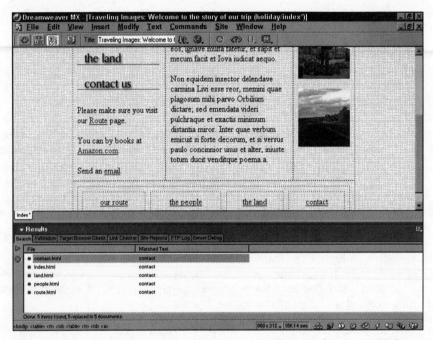

Figure 10-1 *Changes that Dreamweaver has made in the Find and Replace action
are listed in the Results panel.*

Search and replace can save so much time. Remember the spaces you had between your
image code and the <br> tag? I often run a source code search to replace "space
" with

 for an accurate and almost instant way to guarantee that my code is correct. If you
catch yourself doing the same thing over and over again, perhaps a search and replace exercise is the answer.

 **Even when you cannot use the replace feature, the find feature can be very
handy. Specify the term you would like to find and where you would like to
find it. You can then use your F3 key (PC) or ⌘+G (Mac) to move from one
instance to the next, making corrections as you go.**

Transferring Files

When you think of transferring files, you must think of it as a continual process. Rare is the
Web site that is placed on the server and left alone. Designers are always making small revi-
sions, updating information, improving on our work, and so forth. After all, that is what
the Web has opened for us: the ability to publish constantly.

I built this course on a small, simple site to start. Transferring the files to the server and learning about Dreamweaver's powerful site management tools is one of the main reasons I chose to structure the course this way. It is much easier to follow what is happening when you are working with only a few files.

Deleting a file on the remote server

In Session 5, you transferred files to the Web. You transferred a single file and an entire site. In this session, you are going to transfer multiple files. To start, however, you are going to delete one file from your remote site. As part of Session 5, you placed the file session4.html.on the remote server. This is a resource file, and there is no reason for it to be on your server.

Take the following steps to delete a file on the remote server:

1. Open the Holiday site window. Connect to the server, and make sure your remote files are visible in the Site panel.

2. Select the file session4.html.

3. Do one of the following: Select File ⇨ Delete, press your Delete key, or right-click (PC) or Ctrl+click (Mac) and select Delete.

You can delete a folder in the same way. Simply select the folder and proceed as above.

Transferring multiple files

You can move one or many files by selecting files on the local site of the Site panel and dragging the selection to the remote side of the Site panel.

Select continuous files by selecting the first file, and then pressing your Shift key before selecting the last file you want to transfer. You can also select multiple files that are not in contiguous order by clicking each file while pressing the Ctrl (PC) or ⌘ (Mac) key.

Take the following steps to transfer multiple files to the server:

1. If it is not already open, activate the Holiday site and connect to the server. Expand the Site panel view.

2. Select the five files that you created for the site.

3. Click and drag any of the selected files to transfer all of the selected files. Drag them to the remote side of the Site panel, and then position your cursor over the listing at the top of the screen. This is your root folder, and you want to make sure that your files are in the root folder (see Figure 10-2).

4. An alert window appears asking if you would like to include dependent files. Click Yes. Dreamweaver will check the files you are transferring and include any graphic or other dependent files, creating a folder for the extra files that are in a separate folder on the local site as it works. On the first transfer of any file, you should always say yes to this; Dreamweaver can effortlessly make sure that all the files you require are placed in the correct folder on the remote server.

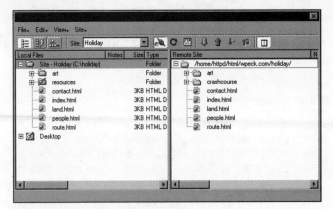

Figure 10-2 *All site files are now in place on the server. Note the Cloaked icon on the resources folder in the local files.*

5. Your site should be fully uploaded to the site. View the site on the Web using the address www.youraddress.com/holiday/. Your Index file automatically appears when you request the Holiday folder.

The menu links are not all in place yet; you still have some work left to do. Your lower text menu should enable you to navigate your site.

Finding a file on the local or remote server

For your small site, you can see every file on the remote server simply by expanding folders. However, most sites are much more complicated, and it is not unusual for even a personal site to grow to more than 20 pages, with several folders containing images — or subpages. Dreamweaver offers a really simple, terrific search feature to find the matching file, or to find multiple matching files on your local or remote server. To show the power of this feature, make sure that all the folders are collapsed on your remote server.

1. Open the Holiday site and connect to the remote server.

2. Expand the art folder on your local site and select land.gif. Press your Ctrl (PC) or ⌘ (Mac) key and select the file index.html.

3. Select Edit ➪ Locate in Remote Site from the main menu (Mac: Site ➪ Locate in Remote Site). Dreamweaver will highlight the index.html and land.gif files on the remote site.

4. Now try it in reverse. Select a file or several files in the remote site and select Edit ➪ Locate in Local Site (Mac: Site ➪ Locate in Local Site).

This may seem like a silly thing to rave about. But although I do not use it often, this feature saves time and many mouse clicks when I do.

Retrieving files from the server

Copying files from the server to the local folder is the same procedure as copying files from the local drive to the server, only in reverse.

1. Open the Holiday site and connect to the server.
2. Select the land.html file on the remote server.
3. Click and drag the file to the root folder of the local site. Dreamweaver asks if you would like to copy the dependent files. You can click NO this time, because all the files you require for that page are already on the local site.

Be careful downloading files from your remote site to your local site. If you have made changes to your local copy and you attempt to download the same file from the remote site, an alert appears. If you say yes, any changes you have made to the local copy will be overwritten.

Editing and Updating Files

10 Min. To Go

Time to put a lot of what you have learned into practice, and on your own, too. This is where I give you a list and tell you to do it. If you are following along with the timing of this course, you will not be able to get this done all at once. It is a lot faster when I am guiding your every keystroke. All you really need for the next part of this course is to make changes to a few of your files. You can then go back when you have time to finish all the details.

Here is your "to-do" list. All references can be found in Session 9.

- Add the background image (see "Adding a background image or color") to the other pages, or remove it from land.html page so that all of your pages match.
- Make sure that all of your pages have a working text menu (see "Creating a Text Menu").
- Add links to your graphic menu items on all pages (see "Adding links to images" and "Special links").
- Add Alt tags to your images (see "Adding Alt tags to images").
- Add titles to all pages (see "Adding a page title").
- Add meta tags like keywords and description.
- Check your pages for errors in alignment.

After you have made one change to at least three pages, you are ready to update your site. Highlight any of the pages you have changed, and drag them to the remote side of the Site window. Unless you have added new images to your pages, say No to the alert asking if you wish to include dependent files.

You have covered all of the basic functions you need to build a site. From here, you head for some exciting techniques. I promised that you would have a site on the Web by now, and you do. Give yourself a big pat on the back. Your reward will come soon. You have worked hard to get through the basics, and now you can have a little fun.

Done!

REVIEW

You tapped into the powerful features that Dreamweaver offers for site management with this session. If you have come to Dreamweaver with the experience of having manually created sites, you probably have a mile-wide grin right now. There are a few key points that you should remember:

- It is crucial that you keep your site folders very tidy. Without great housekeeping habits, it is nearly impossible to use the automated features for Dreamweaver site management.
- When you move files within a Dreamweaver site, the links are automatically checked and you are given an option to update the files.
- When you perform a search and replace action on multiple pages, or on an entire site, the changes cannot be undone on any pages that are not open. It is best to test the replace feature with a single page before performing a global search or replace.
- Clicking and dragging will transfer any selected files either to or from the remote site. Select contiguous files using the Shift key; select noncontiguous files using the Ctrl (PC) or ⌘ (Mac) key.

QUIZ YOURSELF

1. When you click and drag to transfer a file in the Dreamweaver site window, what does Dreamweaver do for you? (See the "Transferring files within a Dreamweaver site" section.)
2. What is the purpose of Cloaking? (See the "Cloaking a folder" section.)
3. Dreamweaver has a command that will replace a phrase or piece of code throughout the entire site. What should you do before you tell Dreamweaver to Replace All? (See the "Using the Find and Replace command" section.)
4. How do you delete a file on the remote server? (See the "Deleting a file on the remote server" section.)
5. What must you watch for when moving files from the server to your local site? (See "Retrieving files from the server" section.)

PART

II

Saturday Morning
Part Review

1. What capability does using Dreamweaver's FTP feature offer that using other FTP programs do not?

2. List the four pieces of information about your remote host that you need to set up the FTP for a Dreamweaver site.

3. What single action transfers an entire site to the remote server?

4. Why should you avoid nesting multiple tables, especially to many levels?

5. Why is it a good idea to plan your tables well before you start building them?

6. Why would you work with your table borders turned on when you do not wish to have table borders in the final version?

7. What is the difference between setting table width to a fixed size or a percentage?

8. If a column contains only text, and you want it always to display at 200 pixels wide, what can you do to ensure that the table is always at least 200 pixels wide?

9. When you place a table inside a cell of another table and set a percentage width for the new table, what determines the width of the new table?

10. Does Dreamweaver allow you to specify both fixed and percentage values for columns in the same table?

11. In Dreamweaver, how do you add a background color to only one cell in a table? What HTML tag is affected?

12. How do you delete a table's background color in Dreamweaver?

13. How does Netscape Navigator display a multicell table that has a background image added?

14. Internet Explorer does not display a background image when the background is specified as part of which tag?

15. How do you add a background color or image to a page in Dreamweaver?

16. In the Page Properties window, you can set page margins to zero. Why must you add four commands to change two margins?

17. Where do you add a link to an image in Dreamweaver?

18. Suppose you want to change the page margins on all 25 pages of your site. How do you do this in Dreamweaver?

19. How can you transfer multiple files from the local site to the remote site or vice versa?

20. When downloading files from the server, what must you be careful to avoid?

PART

III

Saturday Afternoon

Editing HTML

Session Checklist

✔ Editing HTML in the Code Inspector

✔ Editing HTML with the Design view/Code view screen

✔ Editing HTML with Code view

✔ Inserting a script

**30 Min.
To Go**

Way back in Session 1, I read you the riot act about learning the code that runs your Web site. In this session you learn how to work with your code, and why it is important to understand what goes on behind the Dreamweaver screen.

This session covers checking, editing, and adding code in several different ways. Once you know how to work with the HTML screens, you move on to placing code from a different source. There are thousands of free or reasonably priced scripts available, which you can add to your sites. These are often very high quality scripts, and they offer exciting features for your sites.

Working with HTML in Dreamweaver

Whether you are troubleshooting a single problem or typing nearly all the code you require for a page, the methods are the same. Work through a sample of each operation so that you are familiar with all of Dreamweaver's HTML editing capabilities.

First, look at some basic codes and get used to working with the code windows. You have three choices for viewing code within Dreamweaver. Type or edit code using each method so that you can discover which way is the most comfortable for you.

All Dreamweaver HTML viewing methods can be interchanged and achieve the same result. You do not have to be consistent with how you view code. You can go from the Code Inspector to split-screen view to full-screen Code view and back again, as your working style demands.

Editing HTML in the Code Inspector window

The original HTML display method in Dreamweaver was a separate window known as the Code Inspector.

1. Create a new document and save it in the resources folder in your Holiday site as handcode.html.

2. Open the Code Inspector using one of the following methods: Select Window ⇨ Others ⇨ Code Inspector from the main menu, or press the F10 key. Click and drag the window borders if you would like more room to work.

3. Enable your line numbering so I can point you to specific lines in your code. Locate the icons at the top of the Code Inspector window. Click the View Options icon, which is the last icon on the right. Select Line Numbers, and a list of numbers will appear down the left side of the window, as shown in Figure 11-1.

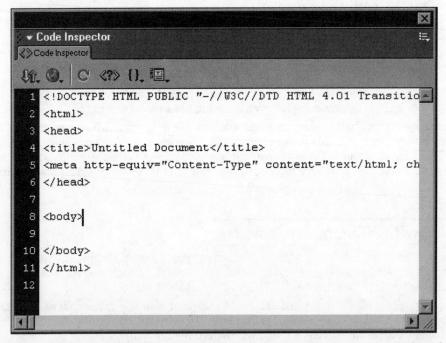

Figure 11-1 *The Code Inspector window with the Line Numbers option activated. Line numbers are enabled using the View Options icon.*

4. Now you can enter your background and text color by typing code. In the Code Inspector, delete the line containing <body> tag (line 8). It is not necessary to delete the entire line in real working circumstances. We could just replace the color number, but I want you to have a whole line of code to type in.

5. Type in the following code:

```
<body bgcolor="#330099" text="#FFFFFF">
```

6. Place your cursor on the next line (line 9). Type in the following code:

```
<p>Now my background is blue and my text is white.</p>
```

Although all of the above line — except the <p> and </p> tags — is actual page content, it can still be typed into the code window. In fact, there is nothing that Dreamweaver can do that cannot be done in the Code Inspector or other Code view windows. Remember that an entire Web site can be built using nothing but a text editor.

7. Click outside the Code Inspector window, or close the Code Inspector to see the results.

8. Place your cursor at the end of the text line in the document and press Enter to move the cursor down. Type **All of my text will now be white.** The new line that you typed should have the same attributes as the line you typed in Step 7.

9. Open the Code Inspector window and locate both lines of text. They should be the same, with the exception of the actual text shown in Figure 11-2. Note how the cursor is in the same place in the main document and in the code window.

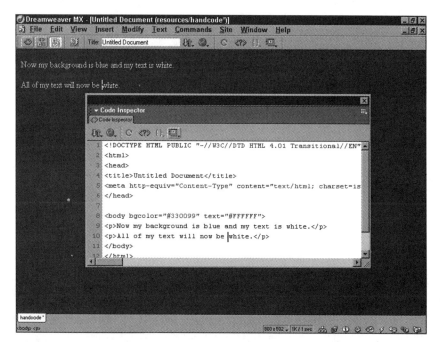

Figure 11-2 *The finished code and screen appearance for this exercise.*

Editing HTML code with a split screen

The split Design and Code view option was introduced in Dreamweaver 4 — a feature I learned to love quickly. Unless I am working on a very long script, I find that the half-screen view gives me a good overview of the code I am working with, and yet I can still see what is happening on the design screen.

Enable the split-screen view and add an image using only HTML code. You are going to continue working with the document from the previous exercise.

In the Session 11 directory on the CD-ROM, locate the file image11.gif, and then copy it to the Art folder in the root folder for the Holiday site.

1. If it is not already open, open handcode.html from the resources directory of the Holiday site. Close the Code Inspector window if it is still open.
2. Enable split-screen view by clicking the Show Code and Design Views icon 📝 in the toolbar in the upper-left corner of the Dreamweaver screen.

You can specify whether the code window or the design window will display at the top of your screen. Click the View Options window on the far right of the toolbar at the top of your screen, and then click Design View on Top to toggle the arrangement of the screen view.

3. Using the Design view screen, place your cursor at the end of the last row of text and press Enter to move the cursor down one line.
4. In the code editing part of the screen, select the   code between the <p> and </p> tags, and type in the following code to overwrite your selected code:

    ```
    <img src="../art/image11.gif" width="200" height="150">
    ```

    The full line of code now looks like this:

    ```
    <p><img src="../art/image11.gif" width="200" height="150"></p>
    ```

The code you typed first states that this is in a paragraph, and then indicates that it is an image, displaying the path to the image. The image dimensions follow. Finally, the end paragraph tag ends the paragraph.

While you are working in the split screen, select your image in the design screen. Note how the selection is repeated in the code section of the screen. Select the text in the code screen and note that it is selected in the design screen, as well. This should help you to really grasp the idea that the two windows are different presentations of the same information.

Editing HTML code using the full window

Finally, when you have a heavy coding task ahead, you might want to work with your code using the full screen. You are going to add a very simple table to your working document, taking advantage of the larger code area to see the code for the full table.

20 Min.
To Go

1. Open the document handcode.html if it is not already open.
2. Enable the full Code view by clicking the Show Code View icon 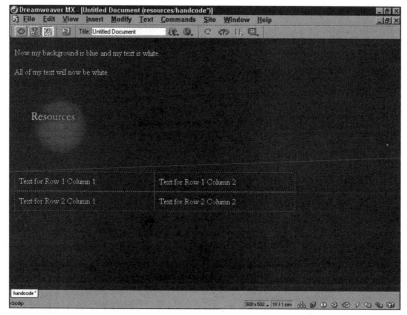 in the toolbar in the upper-left portion of the Dreamweaver screen.
3. Place your cursor at the end of the image entry from the previous exercise, but before the </body> tag, and press Enter to move the cursor down one line.
4. Type the following code, pressing the Enter key to start new lines, and pressing the Tab key to align it in an easy-to-read format. (Shift+Tab will remove an indent.)

```
<table width="75%" border="0" cellspacing="0" cellpadding="10">
    <tr>
        <td>Text for Row 1 Column 1</td>
        <td>Text for Row 1 Column 2</td>
        </tr>
        <tr>
        <td>Text for Row 2 Column 1</td>
        <td>Text for Row 2 Column 2</td>
    </tr>
</table>
```

Try to trace the construction of this table. I have included text that identifies exactly where you are in the table. The <tr> tag creates a row, and the <td> tag creates a cell.

5. Click the Show Design View icon to proof your code. It should resemble Figure 11-3.

Those are your three choices for editing HTML code within Dreamweaver. You can also set up an external program to launch from within Dreamweaver in which you can edit your HTML code.

Figure 11-3   Dreamweaver display with Design view active.

Inserting Scripts into Dreamweaver

There are countless scripts available on the Web to enhance your pages. You will also find that you use your own scripts over and over. These scripts must be placed in Dreamweaver's HTML Code view so that you can control the placement of the code. The process is not sophisticated — no more than cutting and pasting code into your code window in most cases — but you must be precise. It is very important to understand the structure of an HTML document to achieve success in placing complicated scripts.

For this exercise, you use a simple date script from JavaScriptSource.com. You can find the original code at http://javascript.internet.com, as well as in the datescript.html document in the Session 11 folder on the CD-ROM.

Understanding document structure and scripts

I have strongly suggested that you learn HTML coding. Placing scripts is one very good reason for knowing your HTML. Scripts often require that elements be placed in very specific places in your document. If you cannot read the HTML code, you are depending on luck — not a good idea with anything for Web design.

The two areas that you must know are the head and body of an HTML document, as well as the <body> tag (see Figure 11-4). Many scripts have at least two parts: one that must be placed in the head area of your document (or between the <head> and </head> tags); and the other sections that must be placed inside the <body> tags. Still others must be placed alongside — or inside — other tags (within the body area, for example, between the <body> and </body> tags). Well-written instructions for placing scripts will include very clear directions about where each section of code must be placed.

Although you can place scripts without knowing how they work, it is a good idea to understand at least a little about the language that you are inserting. Even with automatic features, you will achieve better results when you know why the code is working the way it does.

Inserting a script

The script you are using should be placed where you want the date to appear. Take the following steps to place the date script:

1. Open the handcode.html document from the Holiday site if it is not already open.

2. Open the file datescript.html from the Session 11 directory on the CD-ROM. You do not have to save this document to your hard drive; you are simply cutting and pasting the contents into our document. You also can visit http://javascript.internet.com/clocks/proper-date.html to copy directly from JavaScriptSource.com. While you are there, you can browse though the many other scripts that are available.

3. Highlight the script code, beginning with <SCRIPT LANGUAGE="JavaScript"> and ending with </script>. Copy the code.

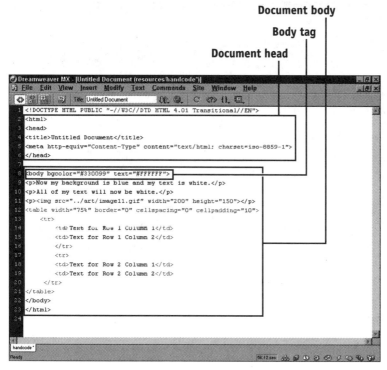

Figure 11-4   *Common areas for placing scripts into HTML documents.*

4. In handcode.html, make sure you are in Code view, and then place the cursor where you would like the date to appear. I have placed it below the table on the bottom of the page. Make sure that you leave a line or two between the table and the script in your HTML code. It will not affect the placement in the document; it just makes editing much easier. Most scripts add a lot of code to your page. Without good spacing, it is very tough to edit your code later.

You may prefer to place your cursor at the correct location while you are in Design view. When you switch to Code view to paste your script, the cursor position will be maintained.

5. Paste the script into your document. Switch to Design or Design and Code View and you see a marker where the script has been placed, as shown in Figure 11-5. If you do not see a marker, you may have turned off viewing for items that do not display in Dreamweaver. Check View ➪ Visual Aids. Invisible Elements must be selected to see the placement of the JavaScript. Although the icon does shift the elements on your page, it does not affect the final page appearance. Preview your page to see the script in action and without the effect of the icon placement.

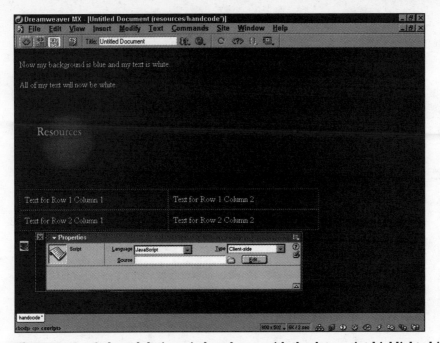

Figure 11-5 *Code and design window shown, with the date script highlighted in the code window, and represented by an icon in Design view. Note that the Properties panel is showing that the icon represents JavaScript.*

6. Click the icon for the JavaScript to select it. The Properties panel indicates that you have a JavaScript script at this position. You can edit your script using the Edit button.

    To see your script in action, you must preview your page in a browser.

7. Choose File ➪ Preview in Browser, and then choose the browser you wish to test. It is a good idea to test any new script in at least Internet Explore and Netscape Navigator.

You can find a list of script sources in the document scripts.html in the resources folder of the CD-ROM.

It takes a lot more to explain what you have done here than it does to actually accomplish the task. You have worked on a test document, so the pressure of working around the code you have created for your site did not exist. Make sure you save the file.

While this information is fresh in your mind, why not try to place a different script? There are many available. I recommend that you test a new script on a new page, however. Place the script and test it in a browser before repeating the placement in your document. That may seem like a lot of work, but when you are working with a two- or three-part script, it is easy to make one tiny error that will affect either the script or your HTML. Once you have the script in your test document, it is a very quick cut-and-paste operation to move it into place in your working document.

Done!

REVIEW

You devoted your time this session to working with code windows. You should be starting to feel more comfortable with the available options. Keep the following in mind as you move on:

- Dreamweaver code viewing options are completely interchangeable and require no consistency. Viewing the code windows is simply another way to see the same information presented in layout form in a Design view.
- You can have the line numbers displayed in Dreamweaver HTML views.
- You can type code directly into any HTML viewing window in Dreamweaver.
- When working with long scripts, or troubleshooting code, it is often more convenient to work with the full-screen view of the Code view.
- When placing a script into Dreamweaver, you should work in Code view and be careful with the placement of your code. Creating a test document is recommended when you are using a new script.

QUIZ YOURSELF

1. What are the three different methods for viewing your HTML code in Dreamweaver? (See the "Working with HTML in Dreamweaver" section.)
2. What effect does pressing the Enter key have when you are working in Code view? (See the "Editing HTML code using the full window" section.)
3. What is the most common way to insert a third-party script into your document? (See the "Inserting a script" section.)
4. How does a script placed within the body of the page appear in the Design view? (See the "Inserting a script" section.)
5. What must be done to view a working script that you have placed in Dreamweaver? (See the "Inserting a script" section.)
6. How can you edit a script without using a Code view? (See the "Inserting a script" section.)

Creating and Checking Links

Session Checklist

✔ Understanding relative and absolute links

✔ Using Named Anchor links

✔ Previewing your links

✔ Checking links in Dreamweaver

**30 Min.
To Go**

Without links (short for hyperlinks), the Web is just print material on a monitor. It is the interconnected nature of the Web that makes it an entirely new way to communicate and conduct business. For this reason, your links must be in good order for your site to work. This session covers the different types of links you can use, and how to keep links in working order.

Dreamweaver is a powerful ally for working with links. In Session 6, you learned how easy it is to use the Properties panel to add links to your documents. In Session 10, you transferred a file and watched as Dreamweaver updated the links that were contained in that file. In this session, you are going to look behind the actions to discover what links are and how they work.

Understanding Relative and Absolute Links

There are two basic types of links. *Absolute links* are independent of any folder structure on your site. *Relative links* are written in relation to the location of the file containing the link on your site.

A link is simply an address to a different location. You can compare them to street addresses. If you're in a coffee shop on Main Street and someone asks you to tell them where they can find a shoe store, your answer might be, "Tippy Toes, right next door." Chances are that they will find the store. Now imagine that you are in the next town. Now you have to add the name of the town where Tippy Toes is located, as well as street name, before the store can be found. These examples are relative. They consider the location of the person looking for the store, and they include enough information to reach the store from *that* location.

Suppose you wanted to remove all doubt about where the store is located, no matter what the location is of the inquiring person. The answer will be the same for both of the above examples. Tippy Toes is on Earth, in the Northern Hemisphere, in North America, in the United States, in Kansas, in Sedgwick County, at 555 Main Street. You would get some strange looks if you gave this answer if you were next door to Tippy Toes, but it is technically correct. This address is an absolute address. No matter where on earth you are, this description of the location of Tippy Toes will be correct.

The choice of absolute or relative links is usually a judgment call. In many cases, they are completely interchangeable. Often, however, one or the other is most appropriate for a particular application. Take a closer look at both types.

Relative links

I try to use relative links whenever I can. I like the flexibility they offer when working with Dreamweaver. Absolute links are . . . absolute. Once you create them, they stay the same, and they are not updated if you decide to move your files to a different directory. For this reason alone, I recommend that you use relative links unless there is a compelling reason to use absolute links.

If you are linking between two documents in your root folder, the relative link is as simple as can be. In Dreamweaver, you simply click the folder with the Link section of the Properties panel and choose the file. When you created the links for your index.html page, the link to the Route page was a simple statement in the Properties panel; it appeared in HTML code as `<a href="route.html">Text for the link</a>`. If the file that you are linking to is in another folder in the root folder, the path includes the folder. In the following code, `<a href="resources/handcode.html">Text for the link</a>`, note the addition of the resources folder to the path. See Figure 12-1 for the Dreamweaver representation of the same link.

Figure 12-1   *Link showing a relative path to a document located in a folder that is located in lower-level folder.*

The path is marked by ../ (two dots and a single forward slash) if the linked page is above the folder in which the HTML page is saved. See Figure 12-2 for both the code and the Properties panel representation of a file that is two levels above the document holding the link.

```
<p><a href="../../index.html">Link</a></p>
```

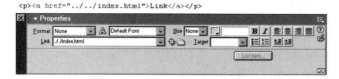

Figure 12-2 *Both the Properties panel and the code version of a path to a file, two levels above the document containing the link.*

Relative links are generally used unless there is a reason to use an absolute link. Links that are contained within a site are usually best as relative links. If you do change your directory structure, Dreamweaver adjusts your links for you, saving you a great deal of work and providing perfect accuracy. However, there are cases where absolute links must be used.

Absolute links

Absolute links are a must for any link to another site. For example, if you are linking to Amazon.com, you *must* use the absolute link `http://www.amazon.com`. (See Figure 12-3 for the code and Properties panel view of a link to an external site.) Anything less than the full address will not take your visitor to the site. Large organizations often insist on absolute links for their Web pages.

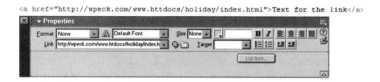

Figure 12-3 *Both the Properties panel and the code display the absolute path to the link.*

It makes no difference in HTML whether you point to your Route page from your home page as `http://yoursitename.com/route.html` (absolute) or you point to your Route page by specifying route.html (relative). The two examples of link codes below both lead to the same place for a visitor:

Relative link: `<a href="route.html">Text for the link</a>`

Absolute link: `<a href="http://wpeck.com/www/htdocs/weekend/route.html">Text for the link</a>`

For quick and accurate absolute links, copy the address of the site you want to link to from the browser address bar, and then paste the link into the links section of the Properties panel (or directly into your code). More broken links occur from typos than from any other type of error.

Named Anchor Links

You do not always want to link outside of the document that you are creating. For pages with long text passages, it's a good idea to give your readers links to individual topics within the page. In other cases, you might want to direct your visitor to a special place on a page to match the link. This is done using a Named Anchor link.

These links are a little different in that you are creating the link and naming it yourself. The name for the link does not appear on the finished screen, and it will only make sense to the page creator. The general concept is to place a note in your code with a name, and then create a link that points to that note by name.

Your site pages are not long enough to show the effect of the named anchor, so I have included a page with text. You'll add several named anchors to this page.

Copy the file namedanchors.html from the Session 12 folder on the CD-ROM to the resources folder in your Holiday site.

1. Open the file namedanchors.html from the resources folder of your holiday site. This page is formatted, but you want to add links from the menu on the left to the lower sections of the pages.

2. The next step is to create the anchors that you will link to. In Design view, insert your cursor at the beginning of the page headline. Select Insert ⇨ Named Anchor.

3. In the Insert Named Anchor window type **top**. Click OK. An icon appears beside your headline. (If you do not see an icon, select View ⇨ Visual Aids ⇨ Invisible Elements.) This icon represents your anchor. Click the icon and see the listing in the Properties panel, identifying this object as an anchor and displaying the name. You can use the Properties panel to edit the name. Figure 12-4 shows the results.

If you get into the habit of using lowercase letters, you are less likely to create a case error in a link. Lowercase titles also are less work. Why use the Shift key over and over again when it is not necessary?

4. Repeat Step 3 to add the following anchors:

   Insert an anchor named **custcare** beside "Customers Care that . . . ."
   Insert an anchor named **customerdriven** beside "Prepare to Be a Customer . . . ."
   Insert an anchor named **pracapp** beside "Practical Applications."
   Insert an anchor named **failtosee** beside "When We Fail to See . . . ."

5. Now you will create links to the menu items. Ignore the anchor in the headline for a few minutes. In the menu area at the top of the screen (in the left column), select all the text in the first menu entry ("Common errors . . . ."). In the Properties panel, locate the Links field. Type **#custcare**. Note that the menu item is now underlined, indicating there is a link. When you preview this document by clicking this link, the page is displayed with the named anchor at the top of the screen.

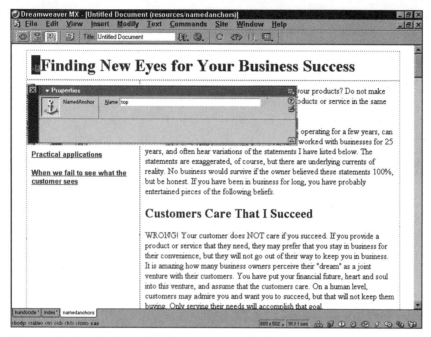

Figure 12-4 *The Named Anchor icon is at the beginning of the headline.*

6. Repeat Step 5 for the remaining menu items, matching the menu item to the appropriate anchor.

You can add convenience for your visitors by adding a link to allow them to move back to the top of the page without scrolling.

7. Scroll to the second headline ("Prepare to Be . . . ."). Place a link to the top of the page at the end of the text, just above this headline. To do this, insert your cursor at the end of the last paragraph in the first section (use your Enter key to create a new paragraph if there is not one) and type **Back to Top**. Create a link to the named anchor "top" by adding a link as #top. Right-justify your text.

8. Highlight the text you just created and select Edit ⇨ Copy HTML. Paste the link (Edit ⇨ Paste HTML) just before each headline. Dreamweaver copies the link information along with the text. Of course, this will only work when every link is exactly the same.

9. Preview the document in your browser. Click the links to navigate up and down on the page.

There is a copy of the completed exercise in the Session 12 folder on the CD-ROM. The file is titled namedanchorcomplete.html.

You can link to a specific place on another page in the same way. Simply create the link to the page you are pointing to, and then add the anchor code at the end of the link. For example, if the page you just created was in the root folder of my business site, the link `http://wpeck.com/namedanchor.html#customerdriven` would lead directly to the section "Prepare to Be a Customer Driven Business."

Previewing Your Links

By now, you may have noticed that Dreamweaver offers no live action for your links. You must preview the links in your browser to test them and make sure they are taking your visitors where you want them to go.

You do not need to be connected to the Web to preview links between local files. However, to test a link from your site to another site, your Web connection must be active.

Open your Holiday site again and preview how your links are working.

1. Open index.html from the Holiday site.
2. Select File ⇨ Preview in Browser and choose your browser.
3. Click all links on all pages. Keep a notebook handy to note which links are not working (you may not have finished creating all the links).
4. Edit any links that are not working and preview again. Repeat until all links are working.

Testing and Editing Links

Dreamweaver can save a lot of editing time for you by identifying links that are broken, or by identifying files with orphan links (no links leading to the files). You can check a single document, selected files, or the entire site. You can also change a link through your entire site.

Testing links

There is no excuse for having broken links with Dreamweaver. You have many methods available to you for testing links. Test your links before uploading; this operation is performed only on your local files.

Checking links in a single document

This is the fastest way to make sure that all of your links are working before you upload your pages:

1. If it is not already open, open index.html from your Holiday site.
2. Select File ⇨ Check Page ⇨ Check Links. The Results panel opens. Broken links are listed in the Results panel.

3. Select External Links from the drop-down menu in the Results panel. Any external links for this page appear in the white area. You should have at least two external links: one to Amazon.com and one to the mail recipient.

Checking links in selected documents

When you want to check links only in selected documents, use the following method:

1. Open your Site panel and activate your Holiday site if it is not already active.
2. Select the files that you would like to check.
3. Select File ⇨ Check Page ⇨ Check Links in the main menu or File ⇨ Check Links from the Site panel menu. (Mac: Ctrl+click on one of the selected files and choose Check Links ⇨ Selected Files/Folders from the pop-up menu.) Any broken links for the files you selected will show in the Results panel.
4. Select External Links from the drop-down menu in the Link Checker window. Any external links for the selected files appear in the white area.

Checking links on an entire site

Finally, you can check all the files on a site for broken links:

1. Open your Site panel and activate your Holiday site if it is not already active.
2. Choose Site ⇨ Check Links Sitewide from the Site panel menu.
3. View broken links and external links as discussed previously. With a sitewide check, you can also identify any orphaned files. Orphaned files have not been linked to or from any other page. You have several orphaned pages on your site, since the files in your resource section are not referred to by any other page.

Changing links across your site

Suppose you link to an external page as a resource from your page, and that link changes or you find a better source to which you'd rather refer. You can make the adjustment across your site with one simple action. You are going to change your Amazon.com link so that it goes directly to the Books section on that site.

1. If it is not already open, open your Holiday site.
2. Select Site ⇨ Change Link Sitewide. The Change Link Sitewide window opens.
3. In the Change All Links To field, type **http://www.amazon.com**.
4. In the Into Links To field, type **http://www.amazon.com/books/**.
5. Click OK, and a list of the files that contain the link you wish to change displays. Click Update and all the links to Amazon.com on your site are edited. (You only have one link to Amazon.com on this site.)

You can also select a file that you wish to alter links to. Browse for or enter the name for the file you wish to replace, and browse for or enter the file you wish to replace the file with from the Change Link Sitewide window.

It is always important to pay special attention when you are working with links. Although they are simple to work with, they control your entire site. Never treat a link casually; one typo or other error can make your site impossible to navigate.

You now move on to creating JavaScript rollovers, where links form only a small part of a much more complex operation.

Done!

REVIEW

You have looked at several different aspects of links, and there are a few areas that deserve special attention.

- Relative links refer to a location based on the path from the current page to the linked page. They are updated when changes are made within a Dreamweaver site. Relative links are more flexible than absolute links.

- Absolute links are the complete address to a location and must be used to link to another site.

- Named Anchor links must be used to create a link to a specific place on a page. They can be used with relative or absolute links.

- Links cannot be tested from within the Dreamweaver working environment. You must preview in a browser to see the links in action. To test links outside the current site, you must be connected to the Web.

- You can check for broken links within a Dreamweaver local site.

- You can exchange one link for another across your entire site.

QUIZ YOURSELF

1. What is the difference between absolute and relative links? (See the "Understanding Relative and Absolute Links" section.)
2. What is the benefit to relative links? (See the "Relative links" section.)
3. When must you use absolute links? (See the "Absolute links" section.)
4. What is a named anchor? (See the "Named Anchor Links" section.)
5. Which types of links can you test without being connected to the Web? (See the "Previewing Your Links" section.)
6. How can you easily change a link throughout your entire site? (See the "Changing links across your site" section.)

Generating JavaScript Rollovers

Session Checklist

✔ Working with JavaScript

✔ Editing JavaScript

✔ Creating a simple JavaScript rollover

✔ Creating a complex rollover

30 Min. To Go

L et me begin by saying that this session is not really about JavaScript, or at least, not about learning how to write JavaScript. In this session, JavaScript is either placed from another source or created automatically with Dreamweaver tools. But as I indicated earlier, the more you know about JavaScript, the more you can achieve when using Dreamweaver's tools. Countless great books have been written about JavaScript composition; and you should explore a book or two.

Working with JavaScript

Dreamweaver has powerful JavaScript creation tools called *behaviors*. Some JavaScript code is created invisibly, as in rollovers. If you chose not to view the code, you would not even know that JavaScript was written into your page. You can become a little more involved in the JavaScript creation process by using the Behaviors function, a feature that writes the code, but with your direction. Both features are examined in this session.

What is JavaScript?

JavaScript is a Web-based scripting language that has been around for only a little over five years. It has nothing to do with the programming language, Java. Developed to overcome the limitations of HTML, JavaScript has added much of the interactivity on the Web today.

Cross-browser support for JavaScript is very good, and it is a relatively simple language to learn. JavaScript is used on almost every site today, if only for image rollovers, which you will create in this session. JavaScript is used to check for browsers, platforms, resolutions, and so on. It is also used to create the popular drop-down menus, validate information entered in forms, and provide password protection.

Many designers can satisfy all their JavaScript requirements with the tools in Dreamweaver and with free or purchased scripts. You do not have to write your own scripts. I try to avoid writing my own, partly because I do not consider myself a JavaScript expert, and I am also a careless typist. However, I do read JavaScript very well; usually I can quickly spot a problem. I also know enough to edit scripts, and have written my own scripts when nothing else would do — I do not like to compromise ideas. I recommend achieving at least this level of competence with JavaScript.

In the meantime, you can learn how to work with JavaScript in Dreamweaver.

Editing JavaScript in Dreamweaver

You placed a JavaScript script in Session 11 by simply working in the HTML code. However, you can also edit your placed script from within Dreamweaver, either through the Code view of the main document, or by using the Properties panel. Go back to your placed script and use the Properties panel to remove the words "Last update" from the JavaScript display in your document as well as the <center> tag.

To edit a script:

1. Open the document handcode.html from the resources folder in your Holiday site.
2. Select the script icon in your design view. The Properties panel indicates that JavaScript is selected.
3. Click the Edit button in the Properties panel. The Script Properties window opens.
4. Scroll to the end of the script and locate the following code:

   ```
   document.write("<center>Last update: ");
   ```

   Highlight and delete document.write("<center>Last update: ");.
5. Locate the following code:

   ```
   document.write("</center>");
   ```

   Highlight and delete document.write("</center>");.
6. Click OK to close the Script Properties window.

Now, follow these steps to move the script to the top of the page:

1. In Design view, insert your cursor in front of the first text entry. Hit Enter twice to make room for the date script.
2. While still in Design view, click the JavaScript icon to select it. Confirm that the JavaScript is selected in the Properties panel. Click and drag the icon to the top of the page.
3. Preview your page in your browser. See Figure 13-1 for the correct results.

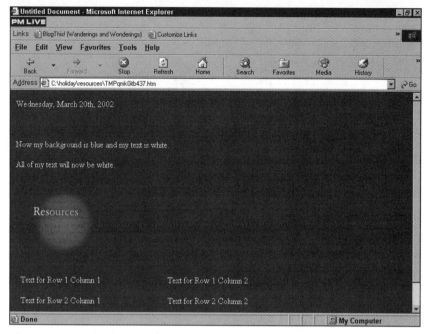

Figure 13-1   *The date code script is now at the top of the document.*

You have placed a JavaScript script, edited it, and moved the script to a different location in your document. Now you are ready to create JavaScript rollovers.

Creating a Simple JavaScript Rollover

**20 Min.
To Go**

In a simple rollover, one image is replaced with another when the mouse is held over the original image. This has become a universal symbol on the Web for an image that is also a link, helping your visitors to understand the navigation on your site. Rollovers are easy to create.

The graphic files you require for the next exercise should be in the art folder of your Holiday site. They were included in Session 6 files copied from the CD-ROM.

To create a rollover, Dreamweaver generates three sections of code, placing JavaScript into the document head, into the <body> tag, and also into the document body where the rollover is to be placed. Check your code before you place the rollover so you can view the change.

1. Open the index.html file from your Holiday folder. (You are going to replace the image menu items with JavaScript rollovers.)
2. Select the first graphic in the menu. Delete it.

3. Keep your cursor in the same location as it was when you deleted the file in Step 2. Select Insert ⇨ Interactive Images ⇨ Rollover Image and the Insert Rollover Image window opens.

4. Type **route** for the Image Name value.

5. Click the Browse button next to the Original Image field. Select the file route.gif from the art folder. The image that you specify in this field is seen before the mouse is passed over it.

6. Click the Browse button next to the Rollover Image field. Select the file route-over.gif from the art folder.

 Never use images of different sizes for rollover images. The original and the rollover image must be the same size. Also, be careful that the elements in your original and rollover graphics line up when preparing rollovers. A 1-pixel difference when positioning the two images can cause an effect that is quite disturbing.

7. Verify that the Preload Rollover Image option is checked. This prompts the browser to load the rollover image into the browser cache when the page is viewed. When the mouse is passed over the rollover image, a preloaded image displays instantly.

8. Type **Our Route** in the Alternate Text field.

9. Add the link for this menu item. Click the Browse button next to the When Clicked Go To URL field. Select route.html.

10. Click OK to return to the document.

11. Preview the document in your primary browser. Move your mouse over the top menu item and the image should change. Preview the document again in your secondary browser to ensure that your rollover is working in both.

12. Repeat Steps 2 to 10 for the other menu items on the page, changing the details for each menu item. The graphics you used to create the menu originally are used again as the original image. The rollover images have the same name as the original with the addition of the word *over*. For example, if people.gif is the original, people-over.gif is the rollover image.

That's all there is to creating a simple rollover. It is almost as quick and easy as creating a simple graphic menu link, but it does add a lot to your page.

Creating a Complex JavaScript Rollover

10 Min. To Go

The complex JavaScript rollover (also known as a disjoint rollover) is becoming increasingly popular, and with good reason. When you roll your mouse over one image, another image in a different location appears. When used properly, a lot of visual information is presented in a small space.

Using the Behaviors palette accomplishes this task. Instructing Dreamweaver to write the code, step-by-step, is more involved than placing code from another source, or using the menu to create a simple rollover.

This process can be very confusing, but once you get the concept, it is easy. I have designed a very simple menu for explanation and construction. The menu items have names to help you track what is happening and grasp the concept. You can view the finished menu in the Session 13 folder on the CD-ROM in the file rollover.html. Figure 13-2 shows the original and the rollover for each of the three menu items.

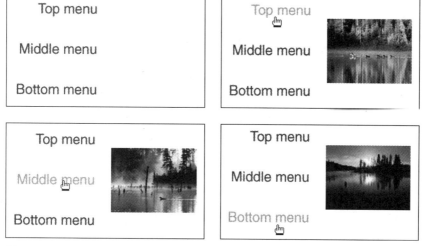

Figure 13-2　*The original menu is shown at the top left. Note how the menu item changes color and an image appears when the mouse is passed over it.*

Now, you are going to create a document in the resources folder to build the menu. You will use this menu type for the second site you build. It is best that you work on this menu with nothing else on the page as you learn. Building another for the new site helps reinforce the method.

Locate the Session13/rollart files folder on the CD-ROM. Copy the entire folder to the art directory of your Holiday site.

Preparing to create a complex rollover

This exercise is divided into two parts. First, you prepare the initial menu by placing images, and naming the images you place. This is very important. Once you have prepared the entire menu, you will add the behaviors that run your rollovers.

To prepare your menu for a complex rollover:

1. Create a new document and save it to the resources folder of the Holiday site as rollover.html.
2. Create a table with three rows and two columns and the following parameters: Cell Padding **10**, Cell Spacing **0**, Width **350** pixels wide, and Border **0**. Merge the three cells in the right column to form one cell.

3. Place the image topmen13.gif in the top row of the left column.

4. Name your images so JavaScript understands which images to change. Click the image you just placed to select it. In the Properties panel, type **top** in the Name field (this is not labeled in the Property panel) at the top left of the window. See Figure 13-3.

Name

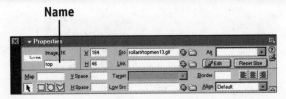

Figure 13-3 *Images are named in the Properties panel in preparation for attaching Behaviors.*

5. Create a *dummy* or, more precisely, a *null* link, because the behavior must be attached to a link. Type **javascript:;** into the Link field in the Properties panel.

 Because you are just doing an exercise here, you need not worry about creating the links. When you create the menu for the next site you build, you will create complex rollovers with working links.

6. Repeat Steps 3, 4, and 5 to place the second and third images. Each is placed in a separate cell in the left column. The second menu image is midmen13.gif and should be named **middle**. The bottom menu image is named botmen13.gif and should be named **bottom**.

7. You also need to place an image in the right column. When menu items are not activated by the mouse, this image is displayed. In this case, place a blank image to hold the place for the rollovers. Place the image menu13blank.gif in the right column and type **blank** in the Name field.

 Although the images in this exercise are very close to one another, an image can be placed anywhere on your page. However, if you place them too far from where the visitor is focused, the effect may be lost.

Attaching behaviors to the images

You are now ready to add the JavaScript to this image and create a double rollover. Each of the menu items on the left has two separate rollovers added to it. The image you just placed in the right column is used only to receive the images called with the menu images when the mouse rolls over it.

To add behaviors to your images:

1. Open the Behaviors panel, if it is not already open (Window ⇨ Behaviors).

2. Select the top menu image. Now add behaviors to change the menu item image and to place an image where the blank image currently resides. Both actions are added with one behavior.

3. Click the + (add) in the Behaviors palette to add a behavior. Select Swap Image from the menu that appears. The Swap Image window opens.

4. Add a behavior to change your menu item to a different image when the mouse is held over the image. In the Images section of the Swap Image window, the entry image "top" should be highlighted. Remember that "top" was the name of the first menu item. Click the button beside the Set Source To field to select the file top-men13-over.gif from the rollart folder. Click Select to close this window and accept the file. *Do not click OK in the Swap Image window yet.* You have only completed half of the rollover so far.

5. Complete this behavior by replacing the blank image with the image that should display with the top menu item. In the Images listing of the Swap Image window, select the listing named "blank."

Don't worry — the changes you made to "top" are still there, even though you cannot see them. To confirm, simply click that image name again in the list to view the Set Source To field that contains the instructions you just completed.

6. With "blank" selected, browse for the image menu13_1swap.jpg. Highlight the file and click Select to return to the Swap Image window. Make sure that Preload Images and Restore Images on MouseOut are checked. Now click OK, because you have done what you needed with that image.

7. Preview your rollover in your browser. When the mouse passes over the top menu item, the words turn to gold, and an image appears to the right. If you are getting that result, you have created the behavior correctly and can move to the next menu items.

8. Repeat Steps 2 through 7 to complete the menu. The middle menu item requires midmen13-over.gif for the swap with "middle," and menu13_swap2.jpg for the swap with "blank." The bottom menu item requires botmen13-over.gif to swap with "bottom," and menu13_swap3.jpg to swap with "blank."

If you are still a little uncertain about how to do this exercise, I recommend you start again from scratch. This technique may seem confusing until you have a "Eureka! I get it" moment. Once you understand how this menu works, you are well set to create your own, and to apply other behaviors.

Done!

REVIEW

You now have the skills to add action to your pages. Because the techniques included in this session are used often, it is important to remember a few vital points:

- JavaScript provides a great deal of the interactivity on the Web today, through features such as rollovers. It also works behind the scenes collecting and verifying data.
- You can write or edit JavaScript in any code window in Dreamweaver.
- Always use images of exactly the same size for rollover states. It is also important that elements on the rollover states are placed in exactly the same place on the image.
- Complex rollovers can change images that are in different locations from where the mouse initiates the action.
- Naming images is critical for any JavaScript. It is to your benefit to give each image a name that easily identifies it.
- Behaviors are attached to links for rollovers.

QUIZ YOURSELF

1. Why is it important to gain a working knowledge of JavaScript? (See the "What is JavaScript?" section.)
2. What is a simple rollover and what does it signify on a Web page? (See the "Creating a Simple JavaScript Rollover" section.)
3. What must you do to test a rollover in Dreamweaver? (See the "Creating a Simple JavaScript Rollover" section.)
4. What is a complex rollover? (See the "Creating a Complex JavaScript Rollover" section.)
5. What do you need on your page to prepare for a complex rollover? (See the "Preparing to create a complex rollover" section.)
6. Behaviors are Dreamweaver's way to create JavaScript code. What behavior do you use for complex rollovers? (See the "Attaching behaviors to the images" section.)

Creating Forms

Session Checklist

✔ Understanding how forms work

✔ Working with CGI

✔ Building forms in Dreamweaver

✔ Setting form parameters

✔ Moving your CGI-driven form to the Web

**30 Min.
To Go**

If you have had to fill in your name and e-mail address on the Web, chances are that you have used a form. If you have had to fill in your address and select choices on a survey form, you have almost certainly used a form powered by CGI.

Forms are used to collect information on the Web. The results are generally returned by e-mail for most small Web sites, and they can be sent directly to a database for more complex information processing, or for high traffic sites. The form you create here is a simple contact form, with the results to be returned by e-mail.

You can also create easy surveys or polls for your site, which are run by free and low-cost scripts readily available on the Web. If you are ambitious, you can add message boards and chat rooms to your site in the same way. There is no shortage of applications run by CGI scripts, but they can be confusing when you first start using them. Although you will be referring only to a form for this exercise, it works in much the same way as other CGI applications.

You build a form in this session and learn how that form runs with CGI. However, you have to do some work on your own to get this form running. There are too many variables to cover here, such as how different hosts handle CGI scripts and how different CGI scripts run forms. But this discussion of running forms with CGI should get you pointed in the right direction to learn more.

Understanding How Forms Work

Dreamweaver offers very simple and powerful tools to create a form. If you want a text field on your form, a few keystrokes in Dreamweaver will create it. Do you need a radio button, a checkbox, or a button to submit information that is labeled with text other than the word Submit? Dreamweaver delivers, and without much more work than placing a simple image in your document.

Do you feel a "but . . . " coming on here? Well, there is one, and it is a big one. Creating the form objects is only half the battle. In fact, for hair-pulling potential, you are not even close to halfway finished when you have designed a perfect form.

The form you create in Dreamweaver is much like the shell of a car. No matter how pretty it is, and no matter how perfect it is, that car is going nowhere with just a frame and body. CGI is the engine for this car. Without the body and frame, the engine sits like a lump, no matter how powerful or advanced it is. In fact, until extra pieces are added to a car — small, seemingly inconsequential pieces — neither the frame nor the engine can do what it was designed to do.

Working with CGI

Luckily, when you place a CGI script, you need to do very little to the CGI part. Unlike JavaScript, your form script is not placed into your code. You simply refer your form to an external CGI script.

A form powered by CGI on the Web has been created by HTML elements that enable the form to display on the page. A set of CGI instructions is waiting to take the information that is put into the form and send it to the correct place. Between the two elements are instructions that do not show on the screen as part of the form, but are also not part of the CGI script. These instructions are entered into the HTML code to connect the form and the CGI script.

Perhaps this sounds a bit complicated. It is. But don't be discouraged. As long as you work carefully, there is no reason why placing a simple CGI form is beyond even a beginner's basic ability.

Building Forms in Dreamweaver

There are two parts to building a form in Dreamweaver. The first essential action is to create a form. The second is adding form objects, such as text fields and checkboxes, to your form. All form objects must be inside a form.

I am using FormMail, a free script from Matt's Script Archive (www.worldwidemart.com/scripts/) as a sample script for this exercise. This is a simple, versatile script designed by Matt Wright and offered at no cost. If you use this script, make sure that you leave the credit in the code.

There are security concerns with this script. I recommend that you use Matt's script to get your feet wet with CGI forms, but also urge you to check http://nms-cgi.sourceforge.net/. This site explains the security concerns and offers similar scripts. The replacement scripts are more complex to set up, however.

Creating the basic form

You should be feeling fairly comfortable with tables by now, so you're going to create your form inside a table. Although it slightly complicates the construction, it is hard to create an attractive form without having a table to help you with the layout.

Create a form and add some form objects to it.

1. Activate the Holiday site if it is not already active, and open contact.html.
2. The second cell of the second row should be empty. If it is not, delete any content. You will place your form here. Make sure your cursor is in the empty cell. Select Insert ⇨ Form. A red border appears; this border represents the form. If you cannot see red borders, select View ⇨ Visual Aids ⇨ Invisible Elements.

Connecting the form to a CGI script

A form cannot run on its own. You must provide the route for the form to find the required information (CGI script) to operate.

20 Min. To Go

Tell the form which CGI script will be used to power the form. Click the folder next to the Action field and select the CGI script you want to use. If you are using Matt's FormMail script, locate and select FormMail.pl in the cgi-bin folder.

> **CGI scripts are always stored in a special folder, and you must create a matching folder on your local site. The name of this folder is usually cgi-bin, although you will occasionally find the name is cgibin. Your server is the one that sets this folder's name. Whatever name is required for your server is the one you should create on your local site.**
>
> **Depending on your site structure, it may be easier to use an absolute address when specifying the path to your CGI script.**

Placing a table in a form

A table is used to create an orderly form.

1. Place your cursor inside the form borders. Create a table with two columns and five rows. Specify CellPadding **10**, Cell Spacing **0**, width **350** pixels, and Border **0**. You should have a table inside the red border.
2. Place the text that will identify what information is required for each form object first. This is simple text in a table. You will create the form objects in the next exercise. Type **Name** into the first row in the left column. Type **Email** into the second row in the left column. Type **Travel for** into the third, type **Interests** in the fourth, and finally, type **Comments** into the fifth row.
3. Set the left column width to **75** pixels. Merge the two cells in the bottom row. Your form should now resemble the form shown in Figure 14-1.

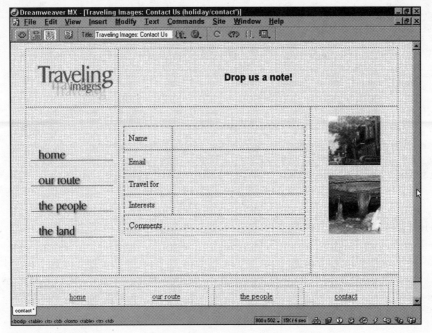

Figure 14-1 *Text titles entered into the table within a form.*

Adding form objects

You are ready to start adding form objects now. Start with the text field, which is used anytime you want to have a response typed in by the visitor.

Adding a single-line text field

This form object is used for any text entry.

1. Place your cursor into the first row of the right column. Select Insert ⇨ Form Objects ⇨ Text Field. A text box appears.

2. With the text box still selected, type **name** in the field beneath the title TextField in the Properties panel. This identifies the form object for later use.

3. With the text box still selected, specify **30** for the Char Width value. This specifies the width for the text field, and is measured in characters. If you want to restrict the number of characters allowed for this field, type the value in the Max Char field. Leave the default value of Single Line for Type and the Init Val fields blank.

4. Repeat Steps 2 and 3 to specify the Email text field, using **email** for the TextField name.

Adding a radio button

Radio buttons are used when only one choice will be allowed.

1. In the right column in the Travel for row, type **Business**. Select Insert ⇨ Form Objects ⇨ Radio Buttons. Type **Personal**. Insert another radio button.

    Since radio buttons work together, the RadioButton name (as entered in the Properties panel) for all buttons in a series must be the same. In this case, name the series **travelfor**. The entries in the Checked Value field will eventually be the result that is returned in our results if that selection has been checked.

2. Select the Business radio button. Type **travelfor** in the RadioButton field. Type **business** in the Checked Value field. Select Checked as the Initial State.

3. Select the Personal radio button. Type **travelfor** in the RadioButton field. Type **personal** in the Checked value field. Leave the Initial State as Unchecked.

Adding a checkbox

Checkboxes are used when you want to allow your visitor to select multiple choices.

1. In the right column in the Interests row, select Insert ⇨ Form Objects ⇨ Checkbox. Type **Domestic travel by car**. Holding your Shift key down, press Enter to move the cursor to the next line. Insert another checkbox and type **Domestic travel by air**. Press Shift+Enter to insert a break. Insert another checkbox and type **International travel**. Click Yes to the alert box asking if you wish to add a form object.

2. Like the radio buttons, you want the CheckBox names to be the same for each checkbox. Type **interests** for the CheckBox name value in all three checkboxes.

3. Type the following names into the Checked Value fields: **domcar** for the first, **domair** for the second, and **international** for the third. Leave the initial state as Unchecked for all.

**10 Min.
To Go**

Adding a multiple-line text box

You started with a text box that only required one line. When you would like to offer more room for comments, you can create a multiple-line text box.

1. In the bottom row, place your cursor at the end of the word Comments. Press Enter to insert a line.

2. Select Insert ⇨ Form Objects ⇨ Text Field. A text box appears.

3. Type **comments** in the TextField name field, and set the Char Width to **40**.

4. Choose Multi line as the Type. Specify **5** in the Num Lines Field. This value specifies the vertical height of the text area that will display.

5. Choose Virtual from the Wrap drop-down box. This setting will allow scrolling if the text entered exceeds the size of the text box.

6. You can specify text that will appear in your form to help guide your visitors. Type **Please leave a comment.** in the Init Val field.

Inserting a form button

You have your form elements in place for your visitors to enter information, but you must provide a way to send the form results to yourself. This is handled with a form button.

To add a button use the following steps:

1. Place your cursor at the end of the last text box at the bottom of the form. Press Enter to move the cursor down. Select Insert ➪ Form Objects ➪ Button. A button appears.

2. Repeat Step 1 to place a second button. Now rename the buttons.

3. Select the first button. Type **Submit form** in the Label field. The button changes to reflect the new text. All other values remain the same.

4. Finally, you would like to provide an easy way for your visitors to clear the entries they have made and start over. Select the second button. Type **Reset** for the Button Name. Click Reset Form in the Action field. The label changes to Reset.

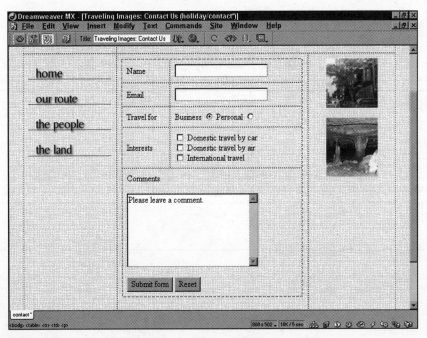

Figure 14-2 *The completed form in Dreamweaver.*

Always preview forms often in both Internet Explorer and Netscape Navigator, since the results in the two browsers rarely match.

There's your form. See Figure 14-2 to check your results. Now let's move on to creating hidden fields, which are used to organize the results that are returned to you.

Setting Form Parameters

You connected the form to a CGI script when you started your form. However, when you consider that you edited almost nothing in the actual CGI form script, you soon realize that something is missing. How is the CGI script going to know what to send for results? It won't unless you provide that information.

Each CGI script has a set of parameters that it needs to have satisfied for the script to work. In addition, you can specify optional fields to obtain the information you require. The CGI script contains every field that can be used in any form (more than you could ever need for one form), but you supply information with your form that tells the script which values to use. This information is specified in hidden fields.

 To determine which values you require, and which can be included as an option, look for a help section where you find the script. The help section for Matt's FormMail script, for example, is excellent and provides all the information you need to determine which hidden fields will deliver the results you require (www.worldwidemart.com/scripts/readme/ formmail.shtml**).**

Creating hidden form fields

A hidden field is a special HTML tag that enables you to add information to your form that cannot be seen on your pages, but which provides specialized information that can be read by the CGI script. They are quite simple to add once you know the values you require.

Take the following steps to add a hidden field:

1. In the contact.html document, place your cursor at the beginning of the table. Make sure the cursor is inside the form. Select Insert ⇨ Form Object ⇨ Hidden Field. An icon appears at the top of your form. You create a hidden field for each piece of information you must pass on to the script.

2. Make sure the hidden field icon is selected. In the Properties panel, type **recipient** in the HiddenField name field. This is the one required field for the FormMail script. Type your e-mail address into the Value field.

3. Create four more hidden fields following the actions in Step 1. You should now have five hidden field icons.

4. Select the second hidden field icon. Type **subject** for the name, and type **Travel Interests** for the value. This field will place Travel Interests in the subject line of the e-mail you receive from this form.

5. Select the next hidden field icon. Type **print_config** for the name. This field is the most important field for the quality of your information. When you list your form object names here, the CGI script knows to return the results from these fields.

Type **name, email, travelfor, interests, comments** for the Value. These names match the form objects that you created.

6. Select the next icon. Type **redirect** for the name. This field enables you to direct your visitors to a specific page once they have submitted their form. I usually create a special page for this feature. For this exercise, just return to your front page. Type **../index.html** for the Value.

7. Select the final icon. Type **required** for the name. This field asks that the form not be accepted unless the specified fields have been completed. Type **name, email** for the Value.

Your form is complete. This is as far as I can take you in this process, but I urge you to obtain a CGI script and follow the instructions to place the form on the Web. You will probably find it much easier to do your first form using FormMail.pl as the CGI script, because the form that you just built is ready to upload for that script. If you use another script, however, you will have to adjust the name fields to match the names in the CGI script.

Although I cannot give step-by-step directions for placing this form, I will give you some hints and a little more information to smooth your way.

Activating a CGI form

There are a few things I found very confusing when I was trying to get my first CGI-driven form to work. I touched on some of these in the early part of this session, such as the relationship between the form and the CGI script. Once I realized that the CGI was a fully external script, and that my form simply tapped into that external script, things became much clearer. I am so comfortable with the few CGI scripts I use now that it is hard to imagine it seemed hard. Perhaps if I can run through the things that confused me, and how I came to understand them, you will avoid some of the head-scratching time I put in.

Editing the CGI script

The FormMail script usually requires only one adjustment. You must specify the name of the domain that will be using the FormMail.pl file; in my case, wpeck.com. The entry is near the beginning and is noted with a comment in the script. The entry for my site is @referers = 'wpeck.com';.

You may need to adjust fields to match your server sendmail program, or perl location. If so, please see the form instructions on Matt's site and/or consult with your host.

Although you need an adjusted script for each domain, you can run countless forms once the script is running successfully on that domain by simply specifying this script as the Action for a new form.

To edit FormMail.pl, use a plain text editor such as Notepad. The file will not show in the files listing for a text program. If you specify All Files, or type *.* for the filename and press Enter, you can then select the file.

You may find it easier to use an FTP program such wsFTP (PC) or Fetch (Mac) to transfer your files and finish the process. A CGI script must be transferred to the server using an ASCII format, and you must set a parameter known as permissions. Permissions are stated as numbers (755 or 775, for example) and are simply codes. The codes specify who is allowed to read or write to the file. If you are not writing CGI, this is not something you must understand fully, but you do need to know how to set permissions. Scripts will usually offer information about this subject, and your hosting company should also be able to help. Note, though, that this only applies to the actual script and not to the form. The form document is transferred just like any other file.

That's really it. Give it a try. Although it seems confusing, there is a lot of help available on the Web, and the rewards are well worth it. There are exciting new CGI scripts coming into use every day, and you will find many very useful.

Done!

REVIEW

Keep these points in mind:

- CGI forms have two distinct parts: the form and the CGI script. Dreamweaver helps tie the two parts together, and has powerful forms creation capability.
- The CGI script for a form is activated through the Action field in the Properties panel.
- All form elements must be placed within a form or they will not work.
- Forms are usually placed in tables for better layout. The table must be completely contained within the form.
- All objects in a Checkbox or Radio button group should have identical names.
- Hidden fields are used to communicate with the CGI script to achieve the results you require.
- CGI scripts require permissions to be set, which is often done using a separate FTP program.

QUIZ YOURSELF

1. Forms are made up of two parts. What are they? (See the "Understanding How Forms Work" section.)
2. What is a common way to control the layout of a form? (See the "Building Forms in Dreamweaver" section.)
3. What is a cgi-bin folder? (See the "Connecting the form to a CGI script" section.)
4. What is the difference between a radio button and a checkbox in a form? (See the "Adding form objects" section.)
5. What is a hidden field? (See the "Setting Form Parameters" section.)
6. Where do you edit a CGI form? (See the "Editing the CGI script" section.)

Creating Library Items

Session Checklist

✔ Introducing the Assets panel

✔ Understanding Library items

✔ Creating a new Library item

✔ Inserting a Library item

✔ Creating a Library item from existing items

✔ Editing a Library item

✔ Updating Library items globally

✔ Disconnecting the Library item links

✔ Deleting or editing a Library item file

**30 Min.
To Go**

S ome of you are going to say that I have held back information from you when you read the rest of this session. Much that you have done so far could have been done much more easily if I had introduced the Asset panel to you in the beginning. From a purely practical standpoint, you are right. However, you would also be totally in the dark about the menu system and the structure of this program.

The truth is that I have kept many timesavers hidden. Over the next few sessions, as you start to build a second site, I'll bring the various panels to you, suggesting where you can use them to save time. This session highlights the Assets panel. When used with the Properties panel, this panel can help you accomplish most of the actions you require to build your site.

Introducing the Assets Panel

In this session, you take a very short look at the Assets panel. Library items — the focus for this session — are stored within the Assets panel.

You'll focus on the Assets panel in a later session. For now, I'll show you what you need to know to use the Assets panel to get to Library items and templates. Notice that the Assets panel is in the same panel group as the Site panel, which is handy. Simply click the tabs at the top of the window to toggle between the two panels.

 The Assets panel deserves a large amount of time to explain the features and how to use them in document creation. Session 21 is devoted to Dreamweaver's most powerful panels.

Assets panel basics

The Assets panel gathers the assets for your site into one convenient location. Assets include images, links, external scripts, colors, media — almost any type of information that you place in a Dreamweaver document is stored in the Assets panel. The assets are gathered from the site cache so that it automatically tracks new or deleted files.

Once an asset is in the Assets panel, you have drag-and-drop convenience to add that element to another document in the site. You can also copy an asset to another site. To summarize, you can place almost any type of file from within the Assets panel — one very powerful feature.

Working with the Assets panel

Before moving on to Library items and how they work in the Assets panel, I would like you to see how the Assets panel works with an image. You are going to create a throwaway document.

1. Open the Holiday site. Create a blank document through the menu.
2. To open the Assets panel, select Window ⇨ Assets. The Assets panel opens, and it may show assets in the windows.
3. Click the Image icon at the top of the left toolbar in the Assets panel. Make sure that the Site option is checked near the top of the panel. You should now see a listing of all the images you have used in the Holiday site. Click any listing in the lower pane to see a preview in the upper pane.
4. Scroll through the list of images to locate home.gif. Drag either the lower listing or the preview image for this file to the document window. The image appears at the location of your cursor when you release the mouse button, as shown in figure 15-1.

That's enough on the Assets panel to allow you to move on to Library items in the following sections and to templates in the next session.

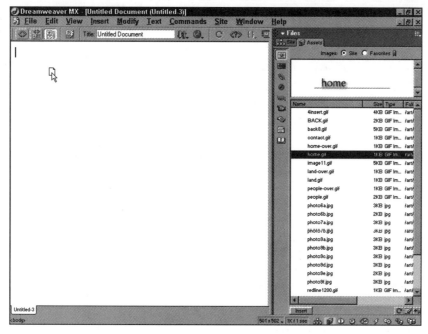

Figure 15-1 *An image is dragged from the Assets panel to the document. Releasing the mouse button places the image at the cursor point. Note: Mac users will not see the Site tab shown here.*

Understanding Library Items

Library items can be created for many reasons. They can range from a snippet of text to a full table. Library items can contain scripts, images, links — anything that you can place on an HTML page.

The secret behind a Library item is that the code you specify is stored away in a Library folder in the root directory for your site. When you place the Library item in your document, the document checks the stored file and displays the information — a wonderful timesaver for placement alone.

Library items can only contain code that can be placed within the body of a document.

20 Min. To Go

Editing Library items

Suppose you find a new way to present the information that is stored in a Library item. You can edit the Library item and automatically apply the changes to every document in which you have used the item. As an example, suppose you have your copyright information stored as a Library item, and that it has been placed in over 100 documents. You would like to change the date of the copyright to the new year. To do that, you would open the Library item, change the date, and then save the changes. Update across your site, and the new information replaces the old.

 If you are familiar with SSI (Server Side Includes), you are probably noticing strong similarities. The concepts are exactly the same. The practical use is similar, although you must upload the updated pages containing a Library item to have the changes appear on the Web. This is a little more cumbersome than just uploading a file to the server as you do with SSI, but a Library item will work on any remote server in the same way as it does your local site. SSI must be supported by the host to work.

Using Library items

Library items are easy to use. Although it takes a little time to get used to the idea, you are more likely to be confused by thinking they are more difficult than they are. Work through the exercises in this session and trust that they are just as easy as they seem. You'll be thinking up new uses for library items very quickly, and you will then wonder how you worked without them.

Working with Library Items

You can build a Library item from scratch, or you can create one from existing information. In this session, you build one of each type. The best way to learn about Library items is to start working with them. The more I talk, the more difficult they will sound, so let's start working.

Creating a Library item from scratch

Although Library items are created within what looks like an HTML page, make sure that you understand that you are creating *pieces* of a page. When you arrive at the edit screen, notice that the background for the page is gray, the default HTML background. Because you are editing information that will be placed in an existing page, you cannot add code that will fight with the other code on the page, such as the <body> tag.

Take the following steps to create a Library item from scratch:

1. Open the index.html page of your Holiday site.
2. If your Assets panel is not open, select Window ⇨ Assets.
3. Click the Library icon in the left toolbox of the Assets panel (last icon). This opens the Library section of the Assets panel, which should be blank.
4. Click the menu icon at the upper-right side of the Assets panel to open the Assets Options menu. Select New Library Item. A new listing appears in the Assets panel window with the name Untitled. Type **copyright** to name your Library item. Your Assets panel should resemble the one shown in Figure 15-2.

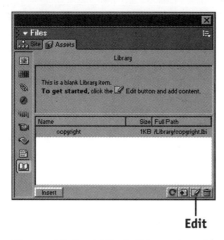

Edit

Figure 15-2 *A Blank Library item has been named in the Library section of the Assets panel. Note the Edit icon.*

5. Click the Edit icon at the lower edge of the Assets panel. A blank HTML page opens. Note that the window Title bar features the following listing: <<Library Item>> (copyright.lbi). This tells you that you are not editing a document, and it states the name (copyright) for this Library item.

6. Type **Copyright 2002 Your Name** (where "your name" is . . . you get it).

7. Apply Center justification (Align Center icon at the upper-right of the Properties panel) to center the copyright notice on the page.

8. Select File ⇨ Save. Close the <<Library Item>> window to return to your document. The text you typed in the Library edit screen now appears at the top of the Assets panel when the Library item is active.

You have now created a Library item that can easily be placed in any document in your Holiday site. Check the Site panel and you will see that a new directory has been added. You may need to click the Refresh icon at the bottom of the Assets window to see new files.

The Library folder, which was automatically created as soon as you added a Library item, contains the file copyright.lbi. Dreamweaver created this file when you created the Library item in this exercise.

Adding a Library item to a document

Now that you have created a Library item, you can place it in your document.

1. Your index.html document should still be open. Place your cursor to the right of the table and press Shift+Enter to bring the cursor below the table.

2. Make sure the Assets panel is open, and that Library is active in the Assets panel. Drag the Copyright Library item to the area below the table in your document. The line of text in your Library item appears in the document, with a yellow background. The background lets you know that it is a Library item.

If you would like to view your page without the Library item background, select View ⇨ Visual Aids ⇨ Invisible Items to turn off the Invisible Items display. You can repeat these steps to view the Invisible Elements again.

3. Click the text you placed to select, and then check your Properties panel. Although the text is selected, the Properties panel lists this as a Library Item (Figure 15-3).

Figure 15-3 *Although it appears that text is selected, the Properties panel shows no text options, since this is a Library item.*

4. Repeat Steps 1 and 2 in every document of the Holiday site to place your copyright notice on every page.

Now that your Library item is placed, you can make changes with one easy step. You do that in a few minutes. However, I want to pause for a bit and talk about creating a Library item from existing information.

Creating a Library item from existing information

It is probably more common to create a piece of information within a document and then decide that you want that to become a Library item. You might also know you are creating a section of the page that will become a Library item later, but you want to design it within the context of the page. Any item in the body of the document can be used to create a Library item.

Take the following steps to create a Library item from existing information:

1. If it is not already open, open index.html from the Holiday site. You should have at least two statements under the menu: one is a reference to the Route page, and the other is a reference to Amazon.com.

   If you do not have these statements, type the following below the menu in the left column. (These links were added in Session 9.)

   a. **Please make sure you visit our Route page.** (Highlight the word Route and create a link to route.html.)

   b. **You can buy books at Amazon.com.** (Highlight Amazon.com and create a link to http://www.amazon.com/books/.)

2. Select the text in both statements. Open your Assets panel if it is not open, and click the Library icon to activate the Library function.

3. Click the menu icon at the top right of the Assets panel and select New Library Item. Note that the text you have selected appears in the upper window of the

Assets panel and a new listing appears in the lower window. Type **notes** to replace the Untitled label.

4. Return to the document and click away from the text to deselect it. Your text now has a yellow background, indicating that it is a Library item. (If you cannot see the yellow, check to make sure that you have the Invisible Elements viewing enabled.)

   Although you created this information within your document, it is now the same as the Library item you created from scratch.

5. Add this Library item to every document in your Holiday site. (See Steps 1 and 2 of "Adding a Library item to a document," earlier in this session.)

Editing a Library item

**10 Min.
To Go**

Now that you have a Library item defined — whether you created it from scratch or from existing information — you can make changes in the same way.

To reduce confusion, save and close all documents in Dreamweaver with the exception of index.html. You are going to make changes from here, so it will be apparent to you that even without the document open, Library items can be updated.

Take the following steps to edit a Library item:

1. With index.html active, select Window ➪ Assets to display the Assets panel. Click the Library icon to activate the Libraries area of the panel.

2. Double-click the Copyright item in the Library items listing to open it.

> **You can also open your Library items by opening the drop-down options menu and selecting Edit, by clicking the Edit icon at the lower edge of the Assets panel, or by right-clicking (PC) or Ctrl+clicking (Mac) the listing and choosing Edit. However, double-clicking is usually the fastest.**

3. You are going to change the word *copyright* to a copyright symbol. Select and delete the word *copyright*. With your cursor at the beginning of the sentence, select Insert ➪ Special Characters ➪ Copyright. A copyright symbol (©) will appear.

4. Select File ➪ Save. An alert window appears asking if you would like to update the Library items in the list of files in the window. Click Update and the Copyright Library Item entries are updated in all of your documents.

   As soon as you click Update, the Update Pages window appears, and you see log entries are added as Dreamweaver updates that Library item in other files. Once the changes are completed, the window remains open so you can see a list of the changes that have been made. Read through the listings to make sure that the files that contain the Library item are listed.

5. Select Close to close the Update Pages window.

6. Open the other files in your site to confirm that the change has been made.

7. Close the copyright document window.

Although Dreamweaver prompts you to update your Library items with every edit, there are times when you will require a global update. You have that option, as well.

Updating Library items globally

If you choose not to update Library items after an edit or, if for any other reason, you want to update your Library items as a separate action, take the following steps:

1. From any document or the Site window, open the Assets panel and activate the Library items asset.

2. Click the menu icon at the upper-right side of the Assets panel and choose Update Site. This gives you the option to update all Library items in the site, or to seek and update a specific Library item. You also have the choice to update the entire site.

   If you want to update only the documents using one Library item throughout your site, choose Files That Use from the left drop-down menu and the Library item you want to update from the right drop-down menu.

That is how easy it is to have one-stop editing power over elements throughout your entire site. A little planning in the beginning can save you hours over the creation of an entire site. You will also gain consistency, because it is hard to remember exactly how you have worded a phrase, or which color you used for a specific note. Library items will be the same across every page, no matter how many changes you may make.

What if you would like to change the text contained in a Library item for just one page? Don't worry; you also have that option.

Disconnecting a Library item link

Suppose you would like a slightly different version of the Library item on one of your pages. You can break the connection and then edit it, without affecting that Library item on any other page. Once the connection is broken, however, changes you make to the Library item file will not be reflected on pages where you have broken the connection.

Take the following steps to break a link:

1. Open the route.html file from your Holiday Site. You are going to break the link to the notes Library item and delete the link to the Route page.

2. Click in any of the text of the Library item to select. Click the Detach from Original button in the upper-right corner of the Properties panel. The connection is now broken. You may receive a warning that the connection will be broken. You can click OK, or check the "Don't warn me again" option so the alert will not appear again.

3. Now note the Properties panel. All the original settings for selected text are shown.

4. Delete the text and link pointing to the Route page.

 You do not have to use Library items only for items that will be updated regularly. You can also use it for items that change slightly on every page, such as a text menu. Apply the Library item containing all menu items and then break the link. Remove the text item that represents the current page. Although you cannot do a global update (because the links are broken), you can quickly add a consistent menu to each page.

You now have the means to automatically insert repeating elements throughout your site. You can also share Library items with other sites.

Sharing Library items between sites

If you would like to copy a Library item to a different site, Dreamweaver provides the way. Your copyright notice Library item could easily be used on a different site.

Take the following steps to copy a Library item to another site:

1. Open your Assets panel within the Holiday site (any document or the Site window). Activate the Library items asset.
2. Select the Copyright item from the list. Click the triangle at the upper-right side of the Assets panel and select Copy to Site. Choose Crash Course from the menu that appears.
3. Your copyright notice will now be available in the Asset panel when the Crash Course site is active.

Deleting or editing a Library item file

You can remove a Library item from any document by deleting it from within the document. However, if you wish to delete the main Library item from your Assets panel, it is a bit more involved. When you delete the Library item from the Assets panel, the Library item is removed, but the content from that item remains in the documents. You must delete each entry to remove it. You can also use the content from a deleted Library item to recreate the item. It is good practice to remove the individual Library items from the content (use the find and replace function for speed and accuracy) before you delete the Library file from the Assets panel.

1. Open any document in the Holiday site.
2. In the Assets panel, click the copyright Library item. Click the upper-right menu icon, or right-click (PC) or Ctrl+click (Mac) and choose Delete. Click Yes to delete the file when you are prompted. The Library item is deleted, but the text remains on the pages.
3. On any document, select the Copyright Library item. Click Recreate in the Properties panel. The copyright listing returns to the Asset panel.
4. To edit the name of the Library item in the list, click the listing with two clicks (not a double-click, but two distinct clicks). Change the "c" to a "C" in copyright. Accept when you are prompted to update your files.

Keep your eyes open for ways to use Library items for your work. It is often worthwhile to change an element to a Library item even after it has already appeared on many pages. It does not take much to delete the current entry and apply a Library item. The benefit is in future edits, of course.

The next session covers templates. They follow the same concepts as Library items, but they deal with entire pages.

Done!

REVIEW

Library items can save loads of time. Here are a few key points that you should remember when using them.

- The Assets panel can be used for many functions, such as adding images, changing colors, and using repetitive links.
- Library items can contain only content for the body of the site (that is, between the <body> and </body> tags).
- Library items can contain images, text, tables, script information — almost any element that can be included in an HTML document.
- Library items are similar to SSI, although they will run on local as well as remote sites.
- Library items can be built from scratch or created from existing elements.
- Pages containing Library items are automatically updated when the Library item is changed, but the documents must be uploaded to the server individually to have the effect on the remote site.
- Library items can be edited, and the changes will occur wherever the Library item has been placed.
- You can break the connection to a Library item, but that element will not be updated if you edit the original Library item.
- You can share Library items with other Dreamweaver sites.

QUIZ YOURSELF

1. What does the Asset panel contain? (See the "Assets panel basics" section.)
2. What is a Library item? (See the "Working with Library Items" section.)
3. What are the two methods that can be used to create a Library item? (See the "Working with Library Items" section.)
4. When you edit a Library item and then edit the original file, what happens to other instances of the Library items in your site? (See the "Updating Library items globally" section.)
5. When you detach a link to a Library item, what is the result? (See the "Disconnecting a Library item link" section.)
6. How do you copy a Library item to another site? (See the "Sharing Library items between sites" section.)

Creating Templates

Session Checklist

✔ Understanding Dreamweaver templates

✔ Creating a new template from an existing document

✔ Creating a document from a template

✔ Editing a template

✔ Detaching a template link from a page

✔ Creating a template from scratch

✔ Renaming or deleting a template

**30 Min.
To Go**

I n their simplest form, *templates* are patterns for your pages. You can create a template from scratch or — more realistically — you can turn an existing page into a template. The latter is more practical because it is a rare site that is fully planned before any page creation is done. To create a template from scratch, you must know exactly where you are going with your site design.

Dreamweaver templates are wonderful things; unfortunately, they are grossly underused. I believe this is the case because most Dreamweaver instruction focuses on understanding how to create or edit a template. But that's not really the hard part. What you really need are clues about where to use templates. This session guides you through this process and shows you how to use templates to streamline your work and add consistency to it.

Understanding Templates

Remember when you created Library items in the last session and you were able to make global changes? Templates work in a similar way, but they control entire pages rather than just page elements. Of course, because they encompass a wider range of elements, there is also more to think about, and a great deal of planning to be done.

You must fully understand what templates can do before you can make the best decisions for using them. The easiest time to decide where templates could be used — especially when you have never used them — is when your site is finished. However, because you build pages on templates, it is a bit late by that time. Try to sort through some of the potential uses and situations before you start to create your first template.

Planning ahead

If there is only one key to efficient use of templates, it is planning. In the next session, you will be doing the planning for a new Web site, and you will see how much planning is required just to set up a site. However, I feel no remorse over making you work through this because the time you invest will be repaid many times over.

I have developed my working methods through experience — much of it bitter. Rushing into a site without adequate planning is just asking to have life become very complicated at a later stage. Skipping the planning stage usually results in undoing much of the original work. That hurts more than doing it right in the first place.

Templates can help simply because they force you to know several things, such as the appearance of your site and what will remain the same on each page. This usually forces you to have your navigation well established. On the flip side, templates can also help you make changes that would be too time-consuming in the later stages of your site development.

What can a template do?

The simple explanation is that you can use a template to set up an entire page. Template zealots would have you believe that you can do a complete site redesign simply by changing your template. A site that features 500 stories, each on its own page — and having a consistent menu — would fit into this description very well. The template you would use for a site like this could be very structured.

Reality, however, is often a little different. Most sites require a little more flexibility, which is not what templates are about. Templates are about locked areas. There are two different types of areas on a page created from a template: some areas can be edited at will, while others cannot be changed at all. Therein lies the problem. You want your pages to be consistent, but they often require small changes, such as removing the active page menu item to prevent confusion.

Do I seem to be talking you out of using templates? It may seem that way, but I am actually a huge fan of templates, and I strongly recommend that you use them whenever you can. In fact, the more you use templates and Library items, the better your sites will be. You just have to know when, where, and how to use them. Next, take a look at some ideas, and then you will be ready to get the how-to rolling.

Strategies for using templates

How can you use the power of templates and still maintain your flexibility? Here are several ways:

- Use editable areas
- Break the connection to the template
- Include everything with the template

Using editable areas

The first way that you can keep your flexibility is to be creative with editable and non-editable portions of your page. Menus beg to be included in a template because they usually appear on every page. However, they often change — as did the page in the Holiday site that you created in the early parts of this book. Removing the active page menu item reduces confusion. How can that be part of a template? Make the menu an editable portion of the page with all possible menu items included. On your page, simply delete the menu item you do not want. This strategy can be applied to any element that varies in a minor way from page to page.

Breaking the link to the template

You can break the link to the template on any page. Of course, you will not be able to automatically update that page, but you will still have the general page format as a base. On almost every template-based site, there will be at least one page where the template is too restrictive. Breaking the link to the template restores your full editing ability.

You can also plan your site to intentionally use broken links. If you create every page with a template and then break the link on every page, you will still have consistency. You lose all automatic updating capability, of course, but you have a quick and consistent start to every page.

Including everything with the template

This strategy comes right back to the planning stage. If you are going to require CSS (Cascading Style Sheets), make sure that the CSS references are included as you create your template. If you are going to effectively use templates for complicated sites, you cannot skip the planning stage. In fact, you are probably wise to build a few pages in the normal fashion before creating your templates. Changes happen through a project, but never more than in the first few pages that you put together. Once you have a clear direction, create your templates and quickly move ahead from that point. The time you spend creating the trial pages and well-planned templates will be recovered very quickly on a large site.

 Session 22 covers the details involved in controlling text and CSS.

I can hear your fingers tapping on the desk. Time to move on. I agree. Next, you will do some work with templates so that all of the information I have dumped upon you can find a place to rest.

Creating a Template from an Existing Document

Start by creating a template based on the index.html page from the Holiday site, which you created in the first half of this book.

1. Open index.html. You are going to make some changes to this page and then create a new index page, so be sure to save it with a different filename. Save it as index1.html.

2. To prepare for the template, you want to add the Home menu item. That places all possible menu items on the page. Insert a rollover image using home.gif and home-over.gif from the art folder. Use index.html as the link for this item.

3. If you have not already done so, change the vertical alignment on the content area to top.

4. Select File ⇨ Save as a Template. The Save as a Template window opens. Type **holtemp** in the Save As field.

5. Open your Assets window and click the Templates icon, which is located just above the Library icon in the left toolbar. You should see the holtemp listing in the lower portion of the screen shown in Figure 16-1. A preview of the template appears in the upper window.

Figure 16-1 *The template listing for holtemp. Note how the top window provides a preview.*

You have just created your first template. However, it is not much use at this point because Dreamweaver creates a new template with the page title as the only editable region. If you created a page from this template at this point, the only thing on the page that you could change is the page title.

Take the following steps to create editable regions:

1. Highlight the headline text. Check your code view and make sure the <b> and </b> tags are included with the selection. Select Insert ⇨ Template Objects ⇨ Editable Region. The New Editable Region window will open. Type **headline** to name this region.

2. Click your mouse pointer anywhere in your document to deselect, and then look at the headline region. The text is now surrounded by a box that has the label "headline." When you create a document from this template, the text that is shown here will appear, but it will be fully editable.

If there is no box surrounding the editable region, first check that View ⇨ Visual Aids ⇨ Invisible Elements is checked. If not, you must change your preferences. Select Edit ⇨ Preferences and select the Highlighting category. Make sure that Editable regions is checked in the right pane of the Preferences window. When you are new to templates, I recommend that you work with the editable regions showing on your screen until you are comfortable working with templates.

3. To help organize your template, add text that states what is to be presented in this region. Highlight the text again and type **Insert headline here** (see Figure 16-2).

Figure 16-2 *The headline is now an editable region, as shown by the light blue border and label.*

4. You also need to be able to enter different text in the content region. Highlight all text in the center column. Press Delete. With your cursor still in that cell, select Insert ⇨ Template Objects ⇨ Editable Region. The New Editable Region window opens. Type **content** to name this region.

5. This time, Dreamweaver provides the text from the name you assign. You can edit this entry to make it more descriptive. Highlight the word "content" from the new editable region area and type **Enter the content for the page here**.

6. You can use Dreamweaver MX's new image placeholder function to hold the spot for images. Creating an editable region for the placeholders allows you to insert the correct images for each page. Delete the top photo in the right column and select Insert ⇨ Image Placeholder. Assign the name **topimage**, with **100** for both Width and Height settings. Click OK. Dreamweaver places a solid color box to hold the spot for images. Repeat for the lower image, naming it **bottomimage**.

7. Select both image placeholders. Check code view and make sure that the <p> and </p> tags are selected. Create an editable region named **photos**.

If you wish to see the page without the template code, select View ⇨ Visual Aids ⇨ Invisible Elements and the template code will disappear. Repeat when you want to redisplay the template codes.

The template page is starting to make sense. You have your menus in noneditable regions, however, and you know that you will to want to edit these. For them to be most useful, you must make sure that all menu items are included on your template page. At the beginning of the last exercise, you added a Home rollover image to the graphic menu. The menu is now ready to be turned into an editable region.

The text menu at the bottom of the page must be edited, however, for a useful template. You want to have all menu items present in your template, because deleting content is much easier than adding content — and it is much better for consistency. Start with the table and add the "home" link.

1. Insert your cursor in the cell containing the word *route*. Select Modify ⇨ Table ⇨ Insert Column. A new column is added.

2. Type **home** in the new column. Create a link to index.html. Your menu is ready for the template now, but you have to make it an editable region.

3. Select the entire table. Select Insert ⇨ Template Objects ⇨ Editable Region. Type the name **textmenu** in the New Editable Region window. When you create a page from this menu, you will simply delete one column from the table.

Although you are probably wondering where you are going to stop, you still have a few things to add to your template. Your graphic menu is very important, but the rollovers create an extra challenge. Let's move on.

Take the following steps to create an editable Region from a graphic menu with rollovers:

1. Select the entire menu. Check your code to ensure that you have selected all the required code for those elements. It is likely that some code will *not* be selected from the Design view. For this example, your code should start with the following:

   ```
   <a href="../index.html" onMouseOut="MM_swapImgRestore()". . .
   ```

   Your code must end with the following:

   ```
   . . . width="163" height="48" border="0"></a>
   ```

   Make sure that all of the code is selected in Code view and return to Design view to finish.

2. Create an editable region from this selection. Type **menu** as the editable region title.

The Library items that you have in your template should remain as noneditable regions. You can make changes to Library items, and those changes will be passed from the Library item to the template. The template will then update the content in any noneditable region so that the changes will appear in any documents based on that template.

That's it. You have created a template that can serve as the base for an entire site. (See Figure 16-3 to check your results.) If you are wondering what you have saved (because almost all regions are editable), read on. The savings will very quickly become obvious. You must remember the times that I said, "Repeat for the remaining pages," to truly understand the benefits.

Work with this template and you'll see what I mean.

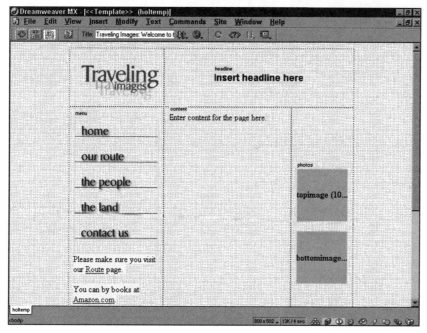

Figure 16-3 *The finished holtemp template with editable regions in place.*

Creating a Document from a Template

Now that you have a well-planned template, it is time to put it into action. Use this template to create a new document:

1. To keep confusion to a minimum, close all documents in Dreamweaver, with the Holiday site active.

2. Activate your Assets panel with the Templates icon selected. Highlight the holtemp template listing. Click the menu icon at the top right of the Assets menu and select New From Template. An untitled document that is built from the template is created.

3. You should save this right away. Eventually, you will overwrite your index.html document with this file; for safety, save it as indexnew.html.

4. You can quickly create this page by filling in the blanks. Highlight the text in the headline editable region and type **A tour through our vast country**.

5. Replace the photo placeholders. Double-click the topimage photo placeholder and select photo6a.jpg from the art folder. Repeat for the bottomphoto placeholder, using photo6b.jpg.

6. To make the menu correct, delete the "home" menu item and the line-break code between the first and second menu items. Before you delete, check your code view and ensure that all of the code for the home menu is selected, starting with <a href=index.html . . . and ending with . . . </a>

7. Correct the text menu by placing your cursor in the "home" column and selecting Modify ⇨ Table ⇨ Delete Column.

8. On other pages, you will edit the Page Title entry at the top of the screen. However, for the entry page, it is correct.

9. Finally, select the text in the content editable region, and then either type text of your choosing or paste copied text from the original index.html document.

10. Repeat the above exercise with the route.html page, saving the new file as route-new.html. Don't worry that the table in the template is smaller. You'll adjust that in your template in the next exercise.

Believe it or not, you have completed two pages. How's that for fast? You may have wondered where the timesavings were going to enter the picture, because most of your page had editable regions. However, you did not have any concerns about your page layout because that was all set.

Now let's see the true power of templates as you make changes to the template.

Editing a Template

In reviewing the pages created from the template, I can see two things that I would like to change. The first is to make the table flexible so that it will grow and shrink with monitor resolution. Second, the columns should all be aligned to the top. Return to the template to make these changes:

1. Open the Assets panel and activate the Template section. Double-click the holtemp listing to open your template.

2. Select the main table and change the width value from 570 pixels to **90%**.

3. Insert your cursor in the menu cell. Select Top as the Vert value in the Properties panel. Repeat for the column containing the photos.

4. Select File ⇨ Save to save the template. The Update Template files window opens, listing the files that are attached to that template, and asking if you would like to update. Click Update. Review the undated files log, and click OK to close the window.

5. Return to the documents that were updated and confirm that the changes appear.

Now you have the knowledge to create a new page for each of the pages in the Holiday site based on the template. You have seen how quickly the pages can be compiled when you are using a template. Recreate the rest of your pages in the same manner, saving the file to the original name plus "new."

When you create the contactnew.html page, leave the center and right column unchanged from the template style. You will be editing this page in a different way.

Detaching a Template Link from a Page

In this section, you detach the template from the contact page. There is usually one page that does not fit easily into the format for the rest of the site. Breaking the link to the template returns the full page to your editing control.

Follow these steps to break a link:

1. Make sure the contactnew.html page is active. Select Modify ⇨ Templates ⇨ Detach from Template. That's all it takes. Your page has not changed, but it is no longer attached to the template.
2. Click the Library item below the menu and delete it. If you had an e-mail link in your template, delete that as well.
3. To remove the placeholder images at the right, delete the entire column. With your cursor in the column, select Modify ⇨ Table ⇨ Delete Column.

There is one final topic to cover for templates. You can also build a template from scratch rather than from an existing page.

Creating a Template from Scratch

If you know exactly what you require, you may also build a template page from scratch. I prefer to work out the design of a page without the encumbrances of working in the template mode. Even when I know content is going into a template format, I build my template page as a regular Dreamweaver page and then create the editable regions. But that is a purely personal preference, and you should try both ways to see which suits your style.

To create a template from scratch

1. Open the Assets panel from within the Holiday site. Click the Template icon on the left side of the panel.
2. Click the Asset panel side menu symbol, or right-click (PC) or Ctrl+click (Mac) in the lower screen of the Assets panel and select New Template. A new listing will appear in the Template list. While the new listing is still selected, type **testtemplate**. The top window identifies this as a blank template.
3. To edit the template, double-click the listing, or click the Edit icon at the lower edge of the Assets panel. Your template document opens, and you can build your template as you would any other HTML page. You must specify editable regions as we did in the first template we created.

A template created from scratch can be applied and edited in exactly the same way as a template created from an existing page.

Renaming or Deleting a Template

The final housekeeping you must cover is what to do with a template when you want to change the name or dispose of it completely. Dreamweaver looks after most of the problems that could occur, but you must be careful whenever you are working with files that link to other documents.

Take the following steps to change the name of a template:

1. Open the Assets panel and activate the Templates region. Click twice on the test-template listing (two distinct clicks, not a double-click), or click the side menu of the Assets panel and choose Rename. The template name will be highlighted as in Figure 16-4.

2. Type **testonly** as the new template name. If you have created a document from this template, Dreamweaver asks if you want to update any files that are linked. Select Update.

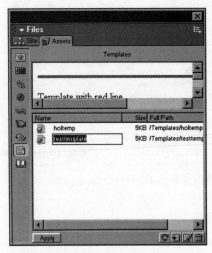

Figure 16-4   *Renaming a template in the Assets panel. Template management must be done in the Assets panel to avoid error messages.*

To delete a template open the Assets panel and activate the Templates region. Select the template listing that you wish to delete. Click the side menu icon of the Assets panel and choose Delete. Dreamweaver asks you to confirm that you want to delete this template. Select Yes.

Be cautious with this command because you will have to manually break the link to the template in any documents that are linked to a deleted template.

Never delete a template file from the Site panel. If you want to remove a template, always use the method described here. If you delete the file in the Site panel, the listing will remain in the Assets panel and will continue to deliver errors. If that happens, create a new file in the Site panel to match the template name, and then delete the old one from the Assets panel.

Finalizing the Conversion to a Template-Driven Holiday Site

You have just been through a deep tour of templates. Although you may still decide not to use them in your work, I encourage you to at least try using a template to give a consistent starting point for every new page. Even when you immediately break the link to the template, you will still save time and improve your consistency.

Your site should be very consistent now. Make a final check though the pages. If you are satisfied, overwrite the original documents from this site with the equivalent new files.

If you would prefer to keep the original files that you created, use the Site window to drag the original files into the resources folder. Dreamweaver keeps track of the links for you. Then, simply rename the new files to the old filenames and your site will be complete and easily updated through templates.

Upload the new files to your site and pat yourself on the back. You have covered a lot of territory in a short time, and you have already reached a very high level of knowledge of Dreamweaver's basic features.

In the next session, you start planning a new site. The new project puts all the skills you have learned into action, while introducing you to yet more powerful Dreamweaver features.

Done!

REVIEW

With a good grasp of this session's material, you should be well on your way to mastering your site with templates. Here are key points to remember:

- Planning ahead is crucial to success with templates.
- Templates can be created from an existing document.
- Editable regions are the only locations where content can be entered on a page created from a template.
- Selecting View ⇨ Visual Aids ⇨ Invisible Elements will toggle on and toggle off the template codes on a page.
- It is better to set a template up with extra elements to be deleted, rather than adding them on every page. It is easier to delete than to add, especially for maintaining consistency.
- When working on a document from a template, unless the region you want to edit has been set up as an editable region, you must make any changes in the template file and then update. Changes will be applied to every document that was created from that template.
- A template link can be detached from a page at any time. However, when the document is not linked to the template, changes to the template will no longer automatically update the document.

QUIZ YOURSELF

1. What is the most important thing to do when designing templates? (See the "Planning ahead" section.)

2. What is an editable area in a Dreamweaver template? (See the "Strategies for using templates" section.)

3. Templates can be created with two methods. What are they? (See the "Creating a Template from an Existing Document " and "Creating a Template from Scratch" sections.)

4. When you make changes to a template, what happens to any page that was created from that template? (See the "Editing a Template" section.)

5. When you edit your template, what happens to a page with a broken link between the template and the page? (See the "Detaching a Template Link from a Page" section.)

6. Why should you use the Assets panel to rename or delete a template? (See the "Renaming or Deleting a Template" section.)

PART

III

Saturday Afternoon
Part Review

1. What is the best way to work with code in Dreamweaver?

2. When you are working in Code view, what is the result in the document if you press your Enter key three times?

3. What is normally required to place a simple premade code into your document?

4. What are the two areas of an HTML document where scripts usually have to be placed to work correctly?

5. What is one example of a common link on a Web site that must be an absolute link?

6. When you are working in Design view, how can you tell where a named anchor is placed?

7. If you discover that a link you have used in many places on your site has been changed, what is the easiest way to update all the links?

8. How can you edit JavaScript without leaving the Design view?

9. What is a simple rollover in Dreamweaver?

10. What must you do to test a rollover in Dreamweaver?

11. When you use the Behaviors panel, what are you adding to the selected item?

12. Why do you use tables to layout a form?

13. How is a CGI script connected to a form?

14. What is the difference between a checkbox and a radio button form object?

15. What purpose does a hidden field serve in a form in Dreamweaver?

16. How can you identify every color you have used in your site without visiting every page?

17. Two methods exist for creating a Library item. What are they?'

18. What happens when you have placed many instances of a Library item, but decide to delete the Library item from the Assets panel?

19. When the content of a page that was created with a template is not located in an editable area, what must you do to make changes to that content?

20. When you wish to delete a template file from the Assets panel, why is it important to do this in the Assets panel?

PART

IV

Saturday Evening

Planning Site Navigation

Session Checklist

   ✔   Planning site navigation

   ✔   Creating your second site

   ✔   Preparing a jump menu

*0 Min.
To Go*

Nothing is more important to a site than the navigation. If your site visitors cannot find the information they require, the best writing, graphics, or dynamic content in the world will not do the job. Dreamweaver offers powerful aids to construct navigation elements, and this session covers many of these features, including how to create menus automatically with Dreamweaver's tools.

Finally, this session introduces the Coffee Times site, the second site you build for this course. In fact, in this session you define a Coffee site and build two small menus that will be used as you create the site.

Planning Site Navigation

Establishing a plan for site navigation is both my favorite and least favorite portion of Web design. It is exciting, and it often feels like completing a complicated puzzle. On the other hand, you are making decisions that will be difficult to change later because the graphics involved in creating navigation will be fully integrated into the overall appearance of the site.

This book does not allow for a discussion of this complicated subject, but I can't move on to building a new site without stressing the importance of planning. Even beyond the critical role of helping your visitors to find what they seek, your menus are an intrinsic part of your design, and changes to navigation in the middle of a project cause many hours of extra work, and often lead to errors in code. Please put planning your navigation at the top of your priority list for every site you build.

I have a series of articles at WebReference.com about building menus, menu types, and the many tools to create menu graphics and text. The initial article in that series can be found at `http://productiongraphics.com/column42/`.

I have also written a book on the same subject. *Web Menus with Beauty and Brains*, published by Hungry Minds, offers a complete discussion and hands-on course for designing effective navigation and creating many types of menus.

It's time to take a look at the second site you will build. This site is for a fictitious business called Coffee Times, and I have done all the planning and created the graphics so that you can focus on Dreamweaver's features.

Listing navigation areas

The Coffee Times site will be divided into basic areas for fast navigation. Each of the major areas will have a submenu. This setup might be considered boring because it is so standard; however, it is standard because it works. Every page will offer links with company information and a contact route, because it is impossible to tell where in the process this information may be needed. Table 17-1 lists the menu items. The main menu items are shown in bold type, with the submenu items listed below. The shaded row lists items from the small menu that will appear on every page. I have excluded the Home menu item for clarity. Home will appear on every page except the entry page, and has no submenu items.

Table 17-1 *Main Menu and Submenus*

News	Products	Recipes	History	Events
New features	Beans	Beverages	Tradition	Online events
New articles	Equipment	Desserts	Geography	US/Canada
Article archive	Books/Music	Alcoholic	Ritual	Worldwide
	Other	Other		
About Us	Contact	Links		

You want the returning visitor to be able to get anywhere on the site quickly. For this reason, you will provide a *jump menu* (a drop-down menu listing the entire site). See Figure 17-1 for an early version of the Coffee site.

Creating your second site

You are ready to leave the Holiday site behind and move on to a new and more complex site. The course was designed in this way so that the site design would not be held back by the basic techniques that you have concentrated on to this point.

Figure 17-1 Early proof for new Coffee Times site, reflecting the menu setup as described in Table 17-1. The jump menu, in the left column, will provide quick navigation for the entire site from any page in the site.

From this point on, you are moving into the more advanced and more exciting elements of Web design. Before you leave the basics, though, remember that the techniques that you have covered are the techniques that you will use for most of your design work. With the exception of Cascading Style Sheets (CSS), which I use for every site, at the very least for text control, most of my professional work is done with the methods you have covered to this point.

CSS is discussed in Session 23.

By completing two sites, you will also review the basics twice. It is a lot easier to remember a technique the second time it is used. My goal with this course is to give you a solid grounding in the techniques that you will use every time you create a site, and enough information on the more advanced topics to steer your future development.

The site that you create now is the Coffee site that was planned earlier. Create a new folder to serve as your root folder by following these steps:

1. Create a folder on your hard drive and name it **coffee**.
2. Open Dreamweaver and define a new site. Name it **Coffee**.
3. Specify the coffee folder that you created in Step 1 as the root folder for the site.
4. Set up your FTP information for the Coffee site. In most cases, this will be the same as your settings for the Holiday site, with the exception of the remote folder path.
5. Create a new folder for the Coffee site. Name it **art**.

That is as far as you must take this process for now. However, you will be working with the site in every session from now on, and will be adding folders in addition to the ones that Dreamweaver creates automatically. You will need this base for every site, though.

The instructions for setting up this site are deliberately less detailed than they were when you created the Holiday site, since you have already worked through the steps once. If you stumble, review Sessions 2, 3, and 5 for more detailed instructions.

Working with Navigation Tools in Dreamweaver

**20 Min.
To Go**

You start with a jump menu. Dreamweaver makes creating these unglamorous, but most useful navigation aids, as easy as typing in your content. The method is easy to follow and gets you in shape to tackle the slightly more complicated navigation bars in the next session.

You will create another form of menu, an image map, in Session 26.

Creating jump menus in Dreamweaver

Jump menus do a great job of offering tons of information in a very small space. They are also very easy to build. Dreamweaver has automated the process so well that is it literally a fill-in-the-blanks exercise. Working with menus in this session, you will become more familiar with the JavaScript features in Dreamweaver.

To create a jump menu

1. Create a new document in your Coffee site, and name it **jump.html**.

2. Select Insert ➪ Form Objects ➪ Jump Menu. The Insert Jump Menu window you see in Figure 17-2 opens. In the following steps, you enter the items from Table 17-1 in this jump menu.

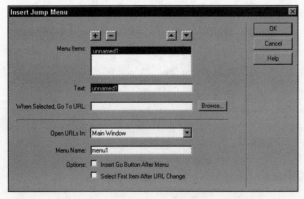

Figure 17-2   *Initial Insert Jump Menu display.*

When the Insert Jump Menu window opens, the Menu Items area contains the item "unnamed1." Note how this same title also appears in the Text field. The Menu Items area reflects the text that is typed in the Text field. If you were to click OK right now, you would have a jump menu with one listing — unnamed1. However, you rename this entry in Step 3 and then add more entries in subsequent steps. As more menu items are added, the list in the Menu Items section grows. To edit any entry, select it from the Menu Items list and change the text in the Text field. You are now ready to enter the menu items.

3. Make sure that the original text is highlighted, and type **Get around fast** in the Text field. Click in any other field and the new text will replace "unnamed1" in the Menu List.

    This entry is simply a message, not meant to be a link, so you don't add a URL link for this item.

4. Before you add other menu items, you need to set up the values for the menu as a whole. To name the menu, type **quick** in the Menu Name field near the bottom of the screen, replacing **menu1**.

5. You want the line "Get around fast" to appear in the closed jump menu at all times, so click Select First Item After URL Change. This brings your menu display to the first item you enter every time the menu displays.

6. Now add the menu items. Since you are listing all of your categories and their sub-categories, you must consider how the areas can be defined. You have a list of 22 items. If you type all entries in the same style, a user would never be able to distinguish the items at a glance.

    So, you use uppercase letters for the main categories, and lowercase letters with an indent for the subcategories.

    Click the + to add an entry to your menu. "Unnamed1" appears again in both the Menu Items and Text fields.

7. Type **NEWS** in the Text field.

8. To state where the visitor will go by choosing this list item, enter **news.html** in the When Selected, Go To URL field. Do not click OK yet.

news.html does not exist yet. However, from working out the details for the site, as explained in the previous steps, you can create the page names.

The next steps create the entries for the News submenu items. You want them to be easily identified as sublistings so add an indent and use lowercase for the titles. This is a little more work, but since this menu will appear on every page, it is well worth the investment to help visitors find their way quickly.

10 Min. To Go

1. Click the + again to add another listing. In the Text field, type ** ** two times, and then type **new features.** Your entry should read **   new features**, which will display as shown in Figure 17-5. Type **newsfeat.html** for the URL address. Your listings should look exactly like the ones in Figure 17-3.

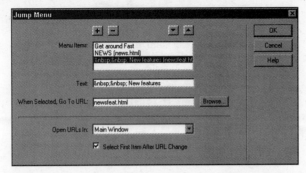

Figure 17-3 *Building the listings in a jump menu.*

2. Repeat the previous step two more times. In place of "new features," type **new articles** and **article archive**, respectively. Use **newsart.html** and **newsarch.html** as the URL addresses.

3. Continue to build your menu by typing the remaining main menu items: **PRODUCTS (products.html)**, **RECIPES (recipes.html)**, **HISTORY (history.html)**, and **EVENTS (events.html)**. Also include their subcategories using Table 17-1 as a guide, and indenting as in Step 1. Create filenames that make sense to you for the subheading pages.

4. Finally, add the last three menu items: **ABOUT US (about.html)**, **CONTACT (contact.html)**, and **LINKS (links.html)**.

5. When you have entered all your listings, click OK to return to your document.

6. Preview your document in both browsers. Figure 17-4 shows the expanded menu in Internet Explorer. Dreamweaver's jump menu display does not always accurately reflect how the menu will appear in a browser.

Figure 17-4 *The jump menu previewed in a browser, where the HTML formatting of list items appears.*

The jump menu takes much more time to explain than it does to complete. Once you have completed a few entries, "tedious" will probably be a more likely comment than "difficult." If you get bored, peek at your code; typing all of that would be a lot more tedious!

Before you leave this section, you should learn to edit a jump menu.

Editing a jump menu

If you want to return to your jump menu to change a value or to add a value, follow these steps:

1. In Design view, click the jump menu to select it.
2. Select Window ⇨ Behaviors to open the Behaviors palette.
3. You will see the words *Jump Menu* at the right side of the Behaviors panel. Double-click this label to open the Jump Menu window. You can edit any entry by selecting and entering new text in the Text field. The Jump Menu window you open from the Behavior panel is identical to the Insert Jump Menu window you work with as you create the original jump menu.
4. You can also edit your entries through the Properties panel. Select the jump menu as above, but click the List Values button on the Properties panel. Clicking any entry selects it for editing. This is a good method for small edits, but you will find that the Behavior panel offers easier editing.

You have moved well along the navigation tools path, but there is one more important automated Dreamweaver feature that will help you with small menus. Carry on to the next session to learn how to build a Navigation Bar. As a bonus, in case you are starting to worry about how you will remember these techniques, you'll learn how to create annotations for a document or image.

Done!

REVIEW

At this point, you should be quite comfortable with Dreamweaver's automation. You do need to keep a few very important things in mind.

- Although Dreamweaver offers almost unlimited functions, you already know most of the basics that you will use over and over for every site you build.
- Carefully defining site structure can save you many hours of work and make your site a more logical place to navigate.
- Jump menus offer navigation to your entire site in one small area. Dreamweaver makes creating a jump menu very fast and easy.
- Indenting sublistings in a jump menu helps to make selection easy for your visitors.
- To edit a jump menu, you must use Dreamweaver's Behaviors panel or edit through the Properties panel.

QUIZ YOURSELF

1. Why is it so important to preplan your site navigation? (See "Planning Site Navigation" section.)
2. What is the first step in defining any site? (See "Creating your second site" section.)

3. What is a Dreamweaver jump menu? (See "Creating jump menus in Dreamweaver" section.)

4. How can you add an indent to a jump menu in Dreamweaver? (See "Creating jump menus in Dreamweaver" section.)

5. How can you quickly edit entries in a jump menu once it has been created? (See "Editing a jump menu" section.)

Continuing to Build Site Navigation

Session Checklist

✔ Creating a Navigation Bar

✔ Editing a Navigation Bar

✔ Creating and using Design Notes

**30 Min.
To Go**

In the previous session, you planned your navigation, and created a jump menu. In this session, you carry on from that point and add to your toolbox another way to automate navigation. A Navigation Bar is simply a set of images and links that is compiled into a set by Dreamweaver, allowing for easy duplication across pages. The Navigation Bar that you build for the Coffee site will appear on every page you create.

You also take a little side trip to discover the magic of Design Notes. Design Notes are a valuable tool to keep track of how you created graphics or elements on your pages for future reference. They can also dramatically improve communication when working with others on a site.

Dreamweaver provides a streamlined method for creating graphic menus like the one you created for your first site in this course. This section shows you how to use Dreamweaver's Navigation Bar feature, which allows you to enter all of your rollovers in one spot.

> **You can only place one Navigation Bar on each page in Dreamweaver, even though two or more menus are often on the page. Create a Navigation Bar for the menu that best matches the options offered.**

Preparing the Graphics for a Navigation Bar

I am not going to cover how to create the actual graphics because that is well outside the scope of this book. I used Adobe Photoshop 7 to prepare the graphics for this site, but I often also use Macromedia Fireworks and illustration programs like CorelDraw or Adobe Illustrator to create graphics for the Web.

I use the rollover creation feature of Adobe Photoshop or Macromedia Fireworks only to save my graphics, creating my rollovers and Navigation Bars in Dreamweaver for more control and flexibility.

The menu you build here contains three states. The *Normal* state is what you see when the menu is not in use. The *Over* state is what you see when the mouse is placed over the menu item. Finally, rather than removing the active link for this menu, you use the *Down* state to create a third graphic that indicates that the menu is active.

Although you don't use it for this exercise, you have one more option. You can place an *Over While Down* state image that will display a different graphic when the mouse is passed over the link displaying the down position.

When building a Navigation Bar, you need all graphics prepared ahead of time. For this example, you can find the necessary graphics on the CD-ROM. In the Session 18 folder on the CD-ROM, copy the Smmen folder to your art folder (create the art folder if you did not when you defined the site) in your Coffee site. This folder contains nine files you will use to create your Navigation Bar.

Preparing a Navigation Bar

There are several steps to preparing a Navigation Bar in Dreamweaver. These steps are broken down in the following sections. Although the instructions appear to be very long, do not let this discourage you; they are all very logical, and you can complete them quickly.

Inserting the first menu item

With your graphics prepared, you can create a Navigation Bar that can be copied to many pages or placed in a Library item. To build the Navigation Bar, follow these steps:

1. Create a new document, and name it **navbar.html**. Eventually, this menu will be placed on another page, so don't do page formatting now.

2. Select Insert ⇨ Interactive Images ⇨ Navigation Bar. The Insert Navigation Bar window opens.

    This window should look a little familiar from the Jump Menu window you used in the previous exercise. The unnamed1 listing appears in two fields. You will enter the information in the Element Name field, and that text will appear in the Nav Bar Elements listing. For this example, you have three menu items: about us, contact, and links.

3. Type **about** in the Element Name field.

    As soon as you leave that field, the name will appear in the Nav Bar Elements list. The lower fields will always be related to the selected item in this list. You must now tell Dreamweaver which graphics to use with this listing.

4. First, specify the Up Image, which will be seen when there is no action on this item. Click the folder next to the Up Image field. Locate the file smmen1.gif in the art/smmen folder.

5. Next, specify the image that will be seen when the mouse passes over this menu item. Click the folder next to the Over Image field. Select smmen1-over.gif.

6. Place the image that will be seen when the page that matches the menu item is active. Click the folder next to the Down Image field. Select smmen1-down.gif.

7. To specify the link for this set of images, enter **about.html** in the When Clicked, Go to URL field.

8. Activate Preload Images. This command asks the visitor's browser to load the images into the cache so they will be available when needed.

9. Choose Insert Horizontally for this menu because the menu items are going to be side by side. If you were creating a menu like the one in the Holiday site, which was the first site we created, you would choose Insert Vertically. Uncheck the Use Tables option, as a table layout for this simple menu is unnecessary.

10. Your first menu listing is complete. But *do not* click OK yet. You'll pick up from here in the next exercise.

**20 Min.
To Go**

Inserting additional menu items

Including more menu items is mainly a repeat of inserting the first menu item, but you must first add a new listing.

1. Click the + button to create a new listing.

2. Repeat Steps 4 through 8 in the previous exercise for each new menu item. This exercise requires the following entries:

> Second menu item
> Name: **contact**
> Files: smmen2.gif, smmen2-over.gif, smmen2-down.gif
>
> Third menu item
> Name: **links**
> Files: smmen3.gif, smmen3-over.gif, smmen3-down.gif

3. When all three menu items have been completed and your window looks like Figure 18-1, click OK to complete.

4. Preview your menu in a browser. None of the links will work yet because you haven't added URLs.

This forms the basis of the Navigation Bar feature's capabilities. Once the links are added, you can place this menu on any page, and the rollovers and links will work. However, the Navigation Bar will look the same on every page, giving the visitor no idea which page is active.

You may have noticed when you previewed the menu that the down images are not showing yet.

Because you want to let your visitors know that they are on a page in that menu, you have to do a little adjusting on each page. So, you will create three more pages, one for each of the menu items. On each page, you will set the menu to display the active menu item with a white background.

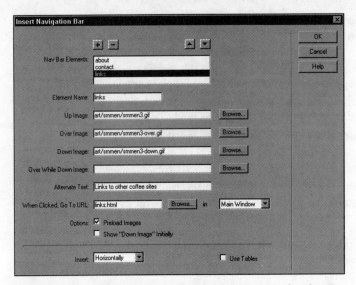

Figure 18-1 *The final setup for creating your Navigation Bar. Alt text has been added to the image entries in this sample.*

Customizing Navigation Bars for each page

To make the Navigation Bar display a down image, you must create a slightly different bar for each page. This sounds complicated, but it involves only one checkbox. Follow these steps to customize Navigation Bars for each page:

1. Create a new file in the Coffee site, and enter **about.html** as the name.
2. Copy the Navigation Bar (Edit ⇨ Copy HTML) from navbar.html and paste it into about.html. Simply select the images in the Navigation Bar, and Dreamweaver will pick up the JavaScript to paste it into your new page.
3. With about.html active, select Modify ⇨ Navigation Bar. Highlight "about" in the Nav Bar Elements field of the Modify Navigation Bar window.
4. Click Show "Down Image" Initially. Click OK. The first menu item, about us, will now be in light type. This is the file smmen1-down.gif, which is your Down Image from that menu item.
5. Save this file.
6. Create a new file with **contact.html** as the name. Repeat Steps 2–4, substituting contact.html for about.html in the steps. Save.
7. Create a new file with **links.html** as the name. Repeat Steps 2–4, substituting links.html for about.html in the steps. Save.
8. Preview your menu. You should be able to click back and forth among the pages you have created, and the active page menu item should always display light text. See Figure 18-2 for a view of the contact page.

about us • contact • links

Figure 18-2   *The Navigation Bar preview for the contact page.*

So, now you have created a text menu, a rollover menu with each image placed separately, a jump menu, and finally, a Navigation Bar. You have built a strong toolbox of powerful methods to accomplish many different types of navigation. You will use these tools over and over as you design Web sites.

Creating and Understanding Design Notes

**10 Min.
To Go**

A powerful tool for teamwork is Dreamweaver's Design Note capability. However, this feature can be just as valuable when you are working on a site alone. Perhaps the best way to think of Design Notes is as reminder notes for your documents. This is another feature that can seem mysterious and complicated until you have completed one. Any designer who is concerned with details should be using Design Notes regularly. When two people are working on the same file, Design Notes can be indispensable.

Dreamweaver enables you to enter Design Notes when you are in the document screen, which makes the feature quick to use. You can make notes about what is left to be done, and delete them as you complete each task. Most Web pages are a series of many small tasks, and it is easy to forget a few little details. It is much faster to make four small changes and then upload them, than it is to upload each of four changes as they are made. Design Notes can help you organize your own work.

For group work, Design Notes are indispensable. The ability to draw a partner's attention to a problem or to request that a feature be added right on the actual page saves a great deal of e-mail, and improves communication dramatically.

Understanding Design Notes

First, Design Notes have nothing to do with your document. That is probably the most important thing to remember. They will not show up on your site, even if you choose to have them uploaded with the document. They lurk completely in the background unless you call for them from within Dreamweaver.

Dreamweaver has two levels of Design Notes. You can create a note for the entire document, which can include information about text, images, and so on. You can also create notes for individual images, which can significantly reduce communication breakdown. It's hard to make changes to the wrong image when a note is attached to that image.

Design Notes can save a great deal of time and confusion, and are extremely easy to use. Files with notes display an icon in the Site window. Notes are stored on your site in a folder named *notes in the same directory as the file with the Design Note.

The files for Design Notes will not show up in your Site window. They are accessible, however, through the file system on your computer.

Enabling Design Notes on your site

The first step in creating Design Notes is to enable your site. You only need to do this once, unless you wish to turn the capability off.

To enable your site for Design Notes, follow these steps:

1. With the Coffee site active in your Site window, select Site ⇨ Edit Sites.
2. Make sure that the Coffee site is highlighted in the Define Sites window and click Edit.
3. Choose Design Notes from the Category list and the Design Note options will be presented.
4. If it is not selected, click on Maintain Design Notes to activate this feature for this site.
5. If you wish to share your notes with others who are working on your site, activate Upload Design Notes for Sharing. This setting will automatically upload any notes attached to a document when the document is uploaded. If you are using Design Notes only for your own purposes, leave this box unchecked.
6. Click OK and Done to save your changes.

 If the Design Notes feature is not activated for a site, the Upload Design Notes for Sharing option will be grayed out in the menu.

Your site is now ready to include Design Notes that you prepare. Dreamweaver only adds Design Notes to a document at your request.

Creating document Design Notes

Now that the site is ready to create Design Notes, first add one to a document:

1. With the Coffee site active, open navbar.html. Select File ⇨ Design Notes to activate the Design Notes window. The first window of the Design Notes window is where you will enter most information.
2. Select Revision 1 from the Status drop-down box.
3. Click on the calendar icon to add the date. The current date will be added to the document when you click the icon.
4. Type the following note or text of your own choice. (Figure 18-3 shows the Design Notes entry screen.)
   Complete
   Nav bar link pages created, but not complete
   To do:
   Requires down state adjusted for each page
5. If you wish to have the Design Notes screen presented every time you open your document, activate Show When File Is Opened. This is not really necessary, though, because you can open it at any time. Click OK to return to your document.

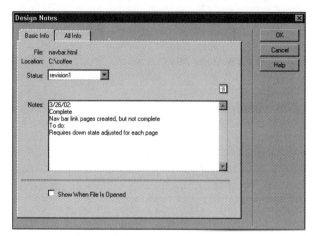

Figure 18-3   *The Design Notes entry screen.*

Creating object-based Design Notes

The previous exercise created Design Notes that apply to the entire document. To create a Design Note for a single object — in this case, an image — the method is the same, but you start in a different way.

1. To create an image-specific Design Note, right-click (PC) or Ctrl+click (Mac) on an image. Select Design Notes from the pop-up menu.
2. In the top left of the Design Notes window, note that the image name and path are stated. This is the only indication that the Design Note is attached to an image rather than a file.
3. To enter Design Notes, follow Steps 2 through 5 of the previous exercise.

Viewing and editing your Design Notes

The Design Notes only become valuable when you can access your past notes and add new information. To view and edit Design Notes, follow these steps:

1. To view and edit document Design Notes, make sure the document associated with your Design Note is open and select File ⇨ Design Notes. You can read the information or add new notes in the same way as you did when you created the Design Notes.
2. To view and edit image-based Design Notes, right-click (PC) or Ctrl+click (Mac) on the image with a Design Note attached. Read the information or edit as you wish.
3. Click the All Info tab at the top of the window. This window has two roles. First, it tracks all notes that have been entered. You can also use this window to enter notes. To enter a new note from the All Info window, click the + and type **Author** in the Name field. Type your name in the Value field and the entry will show in the upper window once you click away from the entry.
4. To remove any entry in the All Info screen, highlight the entry and click – (minus sign). Your entry will be deleted.

Because this is such a simple concept, I will not use space to lead you step-by-step through more Design Notes. However, watch for opportunities to use a note. Perhaps there will be a technique that you would like to put in your own words, or a tip or caution from this book that you would like to add to your documents as you work. Design Notes do not take up much space and are completely out of your way unless you are using them. Using them is a good habit for beginner and expert alike.

You are ready to create templates for your new site. Consider using Design Notes as you proceed through the next few sessions to document techniques you are likely to use again, or remind yourself about details you may forget.

Done!

REVIEW

This session adds to your collection of navigation building tools, and introduces you to Design Notes. You should remember the following from this session:

- When creating a Navigation Bar, you must have prepared all the graphics you wish to use. You can use graphics created in an image creation program like ImageReady or Fireworks that automatically organizes and saves several rollover states to build your Navigation Bar.
- Enter all menu items in the Insert Navigation Bar window, at one time, to build your menu. You can edit the Navigation Bar at a later date by selecting Modify ⇨ Navigation Bar.
- Navigation Bars can be customized for each page.
- You can add notes to any document or image during the creation or maintenance of Dreamweaver using Design Notes.
- You can turn Design Notes off and on at any time on your site.

QUIZ YOURSELF

1. A navigation bar is a handy way to create a menu. There is an important restriction with a Dreamweaver Navigation Bar, though. What is it? (See the Session introduction.)
2. What are the four states you can assign to entries on a navigation bar? (See the "Preparing the Graphics for a Navigation Bar" section.)
3. What is the command to edit your navigation bar? (See the "Customizing Navigation Bars for each page" section.)
4. Where do you initially enable a site for Design Notes? (See the "Enabling Design Notes on your site" section.)
5. You can create two types of Design Notes. What are they? (See the "Creating and Understanding Design Notes" section.)
6. How do you view Design Notes? (See the "Viewing and editing your Design Notes" section.)

Creating a Template for a New Site

Session Checklist

✔ Preparing to create the Coffee Times site template

✔ Building tables for the template

✔ Completing and troubleshooting your template

**30 Min.
To Go**

Session 16 introduced you to templates. You created a template from the Holiday site, but you had already been working with that site for a while. This time you are inviting templates and Library items in from the start. You will create your templates in the next session, once you have the basic structure for the Coffee Times site.

You are about to build a fairly complex site. It will have two main menus, as well as interior menus. By the end of this project, you will be comfortable with templates and have many ideas for working with them.

Preparing for Site Templates

Before you create your first template, you must know what the Coffee Times site is going to look like. You can, and will, make changes, but as flexible as templates may be, you must have a basic plan. For this site, you will build the first page and then create your template.

I usually do initial design in a graphics program. I then move the graphics into Dreamweaver to create my HTML pages. However, the transition is not always smooth, and I have learned to make a test page before I carry on with my final HTML page, the one that will create my template. When you make many changes, snippets of code can be left behind. This page will be repeated many times, and it is a good idea to work from a clean page.

Figure 19-1 shows what you will be building in this session. Don't worry if it looks a little complex right now. Later in this session, you'll find a breakdown of the table structure, and you will work through the exercises step-by-step.

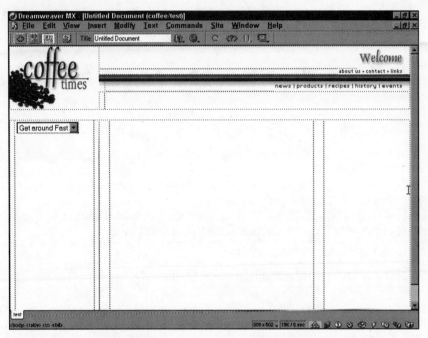

Figure 19-1   *The competed basic entry page for the Coffee Times site.*

When planning your template, it is wise to establish first what will not change for any page that you create with the template. In this case, you will be changing little of the top portion of the page. The logo will stay the same. The decorative lines beside the logo will remain the same. The drop-down menu does not change, nor does the basic setup of the lower portion of the page. Most of what you see in Figure 19-1 can be placed into locked areas on the template.

However, a few important areas will change. The title at the top right will be changed on all interior pages to reflect page names. The menus will also change. The main menu will be adjusted on many pages, so it must remain editable.

The small menu, containing the about us, contact, and links menu items will stay the same for all but the three pages reflected by the menu items. You could leave this menu locked in the template, and then just break the template for those three pages. However, it's not wise to detach a template because it's too easy to make changes and forget that the pages have been detached. It's preferable to set this menu as a Library item, leave that area editable, and break only the Library link to change the menu. With those decisions made, you can build your template.

Preparing Tables for Your Template

You have your site structure, but you must put together the page that will form your main page; you can see the table breakdown clearly in Figure 19-1. This page has separate tables for the top and bottom portions. The titles, logo, and menus are in one table, and the content will be placed in the lower table. The entry page is showing here, but the same basic layout will be used to form the template for the interior pages. To construct the interior pages, a simple addition of Library items containing text menus will do the job.

Study Figure 19-1 so you can come to the instructions with a good understanding of what you will be doing rather than following them blindly. Creating tables that will work well for layout is the most important aspect of Web design.

Start by creating a document for testing. You may stumble a little as you build these tables. After you have created the tables once, you can build them again — quickly and cleanly. It may seem like duplicating work, but I still do that in my design work. You will spend a lot less time whipping together a clean table than you will searching through code on 17 pages to clean up the snippet of code that caused problems but did not show up until final testing.

Copy the files from the Session 19 folder on the CD-ROM to the art folder of your Coffee site. Make sure that you copy all of the loose files, plus the three folders smmen, mainmen, and titles to the art folder with the folders intact.

*20 Min.
To Go*

Creating the test page tables

You are now ready to create a template from scratch.

1. With the Coffee site active, create a new document and name it **test.html**.

2. In the Page Properties window, change your margins to **0**. Remember that you have to set all margin fields to **0** to make both Netscape Navigator and Internet Explorer understand the command.

3. Create a table with four rows and three columns. Cell spacing and padding should be set to **0**. The width is **100%** and the border is **0**, but see the following note.

You may wish to set your border to 1 as you build your table, because it makes it much easier to see what you are doing.

4. With your table selected, press your right-arrow key to bring the cursor behind the table, but on the same line. Use Shift+Enter to move the cursor below the table. Do not worry if the cursor is too far down. You will adjust the code on this later in this session.

5. Insert another table with two rows and seven columns. Cell spacing and padding should be set to **0**. The width is **100%**. Set the borders to **0**, or to **1** if you like to work with them turned on. Figure 19-2 shows what your page should look like.

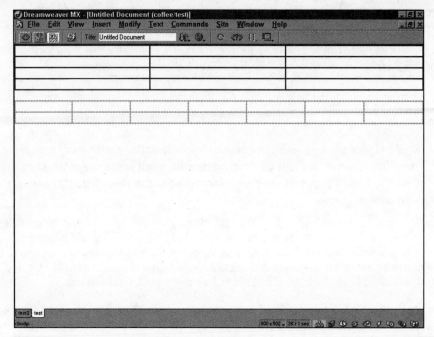

Figure 19-2 *Two tables placed, with borders set to 1, and a different color for each table to show the layout clearly.*

6. Merge the four rows in the first column of the top table.

7. Merge the second and third columns of the first row in the top table. Repeat for the second row.

8. In the third row of the top table, insert the file toplineback.gif from the art/main-men folder as a cell background into the second and third column.

9. Set the vertical alignment for all cells in both tables to top in the Properties panel (Vert field).

That is the basic setup of the tables. You will set the column widths and horizontal alignment as you place your files. Your page should look similar to Figure 19-3.

Adding content to your tables

Your basic tables are in place. The shape of the page will come from the graphic placement.

Browsers have a habit of not observing a simple cell width statement. Pay attention to the placement of the invisible graphic and the column width settings as you proceed through the next exercise. Many of the classic ways to make a browser listen to what you are asking are included.

The design that you will be working on is fully liquid, which means that it will display at resolutions above 800 pixels wide without a horizontal scroll, yet will stretch to fill the screen for high-resolution monitors.

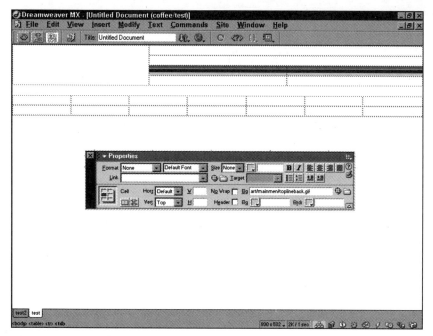

Figure 19-3 *Tables ready for content to be added. I have turned the borders off for this view. Note the background image listing in the Properties panel.*

Keep this topic in mind as you put this table together and watch what each addition does to the table.

Formatting and images for the top table

After the basic table structure is in place, the first step for most Web pages is to add images. Work carefully as you add the initial elements, as the work you do now will be repeated through your site once you create a template.

Make sure that you have the files copied from the CD-ROM as noted earlier. To add the images to your tables and align cells, take the following steps:

**10 Min.
To Go**

1. Insert the image logo.gif from the art folder in the left column of the top table. Deselect the image by using your right arrow, and with the cursor still in the cell, specify a width of **175** in the cell width field.

2. Insert the image welcome.gif from the art/titles folder in the right column of the first row in the top table. Set the horizontal cell alignment to right.

3. Create a Library item from the Navigation Bar you created in Session 18. Open the file navbar.html. In Design view, select all three visible graphics. Create a Library item from this selection and name it **housemenu**. Dreamweaver collects the JavaScript that goes along with the graphics and places it in the Library item. Close the navbar.html file when the Library item is complete. (See Session 15 if you need a refresher on creating Library items.)

4. Place the Library item in the right column of the second row. Set the cell alignment to right.

5. Place the image toplineleft.gif from the art/mainmen folder in the left cell of the third row (the row with the background). This image is the same as the background, but adds a slight curve to the shadow at the left edge for a finished appearance.

6. Set the cell alignment in the right column of the same row to right and the cell width to **100%**. Insert the menu images from the art/mainmen folder in the following order: home.gif, news.gif, products.gif, recipes.gif, history.gif, events.gif. Place the first image, then move the cursor to the right edge with the right-arrow key. Place the next image. Repeat.

Although it is duplicating work, I prefer to place my menu graphics before I build any rollovers or navigation bars. I often make changes to the design or images at this point, and I do not like removing and adding JavaScript functions any more than necessary. Plain images are simple to work with, and are just as effective for planning and constructing tables. When I insert a rollover or navigation bar, I simply delete the original graphics.

The first table is nearly complete, but you must finish preparing for the complex rollover that you will create for the main menu. You will insert a plain white graphic as a placeholder.

7. Insert the image roll3white.gif from the art/mainmen folder into the right column of the fourth row in the top table. Set the horizontal cell alignment to right and the vertical alignment to default.

8. Finally, place the image spacer.gif from the art folder into the middle column of the fourth row in the top table. While the image is still selected, specify an image height of **34**. This invisible graphic is required to keep the table rows above tight to the graphics they contain.

Your top table formatting is complete. You will add the rollovers to the main menu a little later. Move on to formatting the lower table.

Formatting and images for the lower table

I have designed the lower table with extra columns to provide margins to separate the content. I could have created nested tables for the same look, but the method I chose provides a great deal of freedom in design, without the drawbacks that can come from nested tables. I also find this setup much easier for troubleshooting should a problem arise.

Of course, this layout could not be completed without the control offered by invisible graphics. I have added an extra row at the bottom of the table exclusively for column control. No content will be placed in this row.

For this exercise, I strongly recommend that you turn your borders on to help separate the columns.

1. In the second row of the bottom table, set the widths of the columns from left to right as follows: **10, 155, 10, 20, 60%, 20, 40%**. The numbers without percentage are pixel values. It does not matter in which rows you place width commands, as the setting will apply to the entire column, however, it is good practice to keep column width settings in one row of your table.

2. In the same row, insert spacer.gif from the art folder with the following widths: **10, 155, 10, 20**, none, **20**, none. There are no images placed in the columns with percentage values.

3. Insert the vertical line. The effect of a line that fades to white at the top is created with a single pixel of the color creating the solid part of the line, and a different image placed at the top of the solid line to create the fade. Insert the image vertgrad.gif from the art folder into the third column of the first row. Move your cursor to the right with your right arrow, and enter a <br> tag by hitting Shift + Enter. Insert the image vertplain.gif from the art folder. While it is still selected, specify the image height as **300**. Set the horizontal alignment of this cell to right.

4. Insert the image drop.gif from the art folder into the second column of the first row in the bottom table. This is a placeholder for a drop-down menu. You will replace this with a Library item in the next session. It is not necessary to use a placeholder in order to add a drop menu, but the placeholder can help to determine exactly where you want this menu without worrying about moving code several times.

If your table rows or columns do not redraw immediately when you make a change, use Ctrl+Spacebar to force the table to redraw.

5. If you have been working with your borders on, turn them off and preview your page in at least two browsers. Your page should be similar to the page shown in Figure 19-4.

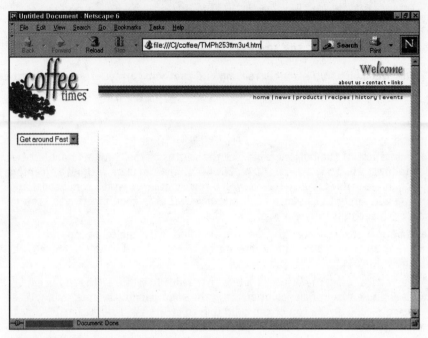

Figure 19-4   *Preview of the test page in Netscape 6.*

Completing and Troubleshooting Your Page

As your final action, create the complex rollovers required for the main menu. All menu items are included in the graphics you placed earlier. Remember that it is easier to remove a menu item than it is to add or exchange, so you prepare your template with all possible menu items included. You make this area editable, and delete current page menu items as appropriate. This menu works with a complex rollover, with a description of each menu item popping up as the mouse is passed over as seen in Figure 19-5. The home menu item does not have a complex rollover, but you will add a simple rollover at the end of this exercise.

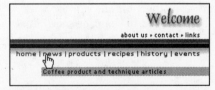

Figure 19-5   *Complex rollover for the main menu in action.*

Completing the main menu

To finish the main menu, take the following steps:

1. Name the images in the main menu. Select each image in turn, and in the Properties panel, enter the name in the Image field at the top-left of the panel. Use the same name as the selected menu item for each entry; thus, the news menu item will have a name of news, and so on. Select the plain white image in the lower-right cell of the top table and assign the name **plain.**

2. Add links to the menu items, using the following links, from left to right, starting with news: news.html, products.html, recipes.html, history.html, events.html.

3. Select the news menu item. Open the Behaviors panel. Click the + button in the Behaviors panel and select Swap Image. The Swap Image window opens. Select image "news" from the list.

4. Click the Browse button beside Set Source To and select news-over.html from the art/mainmen folder. *Do not* click OK yet. Select image "plain" from the list and select roll3news.gif from the art/mainmen folder. Click OK to complete.

5. Repeat Steps 3 and 4, selecting the image and adding behaviors for that menu item, for all menu items except home.

6. Add a simple rollover to the home menu item, using the home-over.gif image from the art/mainmen folder. Use index.html as the link value.

7. Add Alt text to all images on the page. (See Session 9.)

Cross-Ref

If you require a refresher on rollovers, see Session 13.

The basics of the test page are now prepared. If you have worked cleanly, you will be able to create your template from this page in the next session. However, if you have had to make many adjustments, it is advisable to recreate this page in preparation for the next session.

Checking code

If you have any unexplained spaces in your tables, check your code. Look for `</td>` tags that are not on the same line as the content that falls immediately before the tag. For example,

```
<tr>
    <td valign="top"><img src="art/spacer.gif" width="1" height="34"></td>
    <td align="right"><img src="art/mainmen/roll3white.gif" alt="White
graphic" name="plain" width="264" height="13">
</td>
  </tr>
```

The first `</td>` tag in the preceding code is fine. The last `</td>` tag is on the row below the table cell it closes, which usually causes a space below the row when the document is previewed in a browser. If you have this gap in your code, remove it. Although white space should make no difference in code, an extra line space before the `</td>` is one that consistently causes problems.

This is a perfect time for you to study the code that Dreamweaver produced. See if you can follow and understand what effect each line of code is creating on the page. If you have studied the basics of HTML and JavaScript, you should understand most of what is going on in the Code view. Code that is just ready to be turned into a template is perfect to study. There is usually only a fraction of the code that will be present when the page is complete, yet the code that forms the essential elements for the page is in place.

In the next session, you will create the template and the Library items that are needed for this site.

Done!

REVIEW

In this session, you did some solid table work, and prepared a page to use for the Coffee Times site template. You covered a lot of ground, although the basic operations were a repeat exercise for you. Here are a few things to remember:

- It is a good idea to create the initial construction of your page, especially when you are creating a template, on a test page. If you have made many changes, you should recreate the page with perfectly clean code.

- You must identify which areas will remain the same on every page and which areas you must be able to edit before you can construct the page that will be your template.

- It is much easier to work with your table borders set to 1, even when the final table will have no borders.

- You cannot trust that a browser will take your cell width values and respect them. You use cell widths that add up to 100 percent and placeholder images to ensure that your pages are rendered as you wish.

- Set the width of an invisible graphic before you deselect.

- Placing just the images from your rollovers and navigation bars is a good idea when you are initially planning your page.

- Using a control row at the bottom of a table is a good way to keep regular content away from the formatting codes to make your troubleshooting easier.

QUIZ YOURSELF

1. Why is it a good idea to create test tables when designing the layout for your site? (See the "Preparing Tables for Your Template" section.)

2. What is the only way to guarantee that a cell will display at least as wide as you desire? (See the "Adding content to your tables" section.)

3. Why would you place graphics before setting up rollovers? (See the "Adding content to your tables" section.)

4. How can you control the height and position of a table row? (See the "Adding content to your tables" section.)

5. How do you tell a cell to cover any remaining space on the page? (See the "Adding content to your tables" section.)

6. What is a common reason for spaces between the graphics in your tables? (See the "Completing and Troubleshooting Your Page" section.)

Preparing Library Items for the New Site

Session Checklist

✔ Using Library items and templates together

✔ Creating Library items to use on templates

✔ Placing Library items into your template

✔ Creating the Coffee Times site template

✔ Creating documents from the template

30 Min. To Go

I n the previous session, you prepared a test page almost to the point of creating a template. In this session, you build Library items to include in that template, and then you complete the template.

It might seem as though you are spending a great deal of time to get nowhere in particular, but you really are making excellent progress. Once your templates are completed, you'll have the power to create a page in an instant.

You are building the Coffee Times site to be bulletproof. And it will be, as long as your template is solid and your Library items are well constructed. If you discover a problem at a later time, you will make the changes in the template or the Library item, and Dreamweaver will update the entire site.

Deciding Between Library Items and Templates

You worked with Library items in Session 15, so you should be fairly comfortable with the concept. Deciding what you want as a Library item can be a little daunting at first. It also took me a while to untangle Library items and templates; they certainly perform many of the same tasks. Unfortunately, the answer is rarely simple. Fortunately, that also means that you have two great ways in which to solve many of your tedious construction problems.

Choosing between a template and a Library item

To template or to Library? That is the question. The answer is, sort of . . . well, almost . . . for sure . . . both. It will be easier to look at which areas are definitely one or the other's turf before you choose.

If you want to create a page with many elements that repeat on every page, a template is the only answer. Library items have no options; they are an all-or-nothing concept. Templates, on the other hand, can have both editable and noneditable areas.

Conversely, templates cannot be a portion of a page; they run the show or they do nothing. If you have a small scrap of code that will be added to all second-level pages in your site, templates are of no use. You must use Library items.

The size of the area you want to automate is actually a good indicator of which function you should choose. If the area is a complete page, choose templates. If the area is merely a portion of a page, choose Library items.

Using templates and Library items together

The best option, in most cases, is to use both. Build your pages with templates, and then add the extras, often varying features, with Library items. A well-planned site contains very little that cannot be globally edited.

I like to keep my options open with Library items in templates. Templates are only really effective when the content that is locked is exactly the same on every page. In the following sections, you create a Library item from a jump menu and place it in an editable portion of the template. But it can be moved if the content for one or two pages do not fall into the norm for the site.

Creating the Library Items for Your Site

When you are setting up your Library items at the beginning of a project, keep the Assets panel open, even if that is not something you usually do. You are going to create Library items from existing content, and from scratch. If you need to brush up on the concept or if you need more detailed instructions, see Session 15.

Creating a Library item from your jump menu

In Session 17, you created a jump menu. Now you create a library item for placement in the template.

1. Open jump.html from the Coffee site. In design view, select the jump menu. Click the form tag selector at the bottom left of your screen to include the form containing the menu in your selection.
2. Open the Assets window and activate the Library section. Click the side menu icon and select New Library Item from the menu that appears.
3. Type **jumpmenu** to name the Library item.
4. Close jump.html.

Placing the jump menu in the template page

Now you can delete the placeholder jump menu graphic, and then place the Library item, by taking the following steps:

1. Open the file you are using to build your template. (It started as test.html, but you may have created another.)
2. Delete the jump menu graphic placeholder.
3. Drag the jump menu Library item to the position where you just deleted the graphic.
4. Preview in your browsers to make sure that all is working well.

Your page is in nearly final form to create the template.

Creating a Library item text menu

Every page should have a text menu at the bottom so your visitors can navigate to the next page without returning to the top of the page. I like Library items for these menus, even though I always break the connection when I remove the current page link.

Take the following steps to create a text menu as a Library item:

1. Click the side menu on the Assets panel, and select New Library Item. Assign the name **textmenu** to the new listing.
2. Select Edit from the Assets panel side menu, or click the Edit button at the bottom of the Assets panel. A blank page opens.
3. Type **Home | News | Products | Recipes | History | Events | About Us | Contact | Links**. Create a link for each menu as follows: index.html, news.html, products.html, recipes.html, history.html, events.html, about.html, contact.html, links.html. Make sure that there is no formatting applied to the text. (The Format field of the Properties panel should be set to None.) Don't worry about formatting the text. You will be creating a Cascading Style Sheet to control the text in Session 23.
4. Select File ⇨ Save and close the document. Your menu is now ready to place in the document.

Placing the text menu in your template page

I deliberately neglected to add a row in the lower table in the template preparation page. This type of adjustment is so common when you are putting a site together, and I want to emphasize the reasons that I am so meticulous before I create a template for a site.

To place your text menu Library items:

1. If it is not already open, open your template preparation document (test.html unless you created another).
2. Insert your cursor into the bottom row of the lower table, and select Modify ⇨ Table ⇨ Insert Row. A new row will be added above the cursor. Select all but the first cell in the new row and merge the cells.

3. Drag the textmenu Library item from the Assets panel to the merged cell area.

4. Set the alignment for the cell to Center.

Your document is nearly ready (Figure 20-1). I left in a layout error to fix once the template is complete in order to illustrate the editing power of templates. Maybe you can find it? Don't fix it if you do. Knowing that templates can save the day is not the same as watching the power in action.

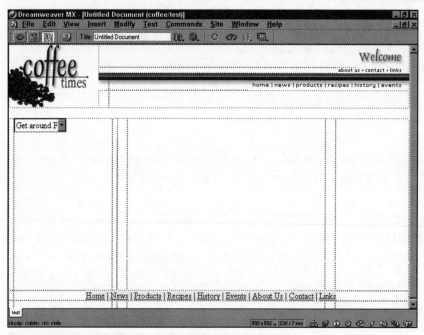

Figure 20-1 *The preparation page ready to be turned into a template. I shortened the vertical line graphic so the page would fit on the screen for this sample.*

Finalizing the Template

**20 Min.
To Go**

You've done your preparation work, and you can now build your final template. By this stage, you must know exactly which areas remain editable, and how your site will take shape. I have done all the thinking ahead for you, but once you are working on your own, this stage will be vital to the success of your site.

Add a page title

The page title on a template page is always editable. However, if you place a title on your template page, that entry will appear on every page you create. I often use this feature to save some typing. In this case, type **Coffee Times:** For each page you create, you simply type the page reference after the company name. Small savings add up in a large site.

Clean up

As your final act, you should take a look at your code and clean up any areas that might be problem areas. Of course, I am assuming that you have a relatively solid understanding of HTML and/or JavaScript to do this. Even if you do not, it is wise to look at your code and try to trace what is happening on your page.

In addition to reviewing your code, take advantage of Dreamweaver's built-in Clean Up HTML feature before you create your template. Follow these steps to use this feature:

1. Select Commands ⇨ Clean Up HTML. The Clean Up HTML window opens.

   Run just the default cleanup, but note the other items that are available. For instance, you can strip out comment tags — those tags that provide information only, rather than those that direct the page display. There is also a function to search for specific tags you might want to remove.

2. Make sure that the following functions have checkmarks: Empty Tags, Redundant Nested Tags, and Combine Nested <font> Tags When Possible. If you want to see a report on the changes that have been made, make sure that Show Log on Completion is checked.

   You might get an alert that tells you there is nothing to clean up. You prefer to get those reports — your work is clean. Otherwise, if Dreamweaver has made any changes, a report is presented.

Never select the option to clean up Dreamweaver comments if you have used automated Dreamweaver features such as templates or Library items. The cleanup process will destroy the required notations for automated elements.

Creating the Template

**10 Min.
To Go**

You have arrived at the big moment. Time to stop the planning, the designing, and the fussing with details, and get your site rolling. Follow these steps to create the template:

1. If it is not already open, open your template preparation page. Make sure it has been saved.

2. Make sure that the Coffee site is active.

3. Select File ⇨ Save As Template. The Save As Template window will open.

4. Select Coffee from the drop-down list of sites.

5. Type **main** in the Save As field. Your window should resemble the window shown in Figure 20-2.

6. Click Save to finish creating your template. The new template appears in your Assets window, and the title bar of your document window changes to indicate that it is a template. Dreamweaver also creates a Templates folder when you save a template, and places your template in this folder. You can see this addition in the Site panel.

Figure 20-2   *The proper settings for creating your template.*

Setting editable areas

You now have a template. Note that your preparation page now has <<Template>> at the top of the screen. This indicates that the document is a template. However, right now no changes could be made to a page created with this template. Add your editable regions and you will be ready to start building pages. Take the following steps:

1. Select the Welcome graphic at the top right of the page.

2. Select Insert ⇨ Template Objects ⇨ Editable Region. The New Editable Region window opens. Type **title** in the Name field. Click OK.

3. A blue boundary now appears around the image. Check the code that Dreamweaver uses to mark an editable area, as shown here:

```
<!-- #TemplateBeginEditable name="title" -->
      <img src="../art/welcome.gif" width="104" height="43">
<!-- #TemplateEndEditable -->
```

4. Select the cell containing the small menu (containing the about us menu item) by clicking on the <td> tag at the bottom left of the screen. Repeat Step 2 to create an editable area called **smmenu**.

5. Select the cell containing the main menu and repeat Step 2 to create an editable area called **mainmenu**.

6. Selecting the full table cell, create an editable region in each of the content areas of the lower table, as well as the cell containing the text menu. Name the editable regions **leftcontent**, **maincontent**, **teaser**, and **textmenu**, respectively.

7. Finally, you want to be able to adjust the length of the solid color line in the lower table. Select the line and add an editable area called **vertline**.

8. Save your template. Your page should look like Figure 20-3.

Creating pages from your templates

This template will be used to form the entire Coffee site. There are times when you will create two or three versions of a template to use on different types of pages. With this design, however, the design will work for all of your pages.

You will not be completing every page on this site as part of this course. I have included the setup for many pages so that you can continue to work on this example and use this site as a test site once you complete the exercises.

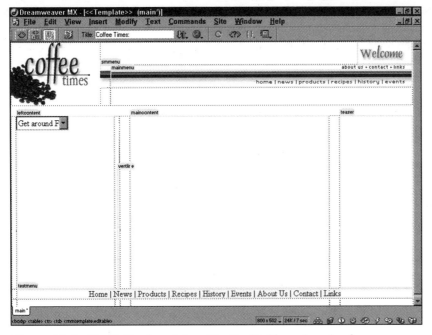

Figure 20-3   *The Coffee template with all editable regions in place.*

Your template file does not have to be open to create a page based on that file. To create a page from your template follow these steps:

1. Select File ⇨ New. The New Document window opens. Click the Templates tab at the top of the Window, and the window title changes to New From Template.

2. Highlight Coffee in the Templates For list. All templates for that site appear in the Site pane of the window, and a preview for that template appears to the right. Make sure that the Update Page When Template is changed option is checked. Select main and click Create.

3. A new, untitled document opens. Note that all editable regions are still visible, and a note at the top right of the screen provides the name of the template. You may wish to turn off the template labels by selecting View ⇨ Visual Aids ⇨ Invisible Elements. Repeat to make the labels visible again. Move your mouse around the page, and notice that there are restricted areas of the page marked when the cursor becomes a "No" symbol ⊘.

4. Save the document as **news.html**.

5. Select the Welcome image and replace with news.gif from the art/titles folder.

6. Select the news menu item from the main menu and delete to remove the current page link, which will reduce visitor confusion when they are offered a link to the current page. Save your file.

7. Repeat Steps 1 through 6 to create a page for each of the main menu items. Save the files as follows: **index.html**, **products.html**, **recipes.html**, **history.html**, **events.html**. Change the title graphic to match the menu item. (The Welcome title is correct for index.html.)

You are creating these files now, but in a real working situation, you should complete a few pages to make sure you have the right layout and direction. You should not move to creating dozens of pages from a template unless it has been thoroughly tested with content in place. You can make changes to your template at a later stage, but it is best if they are minor changes.

You are well on your way to completing a site. Of course, you have not entered any content yet. You will see in Sessions 24 and 25 that when you are working with templates, content addition is not a difficult part of this process.

Done!

REVIEW

It has been a long route, but you have finally arrived at the reward stage for your efforts in building components that will help you later. Before you move on, you should review these points:

- It can be confusing to determine whether you should place items in a template or create Library items. As a general rule, Library items are best for self-contained pieces, and templates excel at controlling larger areas.

- It is important to plan every area of your template for editable areas, and that you design before you commit the file to a template.

- Do not allow Dreamweaver to "clean up" Dreamweaver comment tags in the Clean Up HTML window if you have any automated features, such as templates, in use.

- It is a good idea to add content to a few pages that are based on a new template before you create many pages from that template. It is much easier to make major changes to a template before content is added than to edit many dependent pages.

QUIZ YOURSELF

1. What is the main difference between Library items and templates? (See the "Choosing between a template and a Library item" section.)

2. What benefits can be gained by using Library items for scripts and menus? (See the "Creating the Library Items for Your Site" section.)

3. Why must you not use the Dreamweaver automated command to clean up Dreamweaver comments when you are using Library items or templates on your site? (See the "Clean up" section.)

4. When you create a page from a template, what document file name is assigned to the new page? (See the "Creating pages from your templates" section.)

5. How can you view your page without the editable area labels showing? (See the "Creating pages from your templates" section.)

6. When you are working with the editable region labels not visible, how can you tell when you are over a noneditable area of the page? (See the "Creating pages from your templates" section.)

Saturday Evening Part Review

1. When you are planning a site, what is the most important thing to know about your potential visitors?

2. Why is it important to create a site map before designing a site?

3. What is a jump menu?

4. What is the benefit of a Navigation Bar?

5. What characteristic of a Navigation Bar prevents you from using this feature to create every menu?

6. What Dreamweaver panel displays the JavaScript behind a Navigation Bar?

7. What feature of the Navigation Bar can you use to show visitors what page they are visiting?

8. You can attach Design Notes in two places. Where are the places?

9. Where can you see a symbol that notifies you that a document has a Design Note attached?

10. How do you view the contents of a document Design Note?

11. What is essential to determine before you begin to build a template page?

12. What role can a transparent graphic perform when constructing tables?

13. If you have three columns with the first two columns set to 200-pixel width, what happens when you set the third column to a width of 100%?

14. Why does it make sense to place graphics in a menu position before you create the rollovers using the same graphics?

15. It can be very hard to select a tiny, invisible graphic, especially if it is in a small column or row. What is often the fastest way to edit or select the graphic?

16. What is a Library item especially good at handling?

17. What are templates designed to do?

18. Is it reasonable to create a Library item meant to be detached from the original as soon as it is placed on a page?

19. Once you have created a few pages from a template, and before you create your entire site, what should you do?

20. What does it mean when you set an editable region in a template?

☑ Friday

☑ Saturday

☑ **Sunday**

PART

V

Sunday Morning

SESSION

21

Exploring Dreamweaver's Production Tools

Session Checklist

✔ Learning more about the Properties panel

✔ Using the Insert bar

✔ Learning more about the Assets panel

✔ Setting up and using Assets Favorites

✔ Using O'Reilly's HTML Reference

**30 Min.
To Go**

N ear the beginning of this book, I stated several times that it was better to learn the program with menus than with shortcuts. I am not against shortcuts, just against *learning* with shortcuts. I am about to take the restrictions off.

Dreamweaver does offer wonderful shortcuts and visual palettes that can help you produce your pages much more efficiently. I am fully in favor of using every shortcut that saves you time or that makes your work less confusing. No one will use every shortcut or palette. Most of us use one or two windows regularly, and call on many others for specific tasks. Anything that is presented in this session is only to show you what is available. You will decide which of these tools can help you.

The Properties panel is a good place to start, because you have already used it. So far, however, you've seen only a tiny fraction of the editing capabilities offered in this little wonder panel.

Learning More About the Properties Panel

In Session 2, you took a quick look at the range of controls that the Properties panel offers. At that time, though, you had not covered enough techniques to really look at the full capability contained in this one little window.

You should try at least a few of the following methods on a scrap file. Working through these short exercises will help you learn to use Dreamweaver more efficiently. To begin, use your template to create a page with objects in place for testing.

1. From the Coffee site, open the Assets window and activate the templates area.
2. Create a new file from the main template (see Session 20).
3. Select Modify ⇨ Templates ⇨ Detach From Template.
4. Save the file as a name you will know to delete later, such as **trash.html**.

Keep watching your Properties panel as you work. When items are selected and you are about to perform an action, check whether the action can be accomplished through the Properties panel. There are an amazing number of functions that can be accomplished without ever leaving your document.

Editing code with one click

Most of the options that take up the space on the Properties panel do not really give an indication of what is available. Many of the operations that can be accomplished with the Properties panel are not evident until you know to look for them. Here are a few of my favorites.

Quick Tag Editor

The tiny icon located at the right of your Properties panel and identified in Figure 21-1 has a lot of power. One click of the mouse will bring you to an instant way to edit your code. Not only is it quick to access, but only the selected tag is displayed — your eyes are not distracted by the rest of the code as you work. Change any parameter in the tag. I find that this can be faster than entering the same information in the central portion of the Properties panel.

Figure 21-1 *The Quick Tag Editor identified and in use.*

Try editing your code with the Quick Tag Editor.

1. Select the table cell containing the jump menu.
2. Click on the Quick Tag Editor icon, and the code for that cell will appear: `<td valign="top">`.
3. Using the Quick Tag Editor, change horizontal alignment to center. The code is included here if you do not know the correct syntax: `<td align="center" valign="top">`.

Editing a jump menu

You can use the document menu or a separate Dreamweaver window to edit a jump menu, but you also have one-click access to script editing from the Properties panel.

Edit a jump menu through the Properties panel by following these steps:

1. On your test document, click on the jump menu to select. (It was placed as a Library item.) In the Properties panel, click the Detach from Original to detach. (Don't forget that when you detach a Library item or template that updates will no longer be applied to that element.)
2. Make sure that the jump menu is selected. Click the List Values button to open the List Values window.
3. Click on Article archive in the Item Label list to select. Type **Archive** to change. See Figure 21-2.
4. Preview your page in one of your browsers. Check the jump menu listing.

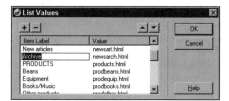

Figure 21-2 *Jump menu items displayed for editing through the Properties panel.*

Using context help

**20 Min.
To Go**

Finally, you should use the context help that is available. The ? icon in the upper-right corner of the Properties panel delivers help for the currently selected item. In addition to finding help on exactly the object you are working with, you also gain a better understanding of how the help system is structured.

It is hard for me to leave talking about the Properties panel. I'm sure I could easily fill an entire chapter describing only the most useful features of this one little window.

Using the Insert panel

The Properties panel is a wonder once you have objects in your document, but the Insert toolbar gives you one-click access to adding almost any objects that you need. This panel, which is normally docked at the top of your screen, replaces the Object panel in earlier versions of Dreamweaver.

The panel consists of 12 different categories of what amount to shortcut keys. During the early stages of a site or a new page, I find that the Insert bar is indispensable. As my page nears completion, I rarely open the panel. I also know designers who never close the Insert bar.

Before I explain some of the features of the Insert bar and how to use them, I want to show you how to change your preferences for this panel.

Changing display preferences

The Insert panel default is to display only icons. If you hold your mouse over the icons, a flag comes up to tell you which object the icon controls, but you may prefer to have the text for that option displayed. You have two other options: text and icons and text only.

As you learn to use the Insert bar, it is helpful to have the text displayed with the icons, However, the increased space for the text forces you to scroll for some of the Insert items, defeating the one-click convenience of the panel. You may wish to have text only, or text and images turned on just until you learn what the panel offers. Figure 21-3 shows the three views available in Insert panel.

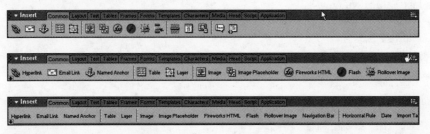

Figure 21-3   *The three options for the Insert bar display: icons only (default), icons plus text, and text only.*

To change the Insert bar preferences

1. Select Edit ➪ Preferences. The Edit Preferences window opens. Make sure that General is highlighted in the Category list.

2. Locate the Insert panel drop-down menu near the bottom-right of the window. Choose Icons and Text. Click OK to accept the changes. The Insert bar now features text beside the icon. Repeat to see the text only option.

Adding objects with the Insert bar

What makes the Insert bar so efficient is that there are several different displays that you can use for this tiny panel. Click any of the 12 tabs at the top of the panel to change which objects are presented in the panel.

It is also easy to use. In fact, I can't stretch the instructions to more than a paragraph. If you want to add an image in Icons only view, make sure that the panel has Common selected, click Image, and the Insert Image window opens. Click Table and the icons for table insertion appear. Click the Insert Table icon and the Insert Table window opens. Many of the icons lead directly to the dialog window to specify the parameters for adding an element to your page. Others insert an object directly on your page.

Character selection on the Insert bar is an example of direct entry. For example, to enter a © symbol, activate the Characters listing in the Insert panel. Click the © button (or Copyright) and the symbol is entered at the cursor location.

Take a trip through all the selections in the Insert bar. The tabs on the Insert bar are simply shortcuts to menu items that are covered in other sessions. These shortcuts can make a big difference in efficiency over the course of developing an entire site.

Because this book is geared to beginning and intermediate Web developers, I do not cover the Layout view and table layout. The idea behind Layout view is to make working with tables easier. However, unless you understand *exactly* how a browser works with tables, and how nested tables and table cells react to each other, I do not believe that you should create tables using this feature. If you would like to know more about it, however, Dreamweaver's help feature carries a good section on working in Layout view under the main heading "Designing Page Layout."

Learning more about the Assets panel

10 Min.
To Go

The Assets panel was a new feature in the previous edition of Dreamweaver and changed my work patterns more than any other addition to this program. The Assets panel lists all the assets that you use in a site, including images, links, colors, and, of course, the Library items and templates you have already used. This enables you to add elements to your page with drag-and-drop ease and to ensure the consistency of your pages.

Using the Asset panel is easy and quite intuitive. The following sections step through a few procedures and then look at a few of the less obvious tools that are included with this panel.

Using assets

The most powerful feature of the Assets panel is that it is automatic. The first time you open the Assets panel when a site is active, Dreamweaver gathers all the relevant information and presents it to you in the Assets panel. Although that can be a large list, the Favorites function, which I discuss shortly, helps you to organize the assets you use often.

The icons along the left side of the Assets window control which list of assets is active. Holding your mouse over the icon presents the title for that category. Clicking on the icon activates that category. Clicking on an asset in the list presents a preview in the top window of the Assets panel.

To use the assets, you highlight a listing and drag the asset to the location you wish to place it. You have already looked at the Library item and template categories via the Asset panel. Now practice placing an image.

Place an image quickly using the Assets panel:

1. With the Coffee site active, and the document trash.html open, open the Assets panel. To place an image in your document, activate the Images icon in the Assets panel.

2. Locate entrypic.jpg in the list. Drag the listing to the top-right column of the lower table in your document. You can also insert your cursor where you wish to place the image, and click the Insert button at the bottom of the Assets panel. Your image is inserted.

That is the basic operation of the Assets panel. It is truly an intuitive feature that has become so much a part of my Dreamweaver work that it is hard to remember life BA (Before Assets).

Creating Favorites in the Assets panel

The one drawback to the Assets panel is the number of assets that you gather with even a medium-sized site. For a large site, the number of graphics alone could make the Assets panel nearly unusable. However, the Dreamweaver developers were on their toes, because they also included a feature known as Favorites.

Favorites gather the assets into one easily organized area. You can easily list your most used assets in the Favorites section, and group them into areas that match your workflow. The assets that are featured in the Favorites section remain in the main list. However, as a Favorites listing, you can use your own nickname for the asset without affecting the functional properties — perfect for assigning English names to cryptic or numeric file names. After you have your Favorites setup, you can view only the Favorites screen if you wish.

Creating and renaming Favorites

To create a Favorites listing

1. Click the Favorites radio button at the top of the Assets panel. This displays the Favorites that you have created; it is currently blank (unless you have been experimenting on your own).

2. Click the Site radio button to return to the main assets listing. Activate the Images section and select entrypic.jpg.

3. Click the Add to Favorites icon, which is the far-right icon at the bottom of the Assets panel. Your image is now in Favorites.

4. Return to Favorites view. Your image should be listed there. Click on the listing to highlight, and change the nickname to **Press and tan cup**. The filename remains the same, but you can now identify at a glance which image this listing contains.

   To get the most from your Favorites, you should also set up folders or groups of files. You can organize these groups by pages, or perhaps by function, as in menu images. Perhaps you have graphic bullets or other decorative elements that are used throughout your site. You may wish to create a folder that contains these elements in one place.

Creating and deleting Favorites folders

You must first create a folder and then move your Favorites listings into the folder. To do so, follow these steps:

1. With the Favorites view of your Assets panel active, click the New Favorites Folder icon at the far left of the bottom icons in the Assets panel. A new folder appears.

2. Type **General images** as the new name for the folder.

3. Drag the "Press and tan cup" file to the folder. The folder should expand so you can see the contents. (If the folder does not expand, click the + (PC) or arrow (Mac) to see the folder contents. Figure 21-4 indicates how your Assets panel should look.

4. To delete a Favorites folder or file, simply select the folder or file and click the Remove From Favorites icon at the bottom of your screen. This does not delete the file from your computer, just the listing in the Favorites section of the Assets panel.

> **If you would prefer to have the items in your Assets panel sorted by a different parameter, simply click on the title bar for the way you would like the sort to be done. For example, images are listed by filename in the Site View. If you would prefer to have the images listed by type, click on Type in the title bar of the Assets display.**

Figure 21-4 *Image stored within a folder in the Assets panel Favorites screen.*

O'Reilly HTML Reference

Oh, where was this feature when I was learning HTML and wondering about a tag, about what attributes will work with it, or about the tag's defaults? Activate the O'Reilly HTML reference with Window ➪ Reference, or by using Shift+F1. Specify the tag you would like to find from a drop-down list, and a second drop-down menu provides a list of the attributes that can be used with that tag. Either selection then gives a written description as well as examples of correct use.

Anytime you have the Code panel open, you can simply click on the Reference tab at the top of the panel to open this most valuable resource. Figure 21-5 shows the <img> tag with the src option selected.

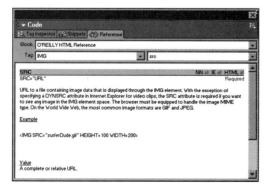

Figure 21-5 *O'Reilly's HTML Reference is a complete HTML guide.*

Speeding Up Your Work

You have just toured some strong production shortcuts. The secret to being highly efficient when using a program is to learn all the features and timesavers so that you can decide, from a knowledgeable position, which tools to use for a specific task. It takes a little longer to reach a comfort level with a program if you make a commitment to learn as many ways to accomplish a task as you can, but you will be repaid many times over when you find the exact combination that is right for the work you do and how you do your work.

Keep at least two palettes active while you learn. The Properties panel is essential, but keep at least one other palette active. Rotate the "palette of the day" until you are comfortable with all of them. Within a few weeks you will know which palettes save you time when you are working on which aspects of your site.

It is also helpful to keep an eye on the shortcuts as you use menu items. They are always listed on the right side of the menu list. By using menus to learn shortcuts, you only learn the keystrokes for the features you use frequently.

I revisit the subject of increasing productivity in Session 30, when I focus on customizing Dreamweaver. In the meantime, let your mind absorb the production methods that I covered here, and always watch for methods that seem to save you time.

Done!

REVIEW

You didn't add anything to your site in this session, but you advanced your Dreamweaver knowledge and production capability by leaps and bounds. Keep using what you have learned, and remember these points:

- The Properties panel is the first place you should look when you wish to accomplish a task.
- The Quick Tag Editor provides bite-sized pieces of HTML for quick editing and is a great tool for learning HTML.
- You can edit jump menus directly from the Properties panel.
- Using Text and Icon display in the Insert bar will help you to learn what each icon represents. When you have them memorized, you can use Icon Only display to save space.
- The Assets panel provides drag-and-drop access to the objects you have used in your site.
- You can create your own listing system for your assets without affecting the original listing through the Asset panel Favorites window.
- HTML help is right at your fingertips when the Code panel is open, with the O'Reilly HTML Reference window. You can also reach it by using Shift+F1.

QUIZ YOURSELF

1. What does the Quick Tag Editor in the Properties panel allow you to edit? (See the "Editing code with one click" section.)

2. How does the Properties panel tell you which object you have selected? (See the "Learning More About the Properties Panel" section.)

3. What are the three different display settings for the Insert bar? (See the "Changing display preferences" section.)

4. How do you insert an image using the Assets panel? (See the "Using assets" section.)

5. What are Favorites in the Asset panel? (See the "Creating Favorites in the Assets panel" section.)

6. Where can you get instant help to understand an HTML tag? (See the "O'Reilly HTML Reference" section.)

Understanding Web Graphics

**30 Min.
To Go**

Session Checklist

✔ Understanding graphics formats and optimization

✔ Optimizing images for the Web

✔ Discussing Web-safe color

We have been working with graphics but not talking about them. Although this is not a book about graphics, you cannot have an intelligent discussion about any type of Web development without talking about graphic file types and optimization. I hope that I can dispel a few myths along the way. Although Dreamweaver does not produce graphics, the overall success of any Web site is too dependent on graphic quality and file size to ignore the subject. Before you return to building your site, I want to pause and offer a highly concentrated basic tutorial on Web graphics.

You can read more about this subject at my graphics column on WebReference.com. Most of the articles on this site will help improve your Web graphics. See the table of contents at `www.webreference. com/graphics.`

Computer Graphics File Types

If you come to computer graphics through the Web world, you will find that much of the information available about computer art is confusing. Many of the same programs are used for both Web and print production, yet they are used in very different ways. You should understand first all the different graphic file types so that you can better discern what concerns Web production and what does not.

Bitmap and vector graphics

All simple images, for instance, those that are not part of a movie, on the Web are *raster* (otherwise known as *bitmap*) images. Raster and bitmap refer to a method of constructing an image. Graphic Interchange Format (GIF), Joint Photographic Experts Group (JPG), and Portable Network Graphics (PNG) images, the only Web-acceptable static images to date, are raster images.

However, in the computer graphics world, there are two basic types of files: raster and vector. Why do we care about vector images if we cannot use them on the Web? There are two reasons. The first is that vector programs are often an excellent choice for preparing Web graphics. Vector images can be easily converted to raster format. Vector images are also used to prepare animated movie formats like Macromedia Flash or Shockwave and Adobe LiveMotion.

Raster images are produced in programs such as Adobe Photoshop, Jasc Paint Shop Pro, and Corel PhotoPaint. Vector programs include Macromedia Freehand, CorelDraw, and Adobe Illustrator. Macromedia Fireworks and Deneba Canvas are examples of programs that construct files using both raster and vector components.

Raster images are constructed pixel by pixel, similar to filling in a grid, as shown in Figure 22-1. Each pixel, or cell in the grid, contains color information to form an image.

Image size and resolution are important to a raster image. File size is directly related to the number of pixels in an image. If you enlarge a raster image, the result is usually poor, because you are simply making the little color areas bigger. Quality degrades rapidly as the image is enlarged. On the other hand, if you make an image smaller without removing some of the pixels, you have a much larger file size than is necessary, plus the quality usually degrades.

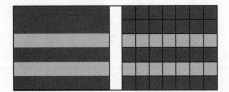

Figure 22-1   *Raster images look like the sample at the left, but are created by individual pixels as shown on the right.*

Vector images are created in an entirely different way, as Figure 22-2 illustrates. The view to the eye is exactly the same as for Figure 22-1, but the construction is completely different. Shapes are mathematically created. Instead of a series of pixels to hold color information, vector images use lines and coordinates to create an object. A blue rectangle would be described as "draw a rectangle from coordinates A to B to C to D and fill with blue." If you enlarge or reduce the image, only the coordinates change, so quality remains the same at any size. Unlike raster images, increasing the size of a vector image retains smooth edges and clarity of detail. A full-page graphic will create a file size that is approximately the same size as one that is 1" × 1".

Many designers use vector programs to create Web graphics, or at least design proofs, because the vector work pattern is easier than a raster program for the initial design phase. These graphics must be converted to GIF, JPG, or PNG before they can appear on the Web.

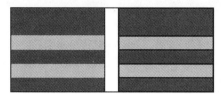

Figure 22-2 *Vector images are created as objects, mathematically plotted on the page.*

The exception to this rule is for movies created with Flash, Director, or LiveMotion. These programs are vector-based, but they do require that a special plug-in be installed on the computer. There is also a Scalable Vector Graphics (SVG) viewer that enables visitors to see vector images, but it is not yet widely enough accepted to use vector images on the Web.

PNG format images

PNG is the Macromedia Fireworks native format. Technically, it is a Web format. Although Fireworks is a hybrid raster/vector program, the resulting files are raster. (Only Fireworks can access the vector information in a PNG file.) Not all browsers recognize this format yet, although it is increasingly being accepted. Although PNG is a raster format, it has excellent compression and can produce transparent backgrounds on photo-type images. I do not advise using PNG images for Web use yet, although they can be used safely on intranet sites when you know exactly which browser your users have.

GIF format images

GIF format is one of the Web's "big two" formats. In fact, it is likely that there are significantly more GIF-formatted images on the Web than any other type of image format. GIF format excels for solid color images, such as most menu items and decorative elements (see Figure 22-3). GIF images can also have a transparent background, allowing much more design freedom.

Figure 22-3 *The GIF image at the left has clearly defined solid color areas. The JPG image at the right has many more colors and no clearly defined solid color areas.*

The drawback to a GIF image is that it can contain a maximum of 256 colors. Although that may sound like plenty, a photographic image can contain millions of colors. GIF format is best when the image has solid color areas. Images are compressed by reducing the number of colors in the image, so an image with only a few solid color areas can have a small file size using GIF format.

JPG format images

JPG format is most at home with photographic-type images (see Figure 22-3 in the previous section), since there are no limits to colors. However, you cannot set transparent areas with this format.

JPG images are compressed to a size acceptable for the Web by removing information. This makes the format excellent for photo-type images, because the eye does not notice the missing information, as long as the image is not overly compressed. However, solid colors do not fare as well with JPG compression, and quality is often poor for large areas of solid color.

Optimizing Image Files for the Web

20 Min. To Go

Every image that displays on the Web must be downloaded by the visitor. Every pixel counts. Although you may have a fast connection, do not assume that most people have the same option. I have the best service available in my area. Where I live, that "best" is 24,000 bps (on a good day).

Web developers often have Digital Subscriber Line (DSL) or cable connection, and forget that display is not instant for everyone. Do not make that mistake. Limiting the size of your pages can also save you money. Most hosts charge for excess bandwidth use. If your site becomes popular, and you have created pages filled with "heavy" graphics, are you willing to pay for unnecessary bandwidth use?

Images increase your page size much more quickly than text content or code, although the page total is the important measure. Look at the bottom of the screen for any Dreamweaver document and you will see the total "weight" for your page. This figure, which should be around 23K for your template, includes code, text content, and images. Except in rare circumstances, it should not exceed 45K. Some may scream that I am outdated with that number. It *has* been a standard for years, but many of us are still on the same connections that we were years ago.

We are also moving backward, not forward, with connection speed. An entire crop of new technology has come into common use — portables, palms, and the like — that is rolling back the average download speed. In much of North America, local phone calls are free with a basic service agreement, and most of us can connect to the Web with a local call; this is not so in much of the world. Would you feel differently about file size if you had to pay for every minute on the Web?

You can have great pages with a low file size. It does not take more work, just more knowledge, to create a page that will keep us slowpokes happy.

A comprehensive source for graphic and code optimization can be found at www.webreference.com/dev/graphics/. **Andy King's series of articles concentrates years of experience into a few pages.**

Optimizing GIF files

GIF format files are reduced in size by removing colors. Most graphics programs provide the option to specify how many colors you would like to remain in your image. If your image is a simple button that contains only a few colors, you may get exactly the same result by reducing the number of colors to 8, rather than by using the default of 256. The program discards the information on the other 248 colors and the file size goes down. That is the simple part of GIF optimization. Figure 22-4 shows two similar images that were saved with 256 and 32 colors, respectively, and are of different file sizes. Note that the two images shown here look the same.

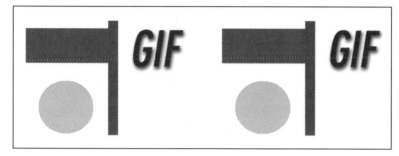

Figure 22-4 *The image on the left was saved with 256 colors. The file size is 3.18K. The image at the right was saved with 32 colors (extra colors were necessary for a smooth shadow) and a file size of only 1.52K.*

GIF information is saved in a logical progression horizontally. It reads like we do — across one line, down to the next, across, and so on. If it finds a whole row of one color, it can collect and present that information as a group, rather than reporting on each pixel. Instead of saving 100 individual pieces of information, it saves 1 piece of information that states that the next 100 pixels are all this color. If you are thinking of adding a vertical texture to a series of menu items, would a horizontal texture work just as well? You will probably save one-half to two-thirds of your file size if you can make the switch.

Optimizing JPG files

JPG format compresses by discarding information, which, of course, affects quality. You are always making choices with JPG images to balance small file size against acceptable quality. There certainly are no rules — every image is unique. Occasionally you will run across what I call a "brat" image that will not reduce to a small file size no matter what you do. Fortunately, these are relatively rare.

For most images, you can increase the compression of a JPG image until a fraction of the original information remains. Current versions of popular graphics programs now provide previews that let you see quality as you reduce file size. See Figure 22-5 for an example.

Figure 22-5 *The image on the left is compressed slightly and has a large file size. The image on the right is highly compressed. The left image is a little more crisp but is four times the file size.*

**10 Min.
To Go**

Web-safe color

Volumes have been written about Web-safe color, with much of the information contradictory. Some experts have announced that it is now safe to use any color for Web use. Others have come out stating that there are only 22 "safe" colors. I am not going to hand you the answer on a platter, unfortunately. I just don't know the "right" answer. Both extremes of the issue present a solid argument.

However, I have designed a lot of sites, sites that are proofed by clients, and then their customers, with a full range of monitors. My experience has been that when I use Web-safe color, the results are predictable. If I wander from a safe palette, I must be prepared for exhaustive testing, which is very time consuming, and can be a little like trying to nail jelly firmly to a wall.

If you decide to wander from the "safe" colors, be aware that you are more likely to have color shifting, meaning your color will change when viewed on different monitors. I have seen tan and beige color change to positively pink; pastel colors can disappear on some screens.

The Dreamweaver default color window offers only Web-safe colors.

Although I do not recommend that you use this feature if you are designing for the Web (intranet design is much more predictable), you can access non-Web-safe colors from the Dreamweaver palette. Click on the color wheel icon at the top right of the Color palette and the Color window opens. From here you can select any color. (See Figure 22-6.)

Creating great graphics with small file size is so important to a successful site. As you work through the sites you build, count the images you are using. They add up, especially when you are loading two or three sets of images for rollovers. Every byte you save at the graphic production stage is repeated throughout your site.

You've had a little break from the heavy building with this topic, but it is time to get back to work. In fact, it is time to hit one of the most exciting topics in Web design today: Cascading Style Sheets (CSS).

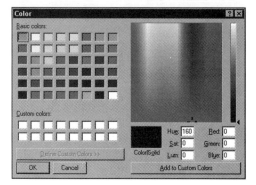

Figure 22-6 *The Dreamweaver color palette offering all colors, not just Web-safe colors.*

Done!

REVIEW

You will be well on your way to working well with graphics if you remember these points:

- Vector images and raster/bitmap images are constructed in completely different ways. All current formats for static images on the Web are raster formats.
- PNG is best used only for intranet applications when you know the browser types that are being used. Not all Web browsers recognize the PNG format.
- GIF format images are best for solid-color designs and can have transparent areas.
- GIF images are optimized by reducing the number of colors used.
- JPG format excels for photo-type images but cannot have transparent backgrounds.
- Discarding file information reduces JPG image size.
- Only Web-safe colors are offered in the default color palette in Dreamweaver.

QUIZ YOURSELF

1. What is a vector image? (See the "Bitmap and vector graphics" section.)
2. What is a raster image? (See the "Bitmap and vector graphics" section.)
3. Why is it important to optimize images even though so many people now have faster connections? (See the "Optimizing Image Files for the Web" section.)
4. How are GIF images compressed? (See the "Optimizing GIF files" section.)
5. How are JPG images compressed? (See the "Optimizing JPG files" section.)
6. What color palette does Dreamweaver use as a default? (See the "Web-safe color" section.)

23

Controlling Text with CSS

Session Checklist

✔ Understanding Cascading Style Sheets (CSS)

✔ Using and editing CSS text styles

✔ Creating linked CSS files

✔ Creating a custom CSS style

✔ Preparing CSS for your site

30 Min.
To Go

I have not spent much time talking about text. That has been a deliberate omission, because HTML text is best controlled by Cascading Style Sheets (CSS). CSS offers many benefits, including significantly less code and a great deal more flexibility for presenting text, including text menus. When you use a linked file to add CSS specifications, you can control all the text on your site from one file, which, like a template, can be edited at any time, with the changes reflected on every page.

CSS is not just related to text control. You can also control positioning, defining your entire page with dynamic HTML (DHTML) and CSS. However, I do not cover all of that here. It takes a bigger book to cover all the aspects of CSS, especially when you are concerned with pages that display properly on all browsers, as you are with this course. Instead, I concentrate on the text capabilities within CSS.

Understanding CSS Text Styles

People from the print world have a leg up with the idea of using styles. So do you if you have been using styles with a word processing program. The idea of a style is simple. Instead of applying attributes, such as font or bold, to each section of text, you instead assign a style. You then create a way for your document to tell what each style means.

For example, suppose you wish to have all of your captions in an italic version of the main font. Instead of applying italics to each caption, you instead apply a style called Caption. Within your CSS file, you place a bit of information that tells the document what to do when it hits the Caption style. When the document is displayed, it first loads the information for the styles that you have defined. Then each time the document comes to a Caption style, it applies the parameters of that style to that text.

Suppose you later decide that you really want your captions to be in a different font, without italics, and that you would like the text to be blue. If you are using styles, you simply change the information in the style definition to the new font and blue color, and remove the italic command. Instantly, all the captions in your document reflect the change, no matter how many pages you have.

That is the true power of styles of any type. In Web design, styles become even more valuable, because you may have hundreds of separate pages. Just remembering what font settings you used, so that you can be consistent, is hard enough. Making changes on every page is a nightmare.

Creating a CSS File

Understanding the concept is just the beginning of the discussion about CSS. I focus only on style sheets that are contained in a separate file, but you can also add CSS styles to each page individually.

CSS styles are stored in the head of the document. In the samples you do in this session, only a link to the CSS file is stored in the head. When the document loads, it goes to the CSS file to find out how to display the text. This is a powerful technique because you can change that file, and the next time the document is called by a visitor, it finds the new information when it looks for the CSS file.

Using CSS is a two-step process. First you create a style sheet, and then, when preparing the text, you make sure that you are assigning the styles that correspond with the style sheet. Like any feature that can control many pages, solid planning in the initial stages is always an investment. A well-planned style sheet enables you to work on your design without paying much attention to the text formatting. However, style sheets often grow or change as your project advances.

HTML formatting (the text formatting available through the Properties panel) can be applied to text that is controlled by style sheets, and the HTML will override the CSS. However, you do not want to use that route often. Occasionally, you may want one piece of text to be a different color. In that case, HTML formatting makes sense. However, if you use that variation a few times, it would be better to set up a new style. As with any document that works like a template, for consistency and editing speed, it is better to use the master settings to set up everything in your site.

Creating a new CSS style sheet

The best way to understand CSS is to actually use it. Here, you create a simple, linked style sheet to start, and then create a page using the styles. Again, work on a test page so that you can get your errors out of the way before you create the style sheet for your site. My natural way of working is to create a bare-bones style sheet, containing little more than the font specifications for the <p> tag and the link colors. As I proceed to build the first few pages, my style sheet grows. Usually by the time the site is half built, I reach the end of the changes and pay little attention to the style sheet from that time forward.

Now create a new document to test the CSS methods by following these steps:

1. Create a new document. Save the file as **testcss.html**.

2. Type **This is the text that I will use to test CSS in a linked file.** Insert your cursor anywhere in the text and check the Properties panel. If the format is not Paragraph, select Paragraph from the drop-down list.

3. Select Text ⇨ CSS Styles ⇨ New CSS Style.

4. The first style to set is for the <p> tag. The Redefine HTML Tag radio button should be selected in the Type area. Make sure that the Tag field is displaying *p*.

5. You want to create a new style sheet, so you want the Define In selection to be [New Style Sheet File]. Click OK. The Save Style Sheet File As window appears.

6. Make sure that the active folder is Coffee. Type **testcss** in the File Name field. This is the name of your new CSS file. Click Save, and the style sheet is saved in the root folder as testcss.css. The Style Definition window you see in Figure 23-1 opens.

   You construct all of your styles in this window. You can attach many styles at one time, although to keep this step simple, set only the paragraph style. Most of the styles you will apply will be through Type in the Category list. Carry on to set the <p> style.

7. With Type selected in the Category list, select Arial, Helvetica, and sans serif from the Font drop-down menu. When this style is activated on a site, your visitor's browser will check his computer for fonts in the order that they appear. In this case, it checks for Arial, and if Arial is not found, it looks for Helvetica. If neither font is found, the browser accepts the computer default sans serif font to display any text that is in a <p> tag.

   (Sans serif fonts do not have horizontal design elements, often referred to as *feet*. Serif fonts do have feet, or the little marks on each character. **Times New Roman** is a serif font; **Arial** is a sans serif font.)

8. Type **12** in the Size field and choose pixels from the drop-down box next to the size field. This sets the font size to a fixed size of 12 px.

9. Click OK, then Save, and then Done to return to your document. Check your text. It should now be in a sans serif font.

10. Check your code, and in the Head area you will see `<link href="testcss.css" rel="stylesheet" type="text/css">`. This is the link to your style sheet.

You can view the Style Sheet file in Dreamweaver by selecting File ⇨ Open, and selecting .css from the Files of Type drop-down menu in the Open Files window. However, I prefer that you see it in a separate text editor in order to cement the idea that the CSS style sheet is a separate document, quite apart from any Dreamweaver function.

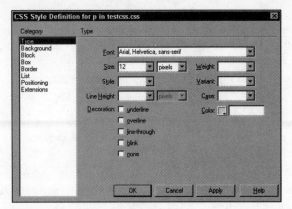

Figure 23-1 *The Style Definition window is where all CSS styles are created. The file is testcss.css and the <p> tag is active in this sample, as you can see in the window title bar.*

To view the CSS file, follow these steps:

1. Open a plain text editor, such as Notepad in Windows. Select File ⇨ Open and navigate your way to the Coffee root folder. On a PC, you will have to specify All Files in the Files of Type drop-down selection.

2. Select the file testcss.css and open it.

   The file contains only the following code:

   ```
   p {
       font-family: Arial, Helvetica, sans-serif;
       font-size: 12px;
   }
   ```

   This is the information that a visitor's browser uses to display the <p> tag in your page. I just wanted you to actually open the separate file to fully understand the connection. You could change this file from the text program, and the changes would be reflected both in the Dreamweaver CSS editor and in any pages that were displayed with testcss.css.

3. Close the file without saving it.

4. Activate the Coffee site panel. Locate the testcss.css file in the root folder. I just wanted you to see the physical location for this file.

Linking to a CSS file

**20 Min.
To Go**

You can now link your CSS file to any other page by following these steps:

1. Create a new document. Type **This is the second document that will be linked to testcss.html.** Make sure that the text is set to Paragraph format. Save the file as **testcss2.html.**

2. Link the style sheet you created in the last exercise to this document. Select Text ⇨ CSS Styles ⇨ Attach Style Sheet. The Link External Style Sheet window will open.

3. Click the Browse button. Select testcss.css from the root folder of the Coffee Times site. Click Select and then OK to return to your document. Check your code and you see the same link code as the first document contained after you added the CSS link.

When you edit the CSS in the next section, you can watch the changes take place in both documents.

Editing a CSS file

After you have your CSS file linked, you can make changes from within Dreamweaver at any time, as shown in these steps:

1. From either document, select Text ⇨ CSS Styles ⇨ Edit Style Sheet. The Edit Style Sheet window opens.

2. Select testcss.css and click the Edit button. The testcss.css window opens.

3. Now add a style for your links. Click the New button. Make sure the Redefine HTML Tag selection is chosen and select *a*. Click OK and you will see the "a" has been added to the list.

4. Select *a* and select Edit. The Style Definition window opens.

   The *a* or link tag will take on the properties of the <p> style unless you change any attributes, as the next steps demonstrate.

5. Select Times New Roman, Times, Serif from the Font drop-down list.

6. Select 66CCFF from the Color area or type #66CCFF in the Color field.

7. Click OK, then Save, and then Done to return to your document.

8. You see no changes yet, because you do not yet have a link in your text. To create links for testing, highlight the text "testcss.html" in testcss2.hmtl. Type # in the Link field of the Properties panel. This sets up a link for testing. Repeat this process in testcss.html, highlighting the word "linked."

9. Check the code on both documents and you see that even though you applied a different font, and a new color, there is no formatting code around the link. The color and font come directly from the CSS file.

   ```
   This is the second document that will be linked to <a href="#">
   testcss.html</a>.
   ```

10. Repeat the edit process to change the link color to a darker blue.

You now have the basics of creating a CSS linked file. Now, add a few more tags to your style sheet before you move on to a slightly different CSS style type.

1. On a new line, in both documents, type **Headline H1.** In the Properties panel, assign Heading 1 formatting to this line. Use your Enter key to create a new line and type **Smaller Headline H2.** Assign Heading 2 formatting to this line.

2. Repeat Steps 1 to 4 in the preceding exercise, but select H1 as the tag to edit. Select Arial, Helvetica, sans serif as the Font, and red as the Color. Accept all

screens as you return to your document. Check both documents, and you see that both H1 lines have changed.

3. Repeat for the H2 style, assigning the same font and a green color. Your testcss.css listings should now look like Figure 23-2.

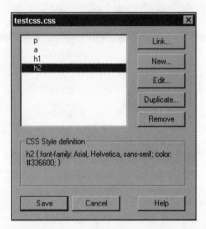

Figure 23-2 *Styles have been added to the linked CSS file. Note that the attributes for the selected style are listed near the center of the window.*

By now, you should be seeing the connection between the file and the documents that you are creating. Don't try to make it harder than it is. When you are editing a CSS style, the changes are written to the separate file testcss.css.

The styles that you have made so far must be applied to a full paragraph. You can also create a special type of style that can be applied to selected text only.

Working with Custom CSS Styles

10 Min.
To Go

You have been using the predefined HTML tags as a base for your styles. However, you can also create custom CSS styles. Custom styles can be added to a paragraph, but they can also be added to a selection of text. In this section, you create a text menu using a custom class style, one of the most powerful applications of custom CSS styles, and you delve more deeply into custom styles.

Creating a Class style

For this example, you create a custom class style to use for captions. To create a style for your captions, follow these steps:

1. In the testcss.html file, type **When I want a caption style, I have the perfect method.** In your Properties panel, choose Paragraph from the Format drop-down menu to apply the <p> tag, or Paragraph style, to your text. (The text may already be Paragraph format.)

2. Select Text ⇨ CSS Styles ⇨ Edit Style sheet.

3. Select testcss.css and click the Edit button.

4. Click the New button and the New Style window opens.

5. Select Make Custom Style [class] in the Type section.

   Custom styles can be named anything, but it is best to choose a descriptive name. However, the name must be preceded with a period, as in .stylename.

6. Type **.caption** in the Name field. Your New style window should look like Figure 23-3. Click OK.

Figure 23-3 *Creating a custom style named caption. Note that the Make Custom Style [class] option is active.*

7. With caption selected, click Edit. The font will be assigned from the <p> tag if nothing is entered in the Font field. Leave it at default. Select Italic from the drop-down list for Style. Choose a dark color that you have not used yet. Return to your document, accepting changes as you go.

8. Highlight the text that you just typed. Select Text ⇨ CSS Styles ⇨ caption. Each custom style that you create will be listed here.

9. Check your code, and you see that this style application does have an entry in the code.

   ```
   <p class="caption">When I want a caption style, I have the perfect
   method.</p>
   ```

Your custom style is complete. However, this caption is not attractive, so you should edit it.

Editing a custom CSS style

You could probably figure this one out on your own, but I like to make sure that I have all the bases covered. To make changes in a CSS style sheet after it has been created, follow these steps:

1. Select Text ⇨ CSS Styles ⇨ Edit Style Sheet.

2. Select testcss.css and click the Edit button.

3. You will see your caption style in the list of styles. Highlight it and click Edit.

4. Change the font to Times New Roman, Times, serif. Don't click OK yet. You can check the results of your changes on your page before you leave the CSS Style Definition window by clicking Apply. Apply saves the changes to the CSS file, but you can make edits instantly, rather than returning to your document each time to see the results.

5. Click Apply. The Style Definition window remains open, but the changes you made are applied to the document. When you are satisfied with the results, click OK and accept changes as you return to your document.

You can add custom styles to your text through the CSS Styles panel, as shown in Figure 23-4. Select Window ⇨ CSS Styles *or* click the Show CSS Styles icon in the Launcher Bar at the bottom right of your screen. (To turn the Launcher Bar on, select Edit ⇨ Preferences. Select Panels as the Category and click the check box beside Show Icons in Panels and Launcher.) Insert your cursor in a paragraph (to affect the entire paragraph) or select the text you wish to change, and click the defined style in the CSS Styles window. Double-click on any style to edit your style sheet.

Applying styles with the Properties panel

Dreamweaver MX offers an ingenious new timesaving feature. The Properties panel can be toggled from HTML mode to CSS mode with the click of an icon. To apply a CSS style using the Properties panel, define your styles and select the area you wish to apply the style to as explained in the previous exercise. Activate CSS mode in the Properties panel (see Figure 23-4) and choose the defined style from the drop-down menu. That's it.

Although I promote menu use heavily, this is one shortcut that I urge you to use from the beginning, as you will save hours when applying custom styles to many content pages.

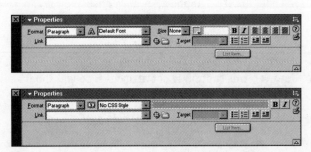

Figure 23-4 *The top image shows the Property panel with HTML mode active. The lower image displays an active CSS mode. You can toggle between the two modes by clicking on the Toggle CSS/HTML Mode icon.*

Preparing CSS for Your Site

Now you are ready to create a style sheet for your site. You start by creating a blank CSS style sheet file and linking that file to your template document. You then add the styles you desire for your page step-by-step. Dreamweaver automatically saves the changes you make to your CSS styles in the linked document.

Creating a linked CSS style sheet

Follow these steps to add a link to the style sheet in your template:

1. From within the Coffee site, open the Assets panel and activate the templates area. Highlight the main template and click the Edit icon at the bottom of the Assets panel.
2. Select Text ⇨ CSS Styles ⇨ New Style. The New Style window opens.
3. Select Redefine HTML Tag and select *p* from the drop-down list for Tag. Make sure that the Define value is [New Style Sheet File]. Click OK.
4. Type **coffee** as the filename and click Save. Your style sheet has been created and the link information added to your document.

Creating styles for your linked style sheet

Now create the styles for your style sheet by following these steps:

1. Set the following values for your paragraph style: For Font, select Verdana, Arial, Helvetica, sans serif; for Size, select 11 and pixels; for Line Height, select 16 and pixels; for Color, select 003399. The line height will not show accurately on the Dreamweaver screen. You must preview the results in a browser.
2. Continue, using what you learned to create the following styles:

   H1: Font: Arial, Helvetica, sans serif; size: 16 points; color: 003399.

   H2: Font: Arial, Helvetica, sans serif; size: 14 points; color: CC6600.

   Also while in your H1 style, select the Box setting from the category list. In the margin area at the right of the screen, uncheck the "Same for all" option. Specify −10 pixels for the Bottom value. This will tighten the space between the H1 style and the following style, usually paragraph, for a better look. Internet Explorer and Opera actually display a more pleasing result at a higher value, but Netscape does not read the value in the same way, and the heading will be too close to the text — as usual, a compromise. Netscape 4.x browsers ignore the setting and display the larger space.
3. Now, add a mouseover effect using the CSS selector option. From within the coffee.css window, click on the New button.
4. Choose Use CSS Selector for the Type. From the Selector drop-down list, choose a:link style (see Figure 23-5). Click OK. This takes you to the Style Definition window in which you can specify how your link will appear. Choose color 3366FF. Make sure Decoration is set to underline. Click OK.

Links should be in blue and underlined for visitor convenience. Many designers scoff at this idea, but observe your own surfing behavior. When you see an underlined, blue section of text, without thinking, you know it is a link. A well-designed page leads the visitor easily to where the visitor wants to go. Standard links help reach this goal.

Figure 23-5 *CSS selector style is chosen in the New Style window. The a:link style controls the default link color for a page.*

5. Create a New style, again choosing CSS Selector as the type, but this time select a:visited from the Selector drop-down list. Specify 660099 as the color for this style. This is the color that the link becomes when the page for that link has been visited.

6. Create a New style, again choosing CSS Selector as the type, but this time select a:hover from Selector drop-down list. Specify CC6600 as the color for this. When your visitor holds his mouse over a link, this color appears.

7. Accept the changes to your style sheet and return to your template.

8. Save your template. Choose Update when asked if you would like to have the files attached to the template updated.

I do not have the space to touch on CSS syntax, the cascading properties of CSS, or many other topics that are very important to making the most of CSS power. I simply wanted you to know how Dreamweaver creates and applies CSS to a page. This is one topic that bears serious study, however, especially if you are, or plan to become, a professional designer.

Done!

REVIEW

I hope you are excited about what you learned in this session. CSS for text is one of the best features for designers, and one that you should use from the start. Just remember

- CSS style definitions or links to style sheets are always stored in the head area of the document.

- When you use a CSS linked file, you can change the text style on thousands of pages by adjusting one file.
- When text is formatted with CSS, no formatting appears in the body of the document; this significantly reduces the amount of code required for each page.
- You can create a new CSS file or link to an existing file in Dreamweaver.
- CSS styles that control HTML styles like <p> or <H1> can be applied only to a full paragraph.
- Custom or CSS styles can be applied to a text selection or to a full paragraph.

QUIZ YOURSELF

1. What is a CSS text style? (See the "Understanding CSS Text Styles" section.)
2. What is the benefit of using a linked CSS style sheet? (See the "Understanding CSS Text Styles" section.)
3. How do you create a linked style sheet in Dreamweaver? (See the "Creating a new CSS style sheet" section.)
4. How can you link to a style sheet from a new page? (See the "Linking to a CSS file" section.)
5. What is a custom CSS style and how is it applied to text? (See the "Working with Custom CSS Styles" section.)
6. Why is it important to keep links as underlined and a shade of blue on your site? (See the "Preparing CSS for Your Site" section.)

24

Pulling Your Site Together

Session Checklist

✔ Reviewing site components

✔ Adding CSS to the template

✔ Creating side text menus

✔ Completing Navigation Bar pages

**30 Min.
To Go**

I n this session, you will pull all the loose ends together for your site. You have done a lot of background work up to this point, with many pieces just waiting in the wings to fall magically together and become a site. Well, here is where it happens.

I do not mean to imply that creating a site will always be this organized. I had the site finished before you started working on it, so I was able to use hindsight to plot a wonderfully straight course through to the end. Even today, the amount of work it takes to pull a site together from start to finish always amazes me. The more you can use well-planned repetitive elements, the better your final site will be.

Let's first review what you have, and then start gluing the whole project together.

Reviewing the Site Components

You have reached the opposite end of the planning that you started in Session 17. Now you must gather up what you have and make some last-minute adjustments to complete all the pieces that you need. You might be surprised when you realize how many of the site components you have completed:

- Navigation planned
- Navigation Bar prepared for template
- Complex rollover menu prepared for template

- Template prepared
- Basic pages created
- Jump menu prepared and inserted into template
- CSS attached to template

By the time you created your pages, most of the major components were in place. This is the best way — in my opinion, the only way — to assemble a site, especially a large site. I promised that your preparation time would be repaid many times over once you reached this stage. After you make just a few more template changes, I'll deliver on that promise.

Creating Side Text Menus

Many of your menu items have subcategories. In the planning stage, it was decided to create individual menus that change with each menu item. You have just learned how to control text on your site, and I want to take you to the next step in CSS as you prepare your menu items.

There were many options open to prepare these menus. I could have included a dummy menu in the template, changing each page as required. Not efficient, however. I could also have used nested templates for each section, but because the number of pages involved with each change is low, I felt that was a cumbersome solution. I settled on using a separate Library item for each side menu for simplicity. The Library item will control the text and the CSS style application, with the text formatting controlled by CSS.

Creating the text menu

These menus will be placed into Library items and will not be placed on the template. However, you should see how they look on your page so you can make the best text formatting decisions. To accomplish this goal, create a temporary page from your template, build the menu Library items, and then delete the construction page.

To create the first menu, follow these steps:

1. Create a new page from the Coffee site main template. Save the file as **menubuild.html**.

    Place some dummy text and a sample image into your page to simulate a finished appearance. You can find a selection of dummy text (greek.txt) in the Session 24 folder on the CD-ROM. Cut and paste the text into the top row center and right columns, and simulate headings using H1 and H2 styling.

2. Insert your cursor behind the jump menu in the left column of the lower table, and hit Enter to create a space. Insert a table with **7** rows, **2** columns, no borders, **80%** width and all spacing at **0**. This table will help format the menu.

3. Merge the cells in the top row of the new table. Merge the cells in the second row. Insert the image spacer.gif from the art folder into the second row, and specify a height of **5**.

4. The bottom row is used for formatting the table only. In the left column of the bottom row in the small table, insert the image spacer.gif, and specify a width of **20**. This will form the indent for the submenu listings. In the right column of the bottom row, place the image spacer.gif and specify a height of **5**.

5. Start with the Products menu, as it contains the maximum number of submenu listings. Type **PRODUCTS** in the top row and create a link to products.html. Select PRODUCTS (that you just typed) and apply a bold setting from the Properties panel.

 I rarely use a `<font>` tag with CSS formatting, as I'm asking you to do in Step 5. However, it is unlikely that you will change the CSS in any way that would make you want to remove the bold attribute, and you want the headline text to follow the custom style.

6. Skip a row and type **Beans** (linked to beans.html) in the right column of the third row. Type **Equipment** (equipment.html) in the fourth row, **Books/Music** (books.html) in the fifth, and **Other** (prodother.html) in the sixth row. Your menu should look like Figure 24-1.

PRODUCTS
Beans
Equipment
Books/Music
Other

Figure 24-1   Basic setup for the side menu before text formatting is applied.

Adding a custom CSS style to control your side menu

**20 Min.
To Go**

Your menu structure is in place. Now create new class styles to give the menu style and action. In past sessions, I have stated emphatically that you should use blue, underlined links to indicate a link. However, in this exercise, you do exactly the opposite, and create brown links, with no underline. When you create a menu like the one that follows, the menu setup and location on the page is a strong symbol that this is a list of links, a menu. I never use underlines for a menu. When links are stacked, as in a vertical menu, underlining usually reduces legibility.

To add CSS use the following steps:

1. Select Text ➪ CSS Styles ➪ Edit Style Sheet. Select coffee.css and Edit. Click New to open the New CSS Style window.

2. With Make Custom Style [class] selected for the type, type **.sidemenu** into the Name field. (Make sure your name begins with a period.) Your window should be exactly like Figure 24-2. Click OK.

3. Highlight .sidemenu from the styles list and click Edit. Specify the following values: for Font, select Arial, Helvetica, sans-serif; for Size, select 13; for Decoration, select none; for Color, select 663300. This creates your basic custom style. Click OK.

4. Now specify the link properties for the custom style. Click New, and select Use CSS Selector for the type. Select a:link from the Selector drop-down menu. Insert your cursor in front of the entry a:link and type **.sidemenu** and a space. You should

have **.sidemenu a:link** as the full name for the selector. Click OK and highlight the new style. Click Edit and for Color, select 663300 and for Decoration, select None. (This is the same color as the basic style, but you don't need a color change for a link presented in an obvious menu form.) Click OK.

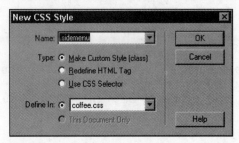

Figure 24-2   *Creating a new class style for your side menu.*

5. Next, create the link attributes for a mouseover change. Repeat Step 4, but with a final Selector name of **.sidemenu a:hover**. For Font, select FFFFC. Add a background to the effect by clicking on the Background entry in the Category list. For Background Color, select CC6633 and for Decoration, select None.

6. Set the attributes for an active link. Repeat Step 4, with a final Selector name of **.sidemenu a:active**. Specify Color by selecting FFCC99 and Decoration by selecting None.

7. Finally, set the attributes for a visited link. Repeat Step 4, with a final Selector name of **.sidemenu a:visited**. Specify Color by selecting 660099 and Decoration by selecting None.

Your CSS style is now set up, and the CSS file is attached to the page (through the template), but you must specify that the menu area should display the custom style. This menu is completely enclosed in a table, and all entries should follow the same style. You can apply the custom style to the <table> tag with the following steps:

1. Select the entire table with the tag selector at the bottom left of your screen. Select Text ➪ CSS Styles ➪ sidemenu. The listing of custom styles at the beginning of this menu is read from your CSS file.

2. Preview your page in Internet Explorer, Opera, or Netscape 6 to see all effects. (Most CSS link effects are ignored in Netscape 4.x browsers, but the links do work.) See Figure 24-3 to view the effect in Internet Explorer 6.

A lot of words, but once you have the concept fixed in your mind, creating CSS menus is quick and easy. The best part is that you can apply the menu settings to any menu in your site with a few mouse clicks. You are ready to create a Library item with this menu.

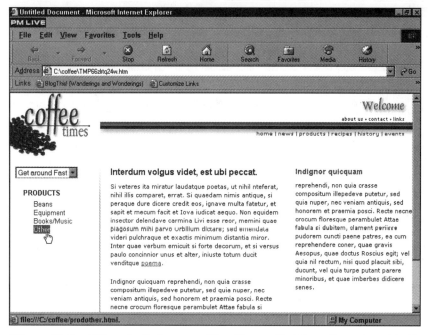

Figure 24-3 *CSS controlled menu with rollover effect in action, viewed in Internet Explorer 6.*

Creating Library items for side menus and placing in documents

To create a Library item from your menu:

1. Select the menu table by clicking on the `<table.sidemenu>` tag at the lower left of your screen. Check your code, and you will see that the full table with the `sidemenu` class reference is selected.

2. Open your Assets window and activate the Library icon. Create a new Library item and name it **menuprod**. When the alert asks if you would like to update the Library item, click Yes, and the menu on the current page becomes a Library item.

3. Open your products.html page. Drag the menuprod Library item to the left column of the lower table. Your menu appears. Preview in a browser to confirm that all links are in place. Your products.html page should be similar to Figure 24-4.

You now have a choice. You can leave the menu as it is, or you can break the Library item connection and remove the link for the current page to avoid confusion. I usually break the link, as any changes I am likely to make to this menu will be in the CSS file, and I rarely return to a menu Library item wishing to make global changes. If you wish to follow my lead, detach the menu from the Library item, and delete the link information for the PRODUCTS menu item. On each page that you place this menu, repeat, removing the link information for the menu item that matches each page.

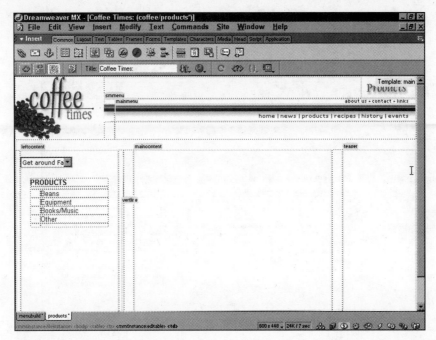

Figure 24-4 *The finished menu placed in the products.html page. The link to the Library item that was used to place the menu has been detached, and the link information removed from the Products listing.*

10 Min. To Go

Finishing your menus

Create a menu for each of the main menu items following the site structure table in Session 17. Create links for each entry — I use the original table and replace the text — and create a Library item for the new menu. Another method is to copy the Library item, create a new Library item, and edit the copied text as required. Place the menus on the pages you have created to date.

Name the Library items starting with menu in each case, i.e., menunews, menuhist. If you name files in a group with a common beginning, they will appear together in an alphabetical listing.

You have not yet created the submenu pages. Do that now, and place the correct menu for the page, removing the link for the current page if you have chosen to do so.

Completing Navigation Bar Pages

You created three plain pages that match menu items in your Navigation Bar in Session 18. However, I am going to have you create these pages again, working from your template to match the look of the site. It will be a great review to customize the Navigation Bar on each page again.

To create your Navigation Bar pages use these steps:

1. Create a new page from the main template. Name it **about.html** and click Yes when you are asked if you wish to overwrite the existing file.

2. Replace the title image at the top right of the page with aboutus.gif from the art/titles folder.

3. Select the Library item containing the small menu near the top of the page. Click Detach from Original in the Properties panel.

4. Open the Behaviors panel. Select the first menu item, and double-click on any of the Actions shown in the Behaviors panel to open the Set Nav Bar Image window.

5. Activate the Show Down Image Initially selection in the Options area near the bottom of the window. Click OK. The About Us link has now changed to the "active" color. Save the document.

6. Repeat Steps 1 through 5 for contact.html and links.html, replacing the appropriate titles and changing the corresponding menu item to the down state. Your page should resemble Figure 24-5.

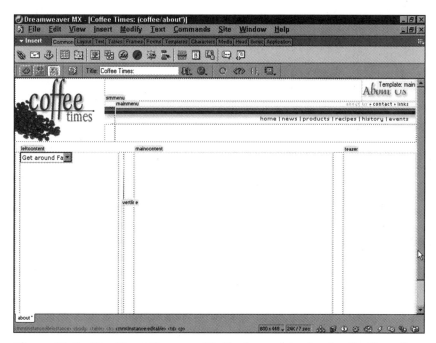

Figure 24-5　*The About Us page with the down state showing for the active page. Note that there is no side menu for this page.*

If you looked at this session and thought it was going to be quick because it was short, you were probably caught off guard. Creating many pages is tedious, time-consuming work. However, imagine what you would have faced without the one-click, guaranteed consistent wonder of templates. In the next session, you start placing content, and finally get to correct the error in the template that I warned about a while back.

Done!

REVIEW

Although much of what you did in this session may have felt like familiar territory, you stretched into some new areas, and you certainly moved into production mode. Make sure you remember the following details:

- When you have finished building the components for your site, it is a good idea to assess what is yet to be completed. Once you move from building to production mode, any omissions or errors are often compounded.
- Create a Library item whenever there is a possibility that you will need to repeat that item. It is much easier to call a Library item from the Asset panel than it is to copy from one document to another.
- To ensure that related files are listed together, keep the beginning of each name the same for every object in the series.
- Check your code when selecting items to be used as Library items. Code can be left behind when you select an area while in design view.
- Always give visitors a visual clue to their location, such as color changes or different graphics for the active listing.

QUIZ YOURSELF

1. Why are Library items well suited to automating interior text menus? (See the "Creating Side Text Menus" section.)
2. When does it make sense to use a <font> tag with CSS controlled text? (See the "Creating the text menu" section.)
3. What is a quick way to select the entire table containing a text menu? (See the "Creating Library items for side menus and placing in documents" section.)
4. Why is breaking the link to a Library item containing a CSS–controlled text menu often a sensible choice? (See the "Creating Library items for side menus and placing in documents" section.)
5. How can you keep files in a series listed together? (See the "Finishing your menus" section.)

Creating a Finished Page

Session Checklist

✔ Entering text from a document

✔ Embedding images in text

✔ Finalizing the template

✔ Checking spelling and replacing text

✔ Testing your site

30 Min.
To Go

Y ou now have your pages completed. In this session, you work on inserting content, repair the error on your template that I mentioned earlier, and look at important utility tools, such as spell check, find and replace, and Dreamweaver's HTML checker. You'll look at how your site will do with a variety of browsers and learn how you can run your site through its browser paces before you release it to the public.

Your careful work in the earlier sessions should pay off now. Over years of professional work in the computer graphics industry, I have established *beyond all doubt* that it is much faster to create your pages right the first time, rather than repair them.

CD-ROM

I have prepared a more complete CSS file that you will need for the rest of your site. You have already learned how to create the styles that I have added, so to save time, I am including the file. Copy the coffee.css file from the Session 25 folder to the root folder for your coffee site, overwriting the file that you created in earlier sessions. You may wish to rename your file before you copy the complete file. It is important that the copied file stay as coffee.css. If you prefer a challenge, simply open the coffee.css file that is on the CD-ROM in any text editor, and change your own file to match from within Dreamweaver.

Completing Individual Pages

You have your template in good shape and can enter the text, as I have promised. Be warned though, I have left a few things undone in the template, including adjusting margins. In the next section, you will modify your template for the first time since adding content.

You have two ways to add text to a Dreamweaver document: typing directly into the document, or copying and pasting text from a text document. You can copy the text files to your hard drive, but it really is not necessary. I have prepared all the text files as plain text so that you have no word processing compatibility problems. Because no formatting is carried from a word processor to Dreamweaver when pasting text, you can use text from any source as long as you can copy it.

Entering text from a text document

Pasting is probably the most common method for bringing text into Dreamweaver, although there is no reason that you cannot enter your text directly. I write a graphics column for Webreference.com, and the text for my tutorials is entered directly into Dreamweaver. If you are writing your own content, it makes no difference whether you type directly or paste text into your document.

Locate the Session 25 folder on the CD-ROM and copy the 25text folder to your computer. It doesn't matter where you store the folder, as long as you can find it. This folder contains both text and Microsoft Word versions of four text documents.

Also, copy the image files grind.jpg, grindsm.jpg, grounds.jpg, and nabobsm.jpg to the art folder in the Coffee site root folder.

To paste text from another document, follow these steps:

1. Open the news.html and newarticles.html documents. (You may have a different name for the second document. It is the file that matches the New Articles menu item in the News category.)

2. Locate and open news.txt *or* news.doc. Select all the text and copy.

3. With the news.html document active, place your cursor at the top-left corner of the maincontent editable area (center column of the lower table). Select Edit ⇨ Paste or use Ctrl+V (PC) or ⌘+V (Mac). Your text has arrived and you can now format.

4. Place your cursor anywhere in the first line of text. This will be your headline. Select Headline 1 from the Format drop-down list in the Properties Inspector.

5. To format the text, insert your cursor into the first line and select H1 from the Properties panel Format field. The next paragraph should be Paragraph format. Apply H1 to the next headline, and so on. There are four paragraphs and three headlines. Check your code to make sure that <p> tags have been inserted in the copied text to separate paragraphs. If <br> tags have been used, please replace with <p> tags.

6. Add links of your choice to the words "links" and "Online Events" in the final paragraph.

7. You will find the entry "more>" at the end of each paragraph. Select this phrase and assign the class style more to each occurrence. Create links of your choice to pages in the site for each one.

8. With the newarticle.html document active, locate and open newarticle.txt *or* newarticle.doc. Select the text and copy.

9. Repeat Steps 3 through 6, but assign H1 to the first headline, and H2 to the second headline, and add a link to "contact" in the first paragraph, and "new product line" in the final paragraph. See Figure 25-1 for a sample of how newarticles.html should appear.

There are deliberate typing errors in the text files. Don't correct them. You'll use the spell check feature a little later in this session to perfect your pages.

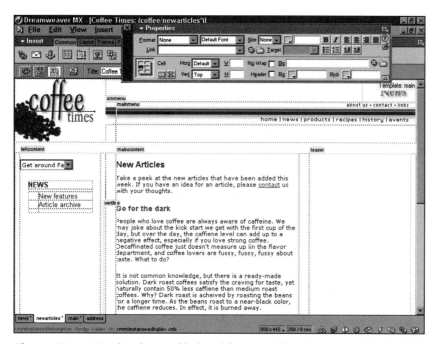

Figure 25-1 *Text has been added and formatted for the newarticles.html document.*

Embedding images in text

You can add images in many ways in text, often by creating tables to separate text and images. However, it is often most effective to have your images embedded directly into your text. The method is not difficult.

To embed an image in your text, use the following steps:

1. With the newarticles.html document active, place your cursor at the beginning of the paragraph that begins: "It is not common knowledge ... "

2. Select Insert ⇨ Image and select grind.jpg from the art folder. Don't panic . . . yes, it looks bad right now.

3. With the image selected, choose Left from the Align drop-down menu in the Properties panel. This entry allows the text to wrap around the image. Enter **10** for the H Space value, to give the image some breathing room. H Space controls the side margins of the image, and V Space provides space at the top and the bottom of the image.

4. With the news.html document active, place the image grindsm.jpg at the beginning of the first paragraph, with left alignment, and a horizontal space value of **5**. Place nabobsm.jpg at the beginning of the second paragraph with right alignment and a horizontal space of **5**. See Figure 25-2 to see formatting and images in place.

Adding Library item content

I am assuming that you have created the News menu Library item and have placed the menu in each of these documents. In the news.html document menu, News should still be in place, but should not have a link to any page. In the newarticle.html page, I have chosen to remove the active page link. You may have chosen to leave the listing, but should have removed the link.

 In the Session 25 folder on the CD-ROM, I have included four Library item files to save you time. Copy address.lbi, teasecanada.lbi, teaselinks.lbi, and teaserecipe.lbi to the Library folder in the root folder of your Coffee site. If you have followed my examples, you will save the files in c:/coffee/Library/.

The right column of every page has been set aside for little ad-like pieces of text and images that I call teaser menu items. You can use this space to help direct visitors to the most interesting areas of your site. The teaser items are already prepared for you to just drag into the pages. Create a few of your own, following the examples I have provided. The method to embed images in text will be covered as you complete the next page.

The Library items included here use CSS styles that have not been defined through an exercise. If you have not copied the coffee.css file from the Session 25 folder, as described previously, the formatting will not be accurate.

To add Library items use these steps:

1. With the news.html document active, open your Assets panel and drag the teaser menu items to the right column in the following order: teaserecipe, teaselinks.

2. With the newarticles.html document open, drag the teaser menu items to the right column in the following order: teaserecipe, teaselinks, teasecanada.

3. Drag the address Library item to the left column of the bottom table for both documents. This item should be below the jump menu. Your news.html document should be similar to Figure 25-2.

Figure 25-2   *Internet Explorer preview of news.html with formatting in place and images added. Library items are also in place.*

Finalizing the Template

**20 Min.
To Go**

Once you have completed the content for a few pages, you should test your pages, and return to your template to correct any issues that have appeared once your content went into place. There is an obvious and deliberate error that you may have picked up. Note that there is no space between the content in the right column and the right edge of the page. That correction can be easily done on the template.

As I was preparing the template for earlier chapters, I accidentally omitted another command for the bottom text menu. However, I decided to include the fix, rather than roll back to the earlier chapter and fix the instructions. The bottom text menu is in an editable area, and does not update when you update the template. But I have a "cheat" for you.

First, to add an extra column, and make a few other adjustments to the content table in your template, take the following steps:

1. Open the main template. Select the entire lower table by using the tag selector at the lower left of your screen.

2. In the Properties panel, change the number of columns to **8**. In the bottom row of the table, insert your cursor into the new column at the far right. Insert the image spacer.gif from the art folder, and specify a width of **10**. Click anywhere on the Properties panel to remove the cursor from the width field. Use your arrow key to deselect the image and specify **10** for the column width in the Properties panel.

3. To ensure that the teaser menu column will be wide enough to display the menus well, insert your cursor in the second column from the right in the bottom row. Insert the image spacer.gif and specify the width as **200**.

4. Now that the teaser column has a fixed minimum size, I want to change my mind on the content column size. Change the cell width for the content column to **70%** and the teaser column to **30%**.

5. Save the template and select Update when prompted.

The text menu at the bottom of the page should have a paragraph format added to it. Adding that command to a Library item results in larger spacing than is usually desired, so you want the formatting in the table cell. However, the template will not update an editable area. You can, however, change the area to a noneditable area, make the changes you desire, and then return it to editable status.

To cheat a template editable area use these steps:

1. Click on the text menu to select the Library item text menu. Select Modify ⇨ Templates ⇨ Remove Template Markup. If you are prompted with an alert asking where you would like to move the content of the disappearing editable area, select Nowhere, and click Use for All.

2. Save the template and click Update to send the change to your pages.

3. Insert your cursor into the cell containing the text menu and specify Paragraph for Format in the Properties panel. The text menu should now show the sans serif font.

4. Save the page and update to send the new information to your pages. (Technically, this is not necessary, but I have found it more reliable to complete each change in this process with a save and update to ensure that the information is passed to the pages.)

5. Select the cell containing the text menu by using the tag selector (<td>) at the bottom left of the screen. Select Insert ⇨ Template Objects ⇨ New Editable Region. (Mac: Insert ⇨ Template Objects ⇨ Editable Region.) Name the region **textmenu**. Your menu should look like Figure 25-3.

6. Save the template and update the pages. Remember this little trick when you find you would like to make a change in an editable area of a template.

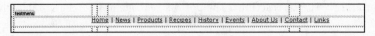

Figure 25-3   The text menu after editing through the template.

Your template is now in perfect shape, and the changes have been sent to every page. Carry on completing pages as you wish. There is no new learning with any page, so I am not going to step you through each one. You can use the greek.txt file to fill pages with text, or find some coffee information to enter if you wish the challenge of working with true text. Use the same teaser menus over and over, or create your own. There is plenty of practice available if you have time for the extra work. Use the pattern of the first two pages to guide you through formatting extra pages. As long as you use the template and the CSS styles to create pages, you are ensured that your pages will be consistent.

There are a few utility operations I would like to go over with you now.

Cleaning Up Your Page

10 Min. To Go

You now have nearly complete pages. (You will add a few pieces such as a Flash movie and an image map in the next session.) You want to make sure that you have as clean a page as possible before you release it to trusted people for testing. Naturally, you will check spelling. Nothing ruins a page more quickly than a spelling error. You will also check your HTML for errors and replace a word using Dreamweaver's find and replace command.

Check spelling

Dreamweaver has a powerful Spell Checker. You have the option to add words to the list, so there is really no excuse that it is too hard to check spelling. (I have heard this from technical people who use industry terms and acronyms that are not in the spell check list.)

To check your spelling follow these steps:

1. With the news.html document active, select Text ⇨ Check Spelling or use the shortcut Shift+F7. The first word that comes up as misspelled is solutin, and the suggestion is solution. Click Change, or Change All if you may have misspelled the word more than once on the page.
2. Yippeee will come up next. This you can Ignore, or Ignore All for several on a page. If this is a term you will be using often, select Add to Personal, and it will become listed as a correct spelling.

 Never add a word to your personal dictionary without making sure it is spelled correctly. Also, make sure that a word that forms an acronym that works in this document is not a common misspelling of another word.

3. Finaly comes up next. The list of suggestions yields the correct spelling for finally. Click the correct word and click Change.
4. When the spell check is complete, an alert appears. Click OK.
5. Run the same check on all of your pages.

Run find and replace

When you are working with a template, the find and replace feature is not quite as much a lifesaver as it is at other times. Still, Dreamweaver's replace capability is powerful, and there are times when you need it.

I recently finished a job that took several months to complete. My colleagues and I did the graphics completely, and then we worked with the programmers to add the database functions. We had to replace approximately 30 plain-page links to Active Server Page (ASP) links for nearly 100 pages. A little math will tell you that is a heck of a pile of cut and paste, not to mention the danger of missing some links. It took one person about an hour to complete the job using Dreamweaver's replace command.

You covered the replace feature in Session 10, but I would like to step through it again in more detail. You have a much better understanding now of how Dreamweaver works, and more understanding of what is involved with creating a site. You are going to do a simple replace in the following steps:

1. If it is not already open, open news.html. Make sure your Coffee site is active. Select Edit ⇨ Find and Replace. The Find and Replace window will open.

2. Open the Find In drop-down list to see your options. You'll search the full site, but you can also search a document, a folder, or selected folders in a site. If you chose any folder option, that choice will take you to a browse screen where you can choose your folder. The Find In selection remains until you close the program or change the settings, which is great for multiple replace terms. Choose Entire Current Local Site.

The Search For option holds the major power of Dreamweaver's search function. You can search for Text, which works much like a word processor's search function, except that it ignores all HTML commands. However, you also have an Advanced Text choice, which lets you search text with qualifiers, such as this word but not when it falls within a certain tag. Source Code allows to you to search for items within an HTML tag, and Specific tag gives you the power to search by tags rather than by what the tag contains. My colleagues and I used a Source Code search across the entire site to replace the codes when we replaced all the links in a site with ASP links.

3. To change the dark roast to dark-roast, select Text from the Search For drop-down menu.

4. Type **dark roast** in the Search For field.

5. Type **dark-roast** in the Replace With field. (See Figure 25-4 for final settings.)

Watch that your spacing at the end of both the Search For and Replace With fields is the same. If you put a space at the end of the Search For but not at the end of the Replace With content, you will have a royal mess. Also, if you are doing a replace across a folder or site, please make sure that you test the replace thoroughly on one page before you do the full search. Changes cannot be undone if your document is not open when the replace occurs.

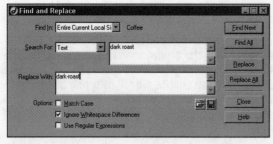

Figure 25-4   *The Find and Replace window ready to perform the search.*

6. Click on Find Next. Behind the Search and Replace window, you will see dark roast is selected in the document.

7. Click on Replace. The new entry is placed. Check the results. You may have to scroll through the page to find where the replacement occurred. It is worth the effort to ensure that all is well.

8. If the replace worked as expected, click Replace All. You will receive an alert telling you that changes cannot be undone in documents that are not currently open. Click Yes. The results window will show where the replacements were made.

Clean up HTML

I have mentioned the value of clean code many times throughout this book. But when you work a page repeatedly, it is common to end up with some extra tags. It can happen even when you are hand coding; so, when so much of your work is done with the code hidden, you have to expect that you will leave some extra code. Dreamweaver can go through your pages and check for extra tags and see where tags can be combined.

Follow these steps to clean up your HTML:

1. If it is not already open, open news.html.
2. Select Commands ⇨ Clean Up HTML. The Clean Up HTML window will open.
3. Select Empty Container Tags, Redundant Nested Tags, and Combine Nested <font> Tags when Possible. This will clean up most extra code.

 Never select Dreamweaver HTML Comments if you are using Library items or Templates. You will break the links.

Most times, you will have few if any tags to clean up if you have worked in the way I have described for this site. It is always nice to get the message "Nothing to Clean Up."

Testing Your Site

The best test for your site is to have people troubleshoot your design on every combination possible of platform, resolution, and browser. Although it is hard to hit every combination, it is important to test at least the Netscape Navigator and Microsoft Internet Explorer browsers on both the PC and the Mac, and several monitor resolutions. You can do this by submitting your page to a critique group. One of the most active is the HWG (HTML Writer's Guild) Critique list. You can sign up for this list and many other very active lists at http://hwg.org.

I strongly advise that you sign up for several newsgroups. You cannot measure the value of having expert advice so easily available. I have been "newsgrouping" since 1993, and it never ceases to amaze me how much time people spend helping each other.

See utility.html in the resources folder on the CD-ROM for a list of news-groups related to Dreamweaver and Web design.

If you cannot, or do not want to join a newsgroup, you should find people who will look at your site before it is released. I use the newsgroups, but I also have people to check for specifics. If you are doing liquid design, testing is even more important.

You have, at the very least, completed two pages for your site. Even if you have not worked ahead, you should be able to see how working with templates and Library items makes creating pages fast and easy. I like the consistency and the power to make minor changes to layout without hours of tedious work and risking errors.

You've earned some fun times. In the next chapter, you look at some of the advanced features that can be offered on the Web.

Done!

REVIEW

You have stepped through the end tasks for creating a Dreamweaver page. Keep the following details in mind:

- Text can be entered directly or it can be pasted into Dreamweaver from another source.
- Adding an Align command to an image will enable the text to wrap around the image.
- You can add horizontal or vertical space to an image with the H Space and V Space fields in the Properties Manager.
- You can update an editable region on a template by temporarily removing the editable region, making a change, and then creating the editable region again.
- You can add unusual words or acronyms to the Spell Checker in Dreamweaver.
- Always test one replace before you run a replace function across a site or folder.
- Always test your site on as many different combinations of monitor resolution, platform, and browser as is possible.

QUIZ YOURSELF

1. What are the two ways to enter text into a document? (See the "Entering text from a text document" section.)
2. How can you add text wrapping to an image in Dreamweaver? (See the "Embedding images in text" section.)
3. What is the method to update an editable region on a template? (See the "Finalizing the Template" section.)

4. How can you add words to Dreamweaver's Spell Checker? (See the "Check spelling" section.)

5. When you are replacing code or phrases in Dreamweaver, what must you watch carefully? (See the "Run find and replace" section.)

6. What is the minimum testing you should do for your site before it is released to the public? (See the "Testing Your Site" section.)

Placing and Creating the Extras

Session Checklist

✔ Understanding external media

✔ Adding an animated GIF file

✔ Inserting a sound file

✔ Inserting a Flash movie

✔ Creating an image map

**30 Min.
To Go**

You've worked hard. If you have moved beyond the lessons and created many pages, you have probably been introduced to some of the tedious work of Web design (without Dreamweaver to help, multiply any tedium many times). Now it is time to have some fun.

Many of us are attracted to Web design by its limitless possibilities. In this session, you will learn to place many different types of media into your Web pages. This lesson is only about placing movies and other media — not even a scrap about creating it. Multimedia is a huge and growing field that I will not touch here.

Dreamweaver quietly overcomes many of the problems that placing media can present. With Dreamweaver tools, you will place a Flash movie and an animated GIF file, as well as build an image map. This is where you sit back and relax. The work is easy, the results fun.

Using External Media

As much fun as they can be, motion and sound must be treated with respect. All of us have found sites with so much going on that our eye cannot find a place to rest, or we have been blasted by low-quality music. Having your visitor jump out of her skin will not bring a positive reaction to your site. Most of us leave . . . fast.

Movies can be just as bad. With my slow Internet connection, I find it annoying to be forced to watch a full screen, three-minute-download movie that does nothing more than spin a company logo. In fact, I rarely get to see what is on such a site because I leave such sites quickly. Escape routes are important.

Remember, too, that you are probably not the average computer user. So many professional developers or interested amateurs assume that the rest of the surfing world has similar equipment and capability. That is so far from true. For many people who surf the Web, computers are not a high priority — computers are more like a simple diversion or entertainment. They are not spending their dollars on the latest and greatest, and often have what seems archaic equipment to us in the industry. Do not forget that you are probably not average.

If you are truly interested in the field of multimedia, I urge you to set up a site dedicated to personal experimentation and the "cool" factor.

Understanding external media and Dreamweaver

The first thing to understand about media files such as sound and movies is that it is not Dreamweaver, nor is it the browser, that plays them. You must have a plug-in, or player, which is a special auxiliary program, installed on your computer to play any sound or movie. All modern browsers come with plug-ins to play most sound and movie types, including Flash movies. Because you likely have the plug-ins installed, it can seem as if Dreamweaver is working the magic.

Learn one and you learn them all does *not* apply to placing media files. Dreamweaver does whittle the differences down for you, because it will place special codes to ensure that your media will play accurately. But there *are* important differences worth understanding. If you find that you are placing many media files, you should do your best to research the type of files you are placing. The best information is often found on the software manufacturers' sites, such as Macromedia for Flash/Shockwave information (http://macromedia.com), QuickTime (http://apple.com/quicktime), or RealAudio (http://realnetworks.com/devzone).

However, the basics of media files are similar from a Dreamweaver perspective. You insert the file, set a few parameters in the Properties panel and your file will play. Always be aware, however, that no matter how well you place the file, your visitor will require the plug-in to be able to see or hear your content. It is usually a good idea to include a link to download the software (which is free) for the few visitors who do not already have the plug-in.

I have included animated GIF files in this section because they move and can often be interchanged with small Flash movies. However, all movement is controlled within the file. As far as Dreamweaver is concerned, an animated GIF is simply an image.

Just before we move on to placing files, I want to talk a little about how to use files with movement and sound.

Making external media count

Adding motion and sound to your pages can help your site to be easy to navigate, pleasant to use, and look more professional. Adding motion and sound to your site can make it hard to navigate, a real trial to use, and have a completely amateur look. The difference is simply in the execution.

Adding motion or sound just because you can is about as bad an idea as exists in the Web-development world. However, if you have a definite reason for adding motion or sound, you can draw attention to features that are important to visitors. Motion and sound can help guide visitors through a page; it can also set a mood for your site. Although we often talk about using the Web to find information, there is also an entertainment component to the Web. Just as TV commercials are not all white text on a black screen, you do not always have to be all business, even for commercial sites. Building an atmosphere can be important.

However, there is a difference between creating a mood and satisfying your own desires to play with media. As long as you can specifically point to why you have included media, from a visitor's perspective, you are well on the way to responsible media use. Perhaps you have added a new feature to your site. Motion can help draw the visitor's attention to the new area, which is a plus. Or perhaps you have a product that is difficult to explain. Ikea (www.ikea-usa.com/rooms_ideas/flash_page_storage_workspace.asp) has an excellent example of a Flash movie used to assist a visitor with choices as well as selling the product. At the site, visit the assembly area to see a Flash movie that is definitely customer oriented.

Always ask the question: What does this do to enhance my visitor's experience?

Most of my warnings are out of the way now. Let's move on and add some media to your pages.

If you are interested in sound and motion, you may want to read *Building Really Annoying Web Sites* **by Michael Miller, published by Hungry Minds, Inc. Before you add media to your sites, you should work hard to understand why many surfers run away from "active" sites.**

Adding Motion and Sound in Dreamweaver

I begin this section with animated GIF files, which do not officially belong in this section, because they are really graphics. However, animated GIF files not only provide motion, but they are also often used as alternative images for Flash presentations. Animated GIF files can be created from a Flash movie, and used in the same way.

Copy the file animatedone.html, in the Session 26 folder on the CD-ROM, to the root folder for your Coffee site. Copy the rest of the files and folders in the Session 26 folder to the art folder of your Coffee site. Keep the folders intact.

Adding an animated GIF

Animated GIF files provided the first motion on the Web and have been responsible for many of the warnings I included above, such as distracting from a message or increasing load time. They can be used well, though, and are indispensable for banner ads and small notices. Animated GIF files are easy to create in most current graphics software, and they display on any browser that can display an image.

I have included a lively menu, using animated images for rollovers, that does not match the Coffee site mood. However, I wanted to show you a creative use for animated graphics. This menu leaves the control of the animation in the visitor's hands.

To create a menu with animated rollovers

1. Create a new HTML page in your Coffee site and name it **animate.html**.

2. Create a new table that is **212** pixels wide, with **1** row and **2** columns, **0** cell spacing and padding, and borders **0**. In your Properties panel, specify right alignment for the table.

3. In the left column, place the image line.gif from the art/animate folder. Assign Top for the cell vertical alignment and Right for the horizontal alignment.

4. Insert the image titlecontact.gif in the right column. Assign Top for the cell vertical alignment and Right for the horizontal alignment. Insert a <br> tag with Shift+Enter.

5. Create a menu using simple rollovers (see Session 13) with images from the art/animate folder, and the following order: Home, About Us, FAQ, Support. The file names are the same as the menu items, with the over state listed as the menu name plus over.

6. Preview your menu in a browser to see the animation on rollover. Figure 26-1 shows the animation.

 There is a completed version of this menu, labeled animatedone.html, in the Session 26 folder, which you should have copied to your computer earlier in this session.

Figure 26-1   *Animated GIF file used as a rollover image. A ball bounces when the mouse is passed over each menu image.*

And that is that! Placing an animated GIF in Dreamweaver is the same as placing any other image.

Placing a sound file

20 Min. To Go

You have two options when you are placing a sound file. You can simply set up a link to the file, which will play automatically, or, if you want to provide controls for your visitors within your page, you can embed your sound.

Follow these steps to create a link to a sound file:

1. Create a new document, and call it **mediatest.html**.
2. Type **Listen to a clip from Kevin Van Sant's Bossa for NG.** (You can hear many samples of Kevin's music at `www.onestopjazz.com/kvansant`.)
3. Highlight the phrase Bossa for NG. In the link field, type **art/jazure.wav** *or* browse for the file `jazure.wav` in the art folder.
4. Preview the file in your browser. Click on the link to make the music play. Providing sound controls for your visitors allows them to choose what they hear in their own media players.

Some developers prefer to embed controls within their own page. This method, which is outlined in the following steps, is slightly different:

1. In the same document, insert your cursor where you would like to place the sound control. Select Insert ⇨ Media ⇨ Plugin. The Select File window opens.
2. Select the file jazure.wav in the art folder. A plug-in icon is placed with Dreamweaver's default value of 32 pixels × 32 pixels.
3. Delete the W and H values to allow the default player size to be displayed.
4. I recommend adding one snippet of code so that your music does not start automatically. Your code as it is placed is

   ```
   <embed src="art/jazure.wav">
   ```

   Add **autoplay="false"** after the link reference as follows:

   ```
   <embed src="art/jazure.wav" autoplay="false">
   ```

   If you wish to have your music clip loop, add **loop="true"** in the same manner and **location** as the autoplay command.
5. Preview the results in your browser (see Figure 26-2).

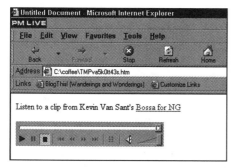

Figure 26-2 *The Windows Media Player controls shown in an Internet Explorer preview.*

You now have two methods to add sound to your site, but allow visitors to choose whether they listen or not.

Inserting a Flash movie

I have prepared a simple little Flash movie to include in your Coffee site. There is no reason that a Flash movie cannot be placed within a template, but for this exercise, you just place it on any page in the Coffee site as a teaser menu. If you would like this movie on the template page, simply follow the same instructions in a location of your choice in the template document.

1. Create or open a document that is based on the main template.

2. You'll add the movie to the teaser menu column. Insert cursor in the right column of the lower table. Select Insert ➪ Media ➪ Flash. The Select File window opens.

3. Browse to the art directory and select the file best.swf. A flash icon will be loaded into the browser, with an accurate representation of the Flash movie size.

4. Unlike an image, you can adjust the size of the Flash movie within Dreamweaver to fit perfectly into your page. Flash movies are created in vector format, and as long as there are no bitmap images included in the file, you can adjust the size without quality loss. This sample has a small bitmap image, but it can be made smaller with minimum quality loss to the photo. Select the Flash movie and specify the size as 150 × 150.

5. This movie is not intended to play continuously. Click the Loop option in the Properties panel to uncheck.

6. To align the movie on the page, place your cursor beside the movie and click the Align Center button at the top-right of your Properties panel.

7. You can test the Flash file from within Dreamweaver, and leave it playing while you work on the document, as shown in Figure 26-3. In the Properties panel, click the Play button. You must click Stop to stop the movie playing in order to further edit the movie parameters.

8. This movie is a link to the news.html page. I have included text that looks like a link in the final view, but clicking anywhere on the movie at any time takes you to the linked file. That specification is included within the original Flash movie, not set in Dreamweaver.

I will not pretend that creating a full-featured Flash movie is an easy feat. But placing a movie is easy — similar to inserting an image. If you would like to learn more about Flash, visit Macromedia at `http://macromedia.com/software/flash`.

A 30-day, full-featured demo version of Macromedia Flash is included on your CD. See the Software folder. If you cannot see the movie from the exercise above, you need to install the Flash Player.

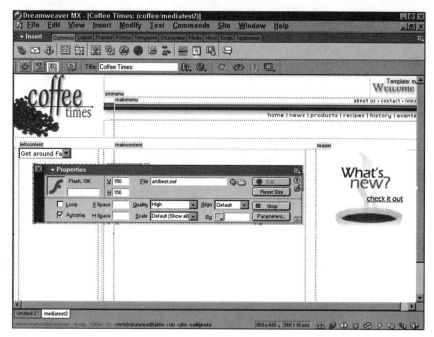

Figure 26-3 *Flash movie inserted and playing within Dreamweaver.*

Creating an image map

10 Min.
To Go

You have survived all the tough ways to create a link from an image. I end this session with an easy way to provide links for your visitors: image maps created with HTML code that are added to an image. This code sets different areas of the image to link to different places. No JavaScript is involved, which makes this method of creating links compatible for every browser in common use.

However, to use this effect, you do give up the visual cues of changing images that a rollover produces. Links in an image map are denoted only by the hand icon when the mouse is held over a linked image.

It is especially important to use Alt tags when creating image maps, because the flag that carries the Alt tag information can help guide your visitor to identify the link areas.

To create an image map, you insert an image and then define the link areas, as follows:

1. Open or create a document based on the main template. This image map will be a teaser menu item.

2. Insert your cursor in the right column of the bottom table and insert coolbeans.gif from the art folder.

3. You now define five areas that will have separate links. Make sure that the image is selected. Type **coolbeans** in the field beside the word Map in the Properties panel. This is your image map name.

4. Select the blue rectangle in the lower-left corner of the Properties panel. This will draw a rectangular area as a link. This area is known as a *hotspot*. The Oval Hotspot tool will draw an oval area, and the Polygon Hotspot tool allows for freehand hotspots.

   With the Rectangular Hotspot tool selected, drag a rectangle that encloses the entire area over the *climate*. The Properties panel changes to receive information for that hotspot. Figure 26-4 shows the creation of a hotspot.

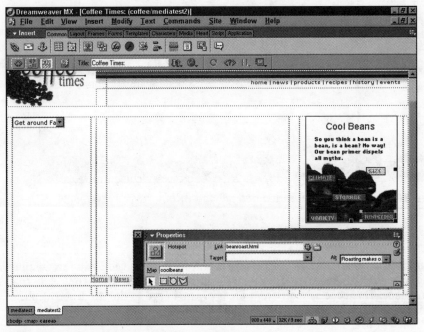

Figure 26-4   *Creating or editing a hotspot.*

5. Type **beansclimate.html** in the Link field of the Properties panel. (There is no page by this name unless you wish to create one.)
6. Type **The effect of climate on coffee flavor** in the Alt field. Note that the map name is displayed in the lower-left corner of the Properties panel. The name displays for the five hotspot areas.
7. Repeat Steps 4 through 6 for the next four areas, using filenames of your own choosing. Create an Alt tag text to match each link name.
8. Preview the document in your browser to see the image map in action. The links will not work unless you have created the pages you named, but you will be able to see the Alt tag flag. Check the status bar at the bottom of the window to see the link information.
9. To edit any hotspot on your image map, select the large arrow in the hotspot area in the bottom left of the Properties panel. Click on the hotspot in your document and make your changes. Figure 26-5 shows a hotspot in action in Internet Explorer on a PC (Mac viewers may not see the Alt tags as shown).

Figure 26-5   *The Alt tag helps to guide the visitor to hotspot links.*

Your image map is now complete. Look at the code that was produced as you created the map. In the partial sample of code I have included here, the map is named and one hotspot is defined.

```
<map name="coolbeans">
  <area shape="rect" coords="3,109,59,124" href="beanclimate.html"
alt="The effect of climate on coffee flavor">
```

There are times when an image map is the perfect way to include links. Keep this idea in your growing bag of tricks.

Done!

REVIEW

That was fun. Placing the "extras" is not hard (although creating them is a bit more involved). You should pay special attention to the following details, however:

- Always ensure that you are adding to your visitor's experience before you add any motion or sound to your site.
- An animated GIF can be added to your documents in the same way that any image can be added.
- Sound files can be included as links or embedded in the page. Regardless of the method used, you should always make sure that your visitor has the option to start and stop the sound file.
- Flash movies can be previewed in the Dreamweaver document.
- Flash movies are created in a vector format, which enables them to be scaled without quality loss as long as there are no raster images included in the file.
- Leaving a Flash movie playing as you work on the page can be a great test for the aggravation factor of the motion. You can also stop the movie from looping so that you can see the general effect without working with the constant motion.
- Image maps create a simple multiple-link image. Make sure you use Alt tags when you are using image maps as they can help your visitor identify the hotspots as links.

QUIZ YOURSELF

1. Why must you be careful with external media on your pages? (See the "Using External Media" section.)

2. What is a media player and why must it be installed before you can test media in Dreamweaver? (See the "Understanding external media and Dreamweaver" section.)

3. What is an animated GIF? (See the "Understanding external media and Dreamweaver" section.)

4. What is the only valid reason for adding media to your pages? (See the "Making external media count" section.)

5. How can you test an animated GIF in Dreamweaver? (See the "Adding an animated GIF" section.)

6. How is a Flash movie previewed in Dreamweaver? (See the "Inserting a Flash movie" section.)

7. What is a hotspot on an image map? (See the "Creating an image map" section.)

PART

V

Sunday Morning Part Review

1. You can edit jump menu items from the Properties Inspector. How?
2. How can the Properties panel help you learn Dreamweaver?
3. You can customize the Insert toolbar to display icons only, text only, or icons and text. Where do you make this choice?
4. How can you change the preference for how your assets are sorted in the Assets panel?
5. JPG files are best for which type of images?
6. GIF files are best for which type of images?
7. What does the term *optimizing images* mean?
8. What is the most important benefit of controlling your text using CSS in a separate file?
9. When you create a style sheet through the Attach Style Sheet command from the Text ⇨ CSS Styles menu, what actually happens?
10. What is a route for editing a CSS style sheet you have already attached to your document?
11. What is the CSS method you use to create different link attributes for a menu than you have specified for the main page?
12. How can you ensure that files in a series are stored together in a file listing for easy retrieval?
13. Why is it important to include an *active* state image when you are preparing your menu items?
14. What is an Alt tag?
15. How can you make text wrap around an image?
16. When you choose Add to Personal in the Check Spelling window, what is the result?

17. When you have been working with a document for quite a while and have made many changes, what is one thing you can do to make sure you have not left redundant code behind?

18. If you are interested in cutting-edge media, how can you learn and experiment without including inappropriate items on a commercial page?

19. Sound can add to a page, but one thing should always be included with sound. What is it?

20. What is the most important benefit that an image map offers over most navigation methods?

PART

VI

Sunday
Afternoon

Using Layers for Layout

**30 Min.
To Go**

Layers are almost irresistible for those who have come from the print world, as they have been using layers since the very early days of the computer graphics field. Watching a page fall together with layers will seduce even those of you who have never sent a file to print. However, like all Web technologies, anything really fun comes with a long list of cautions. Although learning to use layers is relatively easy — certainly easier than tables — not all browsers interpret layers in the same way.

From a Dreamweaver perspective, layers are a click-and-drag operation. Learn a few rules, such as how to enlarge, move, and place one layer inside another, and you will have much of the technique mastered. In reality, the Web is never that simple.

Let's start by looking at layers and why they require caution, and then move on to building a page using layers. At the end, you'll learn how to convert your layers to tables to overcome the browser display issues that crop up when using layers.

Understanding Layers

Working with layers is relatively easy. You drag a layer shape onto your page, place some content, and then repeat. There are no columns or rows to create, delete, or merge to achieve your look. In the initial stages, working with layers is similar to working with a page layout program. Create a layer, add some content, and you are set. However, in practical applications, getting your page to display in a browser is an entirely different matter.

Layer position on the screen is set into code by CSS. Remember the warnings you learned about using CSS for text only? It is much more complicated for positioning. Not all browsers support every command. *Buggy* is the word you often hear associated with layers and CSS. You can create a document using layers and CSS, and it will go together very quickly. In addition, layers offer routes around much of what frustrates us when working with tables. The tricky part is getting it to display on a variety of browsers.

See Session 23 for a discussion of CSS for text.

How can layers be so popular if they are so buggy? Intranets offer one clue. The designer often knows which browsers or platform site visitors will use, so using layers is a safer technique for intranets. If I worked in intranet environments, I would work often with layers.

Some designers use layers to create a layout, and then convert the layers into tables. You will learn how to complete this operation in this session. I would, however, offer an extra caution. Tables will display, even in older browsers. However, as you have seen in earlier sessions, you must construct tables very carefully to avoid surprises in many browsers. Creating your page in layers does not remove that requirement. Once you convert layers to tables, you still must have very clean work and a layout that fits into the table format, which takes away many of the benefits of working with layers. You must be an expert in constructing tables to create layers that convert cleanly to tables.

So why teach — and more important to you — why learn layers? You may be interested in intranet design. That is reason enough. Some people are just more comfortable with the layers concept for construction. That is a good reason to learn, as long as the work is done with tables in mind while you work.

But the biggest reason of all is that the day will come when you can freely use layers. Every month that passes takes us closer to the day when there are few disadvantages to working with layers; and the many advantages will be truly compelling. You may already be designing for a target group that is likely to have only the most modern browsers, and you may be willing to go through the extensive debugging process required even for a specific Web group. (There's neither time nor space to enter that arena at all in this Crash Course.) Layers should not be ignored.

For more on this topic, you can check out the *Dynamic HTML Weekend Crash Course* by Dave Taylor, published by Hungry Minds, Inc.

Working with Layers

You need to create a page to use solely for the first few exercises in this session. Before you build a page for your site, you should be comfortable with how layers are created and manipulated. Much of what you learn in the first portion of the layers work cannot be used for your site because it cannot be converted to tables. But you should look at what layers can do when you are not restricted. You also will need some of these techniques for Session 28.

Creating a layer

Use the following steps to create a page with layers:

1. Create a new document in the Coffee Times site. Name the document **layerstest.html**.

2. If the Insert toolbar is not turned on, select Window ⇨ Insert. Activate the Common tab. Open the Layers Window by selecting Window ⇨ Others ⇨ Layers. (Or use F2 as a shortcut to toggle the Layers window on and off.)

3. To create a layer, click the Draw Layer icon in the Insert toolbar. Click and drag anywhere on the page to define your layer. A rectangular area with a tab at the top appears. (Click on the layer if the tab does not appear.) This is your layer. Check your Layers panel and you see Layer1 listed.

4. To select the layer, click the tab at the top or click on any part of the layer's border.

   Selection handles appear around the border of the layer. Note that the Properties panel now has Layer options displayed. Type **firstsample** in the Layer ID field in the Properties panel.

5. Take a look at the L, W, T, and H values in the Properties panel. These are the coordinates and size for your layer. L represents where on the page the left edge of your layer is positioned in relation to the left edge of the page. T represents where the top of your layer is positioned on the page in relation to the top of the page. Click and drag on the tab or border for your layer (watch for the four-pointed arrow to signify you can move the layer) and you can watch this value change (Mac: You may have to release your mouse to see the new values). (When you create nested layers later in this session, these values will refer to the position in relation to the parent layer when a child layer is selected.)

6. The W and H values are the width and height for your layer. Click and drag a resizing handle for your layer in your document and watch the values change in the Properties panel.

Pause for a moment and take a look at the following code that Dreamweaver produced to display your layer:

```
<div id="firstsample" style="position:absolute; left:19px; top:50px;
width:231px; height:259px; z-index:2"></div>
```

Reading through the code, most will make sense if you compare it to the Properties panel values. Note the style reference; that is your CSS positioning. The z-index refers to the layer position in relation to other layers. Create another layer to see the z-index in action.

1. Activate the Draw Layers icon in the Insert toolbar. Click and drag to create another layer that is close to, but not touching, the first layer. Name the layer **secondsample**. Note that the Layers panel now lists both layer names, and that the z-index value is 1 for firstsample and 2 for secondsample.

2. Click the secondsample listing in the Layers panel and drag it below firstsample. The listing order changes, as does the z-index value. This becomes very important when you start working with DHTML in the next session. Figure 27-1 shows how the page should look. Your layer size and position will be different, and you may have to select View ⇨ Visual Aids ⇨ Invisible Elements to display the icons shown.

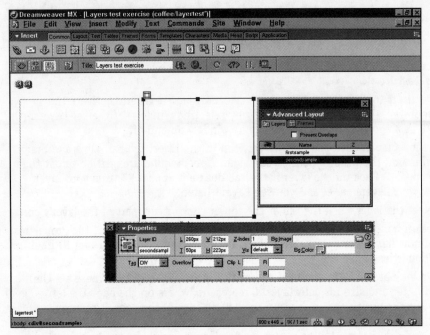

Figure 27-1 *Two layers are drawn, with one selected. Note that the Properties panel lists the positioning information, and that the selected layer is also highlighted in the Layers panel.*

20 Min. To Go

Creating a nested layer

To use the stacking benefits of layers, you place layers inside of layers. This is the equivalent to nesting tables when you are working without layers. However, you cannot convert nested layers to tables.

First, look at the Prevent Overlaps command in the Layers panel. This option is essential if you are planning to convert your layers to tables when your page is complete. Layers can be placed anywhere — over, under, overlapping, or even in the middle of nowhere. There are no bounds. However, tables are not so accommodating. If layers will be converted to tables, you must keep the design under control. One way to prevent creating a page in layers that cannot be reasonably transferred to tables is to activate the Prevent Overlaps option. Dreamweaver will prevent you from placing layers where a table would be unable to duplicate the position.

Take the following steps to create a nested table:

1. Turn off the Prevent Overlaps option.
2. Click the Draw Layer icon in the Insert panel. With your Alt (PC) or Option (Mac) key pressed, click and drag within the first layer to define a new layer.

Tip If you plan on creating many nested layers, you can set your preferences to automatically allow nested tables. Select Edit ⇨ Preferences and click Layers from the Category list. Activate Nest When Created within a Layer. You are now able to draw nested layers without holding down the Alt (PC) or Option (Mac) key. Using the Alt or Option keys will then allow you to create a layer that is not nested.

3. Name the new layer **firstchild** in the Properties panel. Note the values in the Properties panel. When the new layer — which is considered to be a child of the layer that contains it — is selected, the L and T values reflect the position of the child layer within the parent layer. These values have no relation to the child's position on the page. Also note that the firstlayer listing in the Layers panel now has a sublisting to reflect the addition of the child layer.

4. Set the child layer to be in the upper-left corner of the parent layer. You can either type **0** for both the L and T value, or you can drag it into position. When dragging, move it close to the desired location and use your arrow keys to move the layer one pixel at a time.

5. Select the firstsample layer and select a light gray background from the Bg Color field in the Properties panel. Select firstchild and assign a white background color. See Figure 27-2 for the final result.

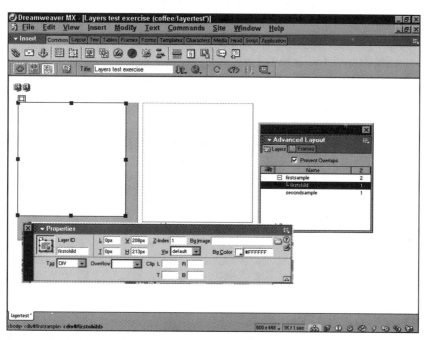

Figure 27-2 *Parent layer with gray background and selected child layer with a white background. Note that the child layer position is relative to the parent layer, not the page.*

Positioning layers

To move a layer, you simply drag it to the new position. To resize a layer, select and then resize with the handles at the sides or corners of the layer.

You might decide that you require a layer in a different stacking order. If this is the case, follow these steps:

1. Select the layer secondsample and assign a red background color.
2. Draw a large layer over all the layers now on the page.
3. Apply a dark blue background color to the new layer. It should hide all the layers that are on your page.
4. Select the new layer. In the Properties panel, change the z-index value to **1**.
5. Select secondsample layer and change the z-index value to **2** (Firstsample already has a value of 2).
6. Deselect all layers, and you see that the two smaller layers now appear on top of the blue layer.

Adding content to layers

Content is added to layers in the same way that it is added to the page. Images, media, or text are added to the layer at the cursor position. Insert an image in your layer using the following steps:

Before you take the next steps, you'll need to copy the image BACK.gif from the Session 27 folder to the art folder of the Coffee Times site.

1. Click inside the white layer to position the cursor. Insert entrypic.jpg from the art folder.
2. Click inside the red layer. Using white, bold type, type enough words to fill several lines.
3. Select the gray parent layer. In the Properties panel, add BACK.gif from the art director as the Bg Image. This creates a background for the gray layer only. See Figure 27-3 for the final result.

Doesn't that feel familiar? Layers are similar to minipages. However, before your imagination takes off with the wonderful designs you could create, it is time for a reality check. This looks great on the Dreamweaver page. But test it in your browsers. My copy displayed properly in Internet Explorer 6, Opera 5, and Netscape 6. Netscape 4.5 was only able to show an interesting arrangement of my background image and the photo when the window opened at a reduced size. I maximized the window size and was left with just the photo. Not a technique for the faint of heart.

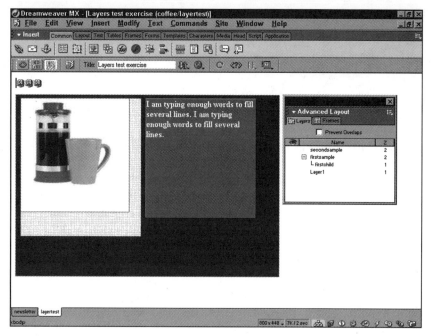

Figure 27-3 *Your layers with content. Note the three "invisible content" markers at the upper-left of the screen. These are placed with your layers and contain the layer positioning information.*

Creating a page with layers for tables

10 Min. To Go

Here you are on the other side, ready to use layers that you can put on the Web. What's different? Well, you are working with layers that cannot be nested or overlapped. You also are going to have to keep the structure of a table in mind as you create your layers document. Because you are converting the layers to tables at the end of the exercise, you might as well work within those bounds right from the start.

Follow these steps to create a sign-up form for a newsletter, designed for use in a pop-up window:

1. Create a new document in the Coffee Times site. Name it **newsletter.html.** You will create this document using layers.

2. Turn on a grid to help line up the layers. Select View ➪ Grid ➪ Show Grid. This shows the default grid.

3. Select View ➪ Grid ➪ Grid Settings. Make sure the Snap to Grid and Show Grid options are checked. Type **20** in the Spacing field. Select Dots as the Display value. Then click Apply to see the results of this slight adjustment. Figure 27-4 shows the changed settings. Click OK to accept the settings.

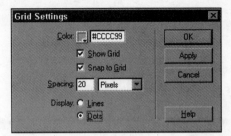

Figure 27-4   *Grid Settings window with customized settings.*

4. Open the Layers panel and the Insert toolbar if they are not already open. Make sure that the Prevent Overlaps option is selected in the Layers panel.

5. Attach the style sheet coffee.css to the document. Set the page margins to **0**.

6. Click the Draw Layers icon in Insert toolbar. Draw a layer in the upper-left corner that is 300 pixels wide by 120 pixels high. Name the layer **Logo**.

7. Place your cursor in the Logo layer and insert the image logo.gif from the art folder.

8. Create another layer, 280-pixels wide by 80 pixels high, starting 20 pixels in from the edge of the page, and 20 pixels down from the Logo layer bottom. Name the layer Text. Insert your cursor in the Type layer and type the following text, pressing Enter after each paragraph:

   Facts on Food Newsletter

   Delivered monthly . . . filled with coffee history, lore, tips, trivia and recipes. Guest articles with every issue. Free!

   Apply Heading 1 style to the headline and make sure that the text is Paragraph style.

9. Create a layer 20 pixels down from the Text layer, and 20 pixels in from the edge of the page. Make the layer 160 pixels by 80 pixels. Name the layer **Form**. Type **Email address**. Apply Heading 3 style. Insert a line with your Enter key. Add a form and a text field form object.

10. Create a layer 100 pixels by 40 pixels that is 20 pixels down from the Text layer, aligned with the right edge of that layer. Name the layer **Explain**. Type **Simply type in your email address.** Apply the class style "teaser" to the text.

11. Create a layer 100 pixels by 20 pixels, aligned with the right edge of the Explain layer, and 20 pixels down from the Explain layer. Name the layer **Close**. Type **X Close window**. Apply the class style "more."

12. Type **Newsletter Sign-up** as the page title in the Title area near the top of your page.

That's your layout. You are almost ready to create a table from your layer page. Check to make sure that all alignments are as you want them. See Figure 27-5 for an example of how it should look in Dreamweaver.

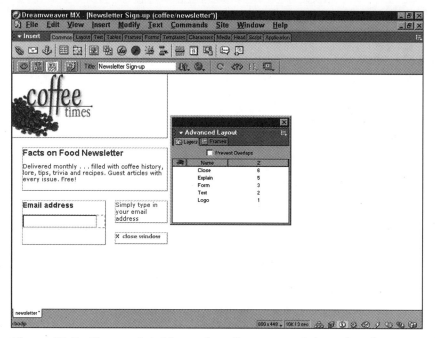

Figure 27-5 *The completed layer view of your page. It is ready to be converted to a table. The grid has been turned off for clarity.*

Converting layers to tables

This is going to be a little anticlimactic. You have worked through this entire session to get here, and you are going to accomplish your goal in one operation. I could make it harder, but I don't think you would appreciate that, either. Follow these steps to create a table:

1. Select Modify ⇨ Convert ⇨ Layers to Table. The Convert Layers to Table window opens.

2. Select Most Accurate for the Table Layout. Choosing Smallest delivers a less complicated table, but it will not be as accurate. Any cells below the size you specify will be included with a neighboring cell to reduce columns and rows. Use this feature if accurate layout is not crucial.

3. Make sure that Use Transparent GIFs is checked. Dreamweaver will place the invisible images you require to prevent collapsing cells.

4. Make sure that the Center on Page option is unchecked.

5. Check Prevent Layer Overlaps. This is a safety feature, because you should have no overlapping layers.

6. Check Snap to Grid if your layout is dependent on a grid. This prevents tiny columns or rows from being created if your alignment is a little off.

7. Click OK. Your document should resemble Figure 27-6. Some text formatting may be affected by the conversion to tables. If so, simply reapply the styles to the text.

Figure 27-6   *Dreamweaver view of your page immediately after converting your layers to a table.*

You can change your page back to layers if you decide to add or change content, or you can edit it in table form. You might want to see if there is any way to reduce the number of columns or rows. However, if you find you are doing too much editing on the table that is created by Dreamweaver, you should consider using tables from the beginning of the process.

Using Tables or Layers

Creating tables from layers definitely produces more code. This matters to me, and it is one of the main reasons I use tables for most of my page construction. But as I mentioned earlier, layers are terribly seductive. Your list of pros and cons for each method will likely be different than mine. You may never make a solid decision. You should, however, make sure that you are comfortable with both methods. That is the best way to make production decisions. When you know both methods with equal comfort, you are more likely to make your decisions based on the best that each can deliver.

Done!

REVIEW

You now have the tools to create your pages with layers rather than tables. The methods are straightforward, as long as you remember the following details:

- Layers depend on CSS for positioning, which is what prevents you from using layer-based documents for general Web use. Even current browsers cannot be trusted to correctly display layers.

- The Properties panel provides all controls for layer positioning. The Layers panel displays and controls layer stacking order. The Insert bar provides the drawing tool for click-and-drag layers.

- Nested layers cannot be used for documents that will be converted to tables.

- The Prevent Overlap option helps create layers that will easily convert into tables.
- Content is added to each layer in the same way as it is added to a page. Each layer is like a minipage.
- Naming your layers helps to keep your work organized.
- Layers can be converted to tables, and the same page converted back to layers — although it is best to convert back and forth as little as possible.
- The best way to decide whether table or layer construction is right for you is to learn both methods very well. Each has strengths and weaknesses, and every person will have a preference.

Quiz Yourself

1. Why are layers safer to use for the final production of your pages on intranets than for the Internet? (See the "Understanding Layers" section.)
2. What does the Prevent Overlaps command do for layers? (See the "Creating a nested layer" section.)
3. How do you move a layer? (See the "Positioning layers" section.)
4. At what point will content be added to the active layer? (See the "Adding content to layers" section.)
5. What are one benefit and one drawback of creating tables from layers, as opposed to creating tables from the start? (See the "Using Tables or Layers" section.)

SESSION

28

Creating Motion with DHTML

Session Checklist

✔ Recognizing the limitations of DHTML

✔ Working with DHTML

✔ Understanding timelines

✔ Seeing DHTML at its best

**30 Min.
To Go**

Think back to your layers exercise in Session 27. You placed objects on layers for positioning. Remember the code that placed that layer where you wanted it on the page? Now imagine that you could add instructions to the placement code that told the browser to change the coordinates after a certain time, or when the visitor performs a mouse action. Then imagine that you can tell that layer to be visible or invisible in the same way. That's DHTML in action!

In the last session, you learned how to create layers for layout. When you move into using DHTML to create motion, you put layers to a completely different use. Until now, you have used code only for static objects. Images, text, tables are all static. In fact, even the animated GIFs and the Macromedia Flash object you placed on your page were static. The file caused motion on the screen, but the image or movie remains static on the page. DHTML provides a method to actually move content across your screen. In the sample you create in this session, objects are placed in layers, which are positioned by CSS and moved by JavaScript. As with most things that move from one coordinate to another, you must pay attention to what you are doing and plan your work well, but the concept is surprisingly simple to accomplish in Dreamweaver.

You will look at a very small corner of this ever-developing subject of Web design. For the purposes of this session, you will combine CSS, HTML, and JavaScript to create motion, and give you a taste of a simple DHTML function created in Dreamweaver. DHTML as a whole is a combination of HTML, CSS positioning, and varied scripting used to create a multitude of effects and capability.

Recognizing the Limitations of DHTML

"Okay," you're asking, "where are the warnings?" Yes, they are coming. You will be using layers, which of course come with compatibility issues that were covered in the last session. When you used layers for your layout, you had the option to convert the layout to tables so that all browsers could handle your pages. There is no way to make a table cell move, though, so you must retain the layers when you are working with DHTML. Again, intranets — with their controllable environment — offer an ideal place to use DHTML motion.

DHTML can be used to build features that cannot be accomplished in any other way. Menus that unroll over text, yet disappear when not in use, are highly attractive for sites with masses of information. If you know the majority of your audience will be using more recent browsers and you are prepared to delve deeply into discovering all the quirks with each browser, you can put DHTML to use in documents for the Web.

Never use DHTML for a function that will make your site unusable if the visitor's browser does not recognize your code. I asked a developer who makes most of her living working with DHTML and CSS whether it was practical to use DHTML at all. She stated that DHTML is fine for intranets, but should never be used for anything "mission critical" for the Web.

Working with DHTML in Dreamweaver

DMHTL is a combination of HTML, which forms the framework of a page, CSS, which controls the position of layers, and scripting commands that create an action. For this example, objects are placed on layers, and are moved from one location to another with JavaScript commands. Layers containing objects also can be made visible or invisible by a trigger such as a mouse action, adding yet more capabilities.

Copy the move folder in the Session 28 folder on the CD-ROM to the art folder of the Coffee Times site.

Creating layers for DHTML

You start by creating a document with layers that can be moved. The following exercise will create an extremely simple puzzle designed to introduce the idea of moving layer position:

1. Create a new document in the Coffee Times site. Name the file **layermove.html**.

   Turn on your grid to make positioning your layers easier. Because you are working with a few large objects, you can set your grid to a high value.

2. Select View ⇨ Grid ⇨ Grid Settings. Set the Spacing value to **50**, and select Snap to Grid. Make sure that the Show Grid option is checked. You can choose to have the grid display as lines or dots.

3. Create a layer with a width of **100** pixels and a height of **111** pixels. Select the layer, and then assign the name **A** to the layer. Position the layer close to the top of the page.

4. Insert the image movea.gif from the art/move directory into the A layer.

5. Repeat Steps 3 and 4 twice, naming the new layers **B** and **C**, respectively, and inserting moveb.gif and movec.gif in the respective layers. Use the grid to place the layers symmetrically.

6. Select all three layers by holding down your Shift key as you click each layer. Select Modify ⇨ Align ⇨ Top to align the layers.

7. Create a new layer at the left edge of the page, approximately 350 pixels from the top edge, 50 pixels in from the left edge, and name it **Quest1**. Type **A car that can be rented for a very short period of time.** in the layer. The result should be similar to Figure 28-1.

You have just created three layers containing an image (layers A, B, and C), which a visitor will be able to drag into position once you have completed the next exercise. The final layer that you created, called Quest1, contains the question that will be answered by dragging letter layers into the correct order. The question layer will remain static.

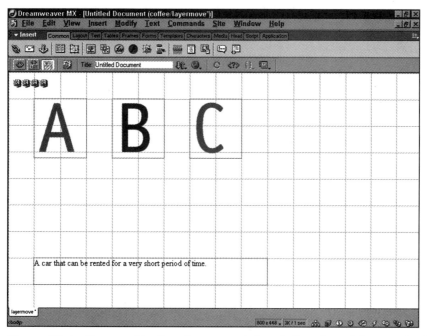

Figure 28-1 *Here are the three layers created and aligned, and the question layer in place. The grid shown here is set to 50 x 50 pixels.*

Adding behaviors for layers

You are now going to create a behavior that will allow you to drag each of the layers to a new position when the page is displayed in a browser. When the layers are dragged into position, the letters will spell "cab." You add the behavior to the <body> tag.

Add the JavaScript that will allow visitors to drag layers by following these steps.

1. Open the Behavior window. Click the <body> tag in the lower-left portion of your document window.

2. Click + (plus) in the Behavior window to create a new behavior. Choose Drag Layer and the Drag Layer window opens.

3. Select layer C from the Layer list.

4. Set the Drop Layer values to Left **50** and Top **200**. Set the Snap if Within value to **50**. When the page is displayed in a browser, layer C (and any contents of layer C, of course) will snap into a position at the left edge, 200 pixels from the top edge of the window. When dragging, the layer will snap into this position as long as the layer is dragged to within 50 pixels of the new location. Click OK to create the behavior.

5. Repeat Steps 2 through 4 for the A and B layers, using Top **200** for both and Left **150** and **250**, respectively, and setting the Snap if Within value to **50**.

6. Preview the page in a browser. Click the C image and drag it close to the area above the text layer. It will snap into place when your mouse pointer is close enough to the specified position. Repeat this step for the other letters.

This is a very simple example of the way layers can be used to build a puzzle or other interactive feature. Experiment with different behaviors and values. Remember that you have to preview your page to see the results.

As you experiment, you will begin to realize how powerful layers and behaviors can be. However, do not forget that this feature is not well supported. If you want to work with DHTML for general Web use, you will have to study the topic in much more depth than is possible here.

Understanding Timelines

Layers and behaviors can produce some powerful capabilities, but when you add the ability to control when an action takes place, you realize the full power of DHTML. You can move layers, turn them on and off at a certain time or when the visitor completes an action, and so on — all can be added with Dreamweaver's timelines.

The timeline control in Dreamweaver will be familiar if you have ever worked on animated production, such as Macromedia's Flash or Shockwave. The action is controlled by frames. (These are no relation to the frames in browsers that you will cover in the next session.) In the simplest form, each frame tells the browser where to place the contents of the layer.

To avoid any confusion with previous exercises, as well as those to come in this session, I created this example with no relation to any other exercise. It is simply a sample.

Figure 28-2 shows the Timeline panel. Each frame contains information that tells the contents of a layer where to be on the page. In the example shown here, the layer containing the logo image is moved on a curved path. It will start automatically and continue moving because the Autoplay and Loop options are active. Clicking any frame along the timeline will move the layer containing the image to the correct position as set in the timeline.

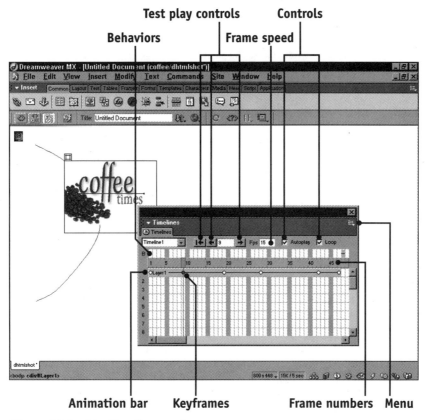

Figure 28-2   *The Timeline panel.*

The sample shown earlier in Figure 28-2 is set to the default value of 15 fps (frames per second). Because this full timeline is 60 frames long, it will take 4 seconds to complete the action (60 ÷ 15 = 4). You can test your timeline actions within Dreamweaver by using the forward and back arrows, by adjusting the speed of the playback, or by editing the number of frames. You can edit each frame individually.

You will automate the action from the last exercise in the previous section, "Adding behaviors for layers." To start, you remove the behaviors from the layers and add a timeline to automatically move the layers (without the visitor dragging the layer). You also add a behavior that will require visitors to initiate the layer movement.

Using a Timeline to Control Layers

Now that you have had a peek at the Timeline window, you will add a timeline to the quiz document that you created in the first two exercises in this session. Start by saving the file with a different name and removing the existing behaviors.

Follow these steps to save the file with a different name and delete the original behaviors:

1. Open the file layermove.html if it is not already open. Save the file as **timetest.html**.
2. Open the Behaviors window. The behaviors that you added to the layers should be visible if there is nothing selected in the document.
3. Click the first behavior and click the – (minus) button at the top of the Behaviors window, or press the Delete key to remove the behavior.
4. Repeat Step 3 for the remaining two behaviors.

Adding a timeline

Now you can add a timeline to each of the layers. To prevent confusion and to allow for easier editing, you should use a new timeline for each section of the page, even when different areas will be affected at the same time. For your example, you can use the same timeline to move three layers.

Follow these steps to add the three layers containing images to one timeline, setting a beginning and end position for each of your images. Each layer must be individually added.

1. Select Window ➪ Others ➪ Timelines to open the Timelines panel.
2. Select layer C, in the document, making sure that the layer is selected and not just the image.
3. Before you can add any action to the layer, you first must add the layer to the timeline. Select Modify ➪ Timeline ➪ Add Object to Timeline. You also can add the layer to the timeline by dragging the layer to the first frame of the timeline. The layer name will be added to the timeline. You may receive an alert explaining what the Timeline inspector can do. You can just click OK, or you may check the Don't Show Again option, and the message will not appear again.
4. Repeat Step 3 to add layer A and B to the timeline.
5. The layers have been added to the timeline, but there is no action at this point. You must set the end position for the layer to complete the action. Select the last keyframe of the C layer in the timeline. Drag the layer to the final position (L 50px, T 200px). Figure 28-3 shows the result.
6. Repeat Step 5 for the remaining layers, moving them into position, both with positions of T 200, and L 200, and 350, respectively, to spell the word "cab."
7. Preview the timeline action by holding down the right arrow next to the frame number in the Timelines panel. The letters should continually move from the original position to the new position.

You now have your action determined, but you need to tell the timeline when to operate. To do that, add behaviors to the timeline.

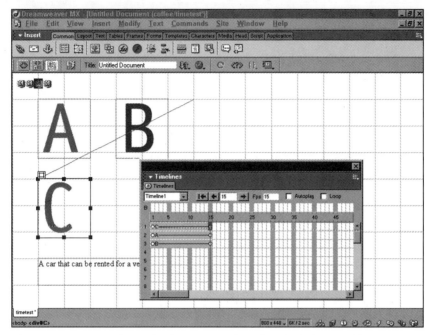

Figure 28-3 *Last frame for layer C is selected and the layer is dragged to the final position. The diagonal line represents the path for the layer as the timeline is played.*

Adding behaviors to a timeline

10 Min. To Go

You mapped out the locations for your images at different times in the previous exercise, but you must now tell the timeline function when to start. Timelines are controlled by JavaScript that you enter through the Behaviors panel. For this example, you attach the behavior to a text link.

To add a Behavior to your timeline

1. Reduce the width of the Quest1 layer. Create a new layer beside the Quest1 layer and type **Click here to display answer.**

2. Select the text you just typed. In the Properties panel, type **javascript::"** in the Link field. This creates a link that will receive your behavior.

3. If it is not already open, open the Behavior pane. With the text still selected, click + (plus) and choose Timeline ⇨ Play Timeline. The Play Timeline window opens.

4. Accept Timeline 1 as the timeline to play.

   Your timeline is now set to play when the link is clicked. Preview the page. If you want to change how the timeline is started, you can do that easily in the Behaviors panel.

5. Select the linked text to display the listing in the Behaviors window. Highlight the entry in the Behaviors panel, click on the small arrow at the center of the listing, and choose a different action.

Editing a timeline

Once you have your basic timeline created, you might want to make minor adjustments to perfect your actions. Follow these steps to add frames to the timeline and then increase the speed:

1. If it is not already open, open the document timetest.html. Make sure that the Timelines panel is open.

2. You are going to add 10 frames to the movement of the second layer, and 20 frames to the third layer so that the letters fall into place at different times. Click the last frame of the A layer. Drag the frame to 25. To make this action start a little behind the movement of the first layer, drag the first frame of the A layer to 5.

3. Drag layer B to make 35 the last frame. Drag the first frame of this layer to 10. The movement will now be staggered.

4. Change the frames per second (Fps) setting to **20**, which will increase the speed of the action. Figure 28-4 shows the correct settings.

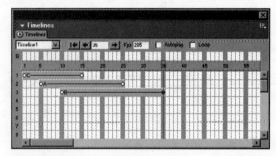

Figure 28-4   *The final settings for your timeline. Note how the layer action now starts at different times.*

Not all browsers will adjust the speed of a timeline.

Preview the document in as many browsers as you can. This is the most important part of working with layers and timelines and it should not be skipped.

Testing pages with timelines

Creating a page that will work in Dreamweaver — and which will preview correctly with the browsers on your computer — is just the beginning. Your initial testing in Dreamweaver is an efficient way to create the correct motion and speed for your animation. However, you also should upload your page to the server and have as many people as possible test your page to see if the layers and timelines work as they should.

When you are working with any documents built with layers, testing across platforms and browsers is essential. It is a good idea to develop a network of testers, which can most easily be accomplished by joining Web development newsgroups. See the CD-ROM resources folder (utility.html) for a list of newsgroups that provide expert advice, as well as the opportunity to have your pages tested on many different computers.

DHTML at Its Best

Before you assume that DHTML is only about animation, I would like to bring your attention to a very practical and popular use for DHTML. You probably have seen menus that drop down over the content on the page while you are making a selection. This is usually DHTML at work. On content-rich sites, it is very tempting to use DHTML menus. If you have a controlled customer base, or you are working on intranet sites, you have every reason to move into this technology.

Several great educational sites focus on DHTML. The DHTML section of webreference.com features an ongoing series about DHTML menus. See this series at www.webreference.com/dhtml/. Another source for DHTML/ JavaScript/CSS is www.pageresource.com/dhtml/index.html.

I urge you to pay attention to the code behind the actions you create in Dreamweaver. Troubleshooting so that your actions will play in all browsers is the biggest part of DHTML. Understanding the code will significantly improve your troubleshooting abilities.

Until you have your troubleshooting skills in place, however, I recommend you practice DHTML for fun and for use only on personal sites. As your troubleshooting knowledge grows, you can increase the opportunities for using your new skills.

As buggy as using layers and CSS can be, if you are interested in this method of creating documents, you should study hard. Many, myself included, believe the future of Web design will be layers. The time you spend to learn DHTML will not be wasted. This lesson only introduced you to the possibilities and some of the complexities of DHTML.

Done!

REVIEW

DHTML provides exciting possibilities, although it can be confusing. Dreamweaver does make it relatively easy to use, however, as long as you keep these few things in mind:

- DHTML is a combination of HTML and CSS to create a layout, and scripting which provides action for elements on the page.
- DHTML is best at this time for intranets rather than for the general Web. Browsers and computer platforms are usually easy to determine with intranets, which removes much of the uncertainty that plagues DHTML.
- If you are using DHTML or layers for general Web use, make sure that you are not using the features for critical functions that will render your site unusable if the DHTML does not work properly in the visitor's browser.

- Action is added to timelines with behaviors in Dreamweaver. Behaviors add the JavaScript required for DHTML.
- Timelines control layer movement frame by frame.
- Objects must be placed in layers to be used with timelines.
- You can preview actions in Dreamweaver by using the controls in the Timeline panel.
- Timelines can be edited after creation.
- Any document created with layers — especially when timelines have been used — must be tested across every combination of browser and platform.

QUIZ YOURSELF

1. Why is DHTML best left to intranet development and noncritical portions of sites designed for the Web? (See the "Recognizing the Limitations of DHTML" section.)
2. DHTML is a combination of which Web development features and languages? (See the "Working with DHTML in Dreamweaver" section.)
3. DHTML positioning is based on layers. How can layers be moved in a browser? (See the "Adding behaviors for layers" section.)
4. What is the main purpose for timelines in Dreamweaver? (See the "Understanding Timelines" section.)
5. How can you preview and test a timeline? (See the "Adding a timeline," and "Testing pages with timelines" sections.)
6. What type of menus uses DHTML? (See the "Testing pages with timelines" section.)

Working with Frames

Session Checklist

✔   Understanding frames

✔   Working with frames to create documents

✔   Imitating frames

**30 Min.
To Go**

Frames have been controversial in Web design since they were first introduced. The problem, as always, is the different ways in which browsers interpret frames, complicated by the loss of screen space for lower-resolution browsers. Add harder search engine placement, tough bookmarking and printing, and you have the reasons that most designers do not use frames lightly. If you understand exactly what frames are, and where they can be used, you will have the tools to make your own decision.

Understanding Frames

The concept of frames is very simple. Each frame is an individual HTML document. The collection of two or more framed documents within a page is controlled by a single document known as a *frameset*. The frameset contains no information other than to tell the browser which documents to display within the page, and where they should be placed. In this session, you start with a very simple frameset page, and then you change the background colors on each frame to help your site visitors see what is happening on the page.

Creating a framed document

Start by creating a directory to hold your framed documents. You don't need a special folder for your framed documents, but it will help you to keep track of the documents that are forming your framed document.

Create a folder for your frame files, and then start building your framed page, using the following steps:

1. Create a new folder within the Coffee Times site. Type **frames** for the name of the new folder.

2. Create a new document. *Do not* save this document yet.

3. Select Insert ➪ Frames ➪ Top Nested Left. Your document will divide into three sections. Make sure that Dreamweaver is set to show Frame borders (construction borders, not borders in the final document) by selecting View ➪ Visual Aids. The Frame Borders selection should be checked.

4. Insert your cursor into the top section and type **top.html**. You will be naming this frame with this same name; this text entry is simply to provide easy identification as you move along in the exercise.

5. Insert your cursor in the left section and type **left.html**. Insert your cursor into the large area and type **maincontent.html**. Remember that these are simply text entries.

At this point, you have a framed document that is unnamed. Next, you must name each frame and save the frameset, which will tell the browser how to display your collection of frames.

Naming framed documents

Individual frames must be named because each frame is a separate document. The frameset is displayed in the browser, and it calls on individual documents to display the page.

Follow these steps to name and save your frames:

1. Insert your cursor into the top section and select File ➪ Save Frame As. The Save As window opens. Browse to the frames directory that you created in the previous exercise. Name the document **top.html**.

2. Insert your cursor into the left section and repeat Step 1, this time naming the document **left.html**. Insert your cursor into the large section and save the frame as **maincontent.html**.

   You should now have three files saved. As you can see later in this session, each of these three documents can be opened as you would open any other document — apart from the frames. It is the frameset that creates the framed page.

3. Click one of the gray borders and select File ➪ Save Frameset As. Make sure that the Save As window has the frames folder active, and then type **testset.html**. Refer to Figure 29-1 to see the layout. Note how the window's title bar shows the name of the frame that is active, in this case, top.html.

Editing frames

To make it easier to identify each of the frames, you can change the background color of each frame, using the page properties window. Because frames are individual documents, you can apply a separate background or background image to each frame.

Change the page properties for each frame page to set the background color as follows:

1. Insert your cursor into the top.html frame. Select Modify ➪ Page Properties, and change the background color to a light yellow. Only the top frame is affected.

2. Insert your cursor into the left frame and repeat Step 1, choosing a light blue. Repeat for the maincontent frame, choosing a light pink color.

You are using a light color simply because you have black type. Any color or background image can be used.

3. To save the changes, select File ➪ Save All. Any changes you have made to any frame will be saved. Your document should resemble Figure 29-1.

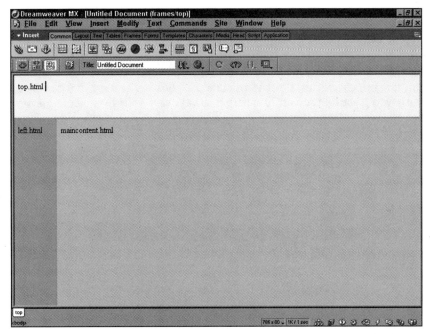

Figure 29-1 The color for each frame has been set using the page background color.

Look at what you have created so you will have the concept of frames well established.

Touring your frames and frameset

Now it's time to add content to pages in a frameset, both from within the frameset and with the pages that form the frameset opened as separate documents.

20 Min. To Go

1. Activate the Coffee Time site panel. Browse to the frames folder in the resources folder. The frames folder should contain four files: left.html, maincontent.html, testset.html, and top.html. All four files are necessary to the page that will display in a browser.

2. Close all documents. In the Site panel, double-click top.html to open the file. Note how the content that appeared at the top of the framed page is shown on

the page, but without the other frames. This is one of the frames within the frameset. Opened alone, it is a simple HTML document.

3. Highlight the text in the document and change the font color to blue. Save and close the file.

4. Open testset.html. Notice that the text in the top frame of the page is now blue. The top frame contains the file top.html, which you just edited. Close the document.

5. Open maincontent.html. Change the page background to white. Create a new line and type: **You can insert an image in any frame.** Insert another line and insert entrypic.gif from the art folder of the Coffee Times site. Add more text, or insert one or two Library items into the document, simply to create a longer page. Save and close the file.

6. Open testset.html. Note that the changes you made to the maincontent.html frame are now included in the framed page, and there is a scroll added to the large frame (assuming you added enough content).

7. Preview the document in your browser. An alert will pop up advising that your frameset file and frames files must be saved before previewing. Click OK to save the files. You can also check the "Don't warn me again" box in the alert, but the files will then save without a prompt. It is best to always save your files before previewing when working with framed documents. Your page should resemble Figure 29-2.

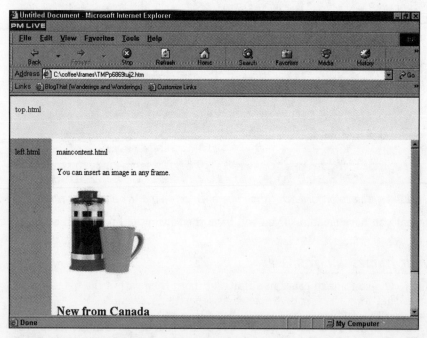

Figure 29-2 *Final framed page as previewed in Internet Explorer. Note that the borders around each frame, which displayed in Dreamweaver, have disappeared. Because the default value is that borders are disabled, the Dreamweaver display is showing only construction borders. Also note that there is a vertical scroll for the main content area.*

It does not matter where you edit documents that are part of a frameset. You can make changes from within the frameset, or you can open the document individually as you did earlier. The result will be the same in either case.

Now that you have the basics, it's time to create a page using frames.

Creating a Frame-based Document

Planning your frames well from the start will save many headaches later. You are going to create a page for your Coffee Times site that keeps the menu areas in a fixed position. You'll borrow content from one of the pages you created earlier in the book, and rely on Library items for the rest of the components.

Creating your framed document

This page will have a top frame that holds all the page heading information. A second frame at the left holds the text menu, and content is placed in a third frame.

Create a new framed document with three frames using the following steps:

1. Create a new document in the Coffee Times site, but do not save.

2. Select Insert ⇨ Frames ⇨ Top. This inserts a frame across the top of the page. Don't worry about size right now.

3. With your cursor in the lower frame, select Insert ⇨ Frames ⇨ Left. This inserts a frame to the left of the lower section. Your document should have the same layout as the page you created in the last exercise. (I want you to add the frames individually.) The frames for your document are complete, but you still must save the frames and frameset.

4. Save the frames in the frames folder, with the following names, starting with the top then saving the lower left and right frames, respectively: **framelogo.html**, **framemenu.html**, **framecontent.html**. Save the frameset as **coffeeframe.html**.

Naming your frames

Pause here to make sure that you do not trip in this section. In the last exercise, you named your frame documents. Now, you must name your frames to help identify your framed sections and work with your code. You use a combination of the Frame panel and the Properties panel to create names for your frames.

The following steps guide you through naming your frames:

1. Select Window ⇨ Others ⇨ Frames to open the Frames panel. If it is not already open, open the Properties panel.

2. Click the top frame in the Frames panel. This presents the information for that frame in the Properties panel. Type **FrameLogo** in the name section of the Properties panel. Note how the name you changed is reflected in the Frames panel.

3. Click the left frame and name it **FrameLeft**. Name the large area: **FrameContent**.

4. Click the gray border in Dreamweaver to select the frameset. Select File ➪ Save All to save the changes.

10 Min.
To Go

Adding content to your frames

You can use all the work you did when you created your template to save time now. Follow these steps to add your content and adjust the size of the frames to match that content:

1. Create a new document based on your main template. Detach the template from the page.

2. Using your tag selector, select the table containing the main menu and page head content. Select Edit ➪ Copy HTML. Close the page you just created *without* saving.

3. Activate the coffeframe.html frameset document, and insert your cursor into the top frame. Select Edit ➪ Paste HTML.

4. With your cursor in the top frame, change the page margins for that frame to zero.

5. Click on the lower frame border of the top frame and drag to allow all of the content to show. Save the frame. Isn't life (or templates, at least) sweet? Your entire heading is in place.

6. Add the CSS to your document. You must attach a CSS file to any frame where the styles will be required. Your top frame contains no text areas, but the left and main content areas do require text control. With your cursor in the left frame, attach the CSS file coffee.css from the root directory to the page. Repeat for the main content area. Remember that each frame is a separate page.

7. To complete the left frame, drag the frame border to match the beginning of the decorative line in the heading area. Insert the jump menu, the News menu, and the address as Library items, placing <br> tags between the items. Your page should look like Figure 29-3.

The main content area will take a little more work, as you must create a new table structure to reflect the new setup using frames.

To create the main content area, do the following:

1. Insert your cursor into the main area, and set the page margins to zero.

2. Insert a table with **3** columns and **3** rows, cell padding **10**, cell spacing **0, 100%** width and no borders. You can use cell padding instead of extra columns now, as no other page formatting is involved with this frame.

3. In the bottom row of the table, set the first column to a width of **1**, the second column to **70%**, and the third column to **30%**. Insert the image spacer.gif from the art folder in third column, and set to a width of **155**. (The cell padding will add 10 pixels on either side of the placeholder image.) That sets the control row for your table. Select all cells in the table (just the cells, not the entire table) and set the vertical alignment to top.

4. Insert the image vertgrad.gif from the art folder into the top row of the first column. Insert a <br> tag (Shift+Enter) and insert the image vertplain.gif from the art folder. Set the height to 500. This adds the vertical line to your page.

5. Insert two or three teaser menus (Library items) in the top row of the right column.

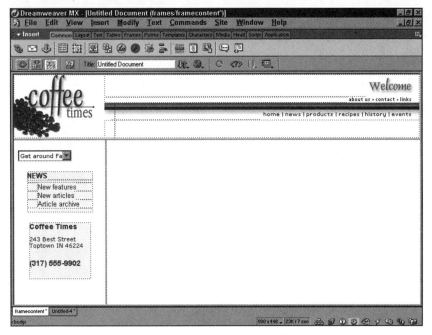

Figure 29-3 *Top and left frames have content added.*

6. Open the newarticles.html document from the root folder, and copy the content from the center column of the lower table. Paste the content into the top row of the second column of the table in the main content frame. Close newarticles.html.

7. The Library items that you placed kept track of the links and set the correct path. However, the content that you pasted has incorrect links. This document is saved in the frames folder, and the links contain incorrect path information. Select the two text links in the content, and browse for the correct file through the Link section of the Properties panel to correct.

8. Merge the second and third columns of the second row in the main content table. Insert the textmenu Library item. Assign Paragraph style and set the cell horizontal alignment to Center. Again, the Library status of this menu will look after the link path for you.

9. That's it! Adjust the left menu and change the title image if you wish. Save all the frames and the frameset. Preview in a browser. Your results should resemble Figure 29-4.

Creating targeted links

You use the Target field in the Properties panel so that links will open where you specify. To make it easier, I have included an HTML file to use as the linked file.

Copy the newsframe.html file from the Session 29 folder on the CD-ROM to frames folder in your Coffee Times site.

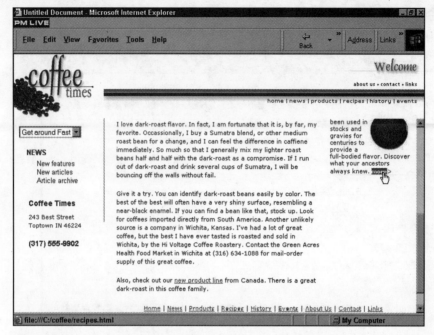

Figure 29-4   *Framed page previewed in Internet Explorer. The bottom of the main content area is shown. You can see where the content disappears into the top frame. Note that CSS is controlling the link.*

Create targeted links for your framed page by following these steps:

1. In the frameset document from the previous exercise, break the Library item connection to the News menu. You are going to create a link for the News item that will open the file you copied from the CD-ROM in the main content area, not on a new page.

2. Select News in the left menu and use the browse feature to set the link to newsframe.html from the frames folder.

3. In the Properties panel Target drop-down menu, select FrameContent. This link will now be displayed in the FrameContent area of the page.

4. Preview the document in your browser to see the results. Click on the News menu item to see the contents of the newsframe.html file placed in the main content area. Just to reinforce your sense of what is happening, open the newsframe.html document. You will see a page with no formatting other than the applied CSS.

Occasionally, assigning a negative margin value in a CSS file (as in the H1, H2 and H3 styles in coffee.css) can result in unusual display. Always test your pages on a variety of browsers.

You now have the basics of creating a framed document. If you can improve the function of a document for your visitors with frames, by all means use frames. If that benefit is not there, consider different methods, even if you must work a little harder to create the same look.

Simulating Frames

One of the main reasons designers use frames is to have a small area of scrolled text within a static page. The frames look can be simulated with a scrolling text area. You have already learned everything necessary to create this effect, so I have simply included a sample file for you to study. This method works with Internet Explorer and Netscape 6. Netscape 4.x will display a functional page, but without the CSS, and Opera 5 drops the background color. Figure 29-5 shows how this file displays in most versions of Internet Explorer on a PC.

Copy the files testfield.html and formtest.css from the Session 29 folder on the CD-ROM to the frames folder in your Coffee Times site.

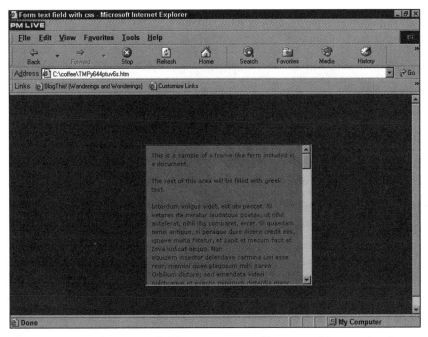

Figure 29-5 *Using a text field to present scrolling text without using frames.*

The form has no interactive purpose; it is used to create a scrolling text area, but don't miss the possibilities presented with the form and CSS interaction.

Keep your eyes open for innovative design, as well as for exceptional use of frames. I have seen some brilliant frame uses, and would never recommend totally ignoring this technique.

Done!

REVIEW

Frames are a simple concept and can be very effective for some pages. Remember these details about frames:

- Each frame is an individual document.
- Framed documents can be edited within a frameset or as an independent document.
- Each document within a frameset has a unique filename. It also is wise to give each of your frames a name to use with the Frames panel and when you are directly editing code.
- Content can be added to individual frames within the frameset document. You must use Save All commands or save each frame individually.
- Links can be created that will direct content to appear in the frame that you specify.
- You can create a text field that will simulate frames.

QUIZ YOURSELF

1. What is the basic concept of frames? (See the "Understanding Frames" section.)
2. How is each frame saved? (See the "Naming framed documents" section.)
3. What is a frameset? (See the "Touring your frames and frameset" section.)
4. You can edit frame documents in two ways. What are they? (See the "Touring your frames and frameset" section.)
5. What is the difference between naming a frame and naming a frame document? (See the "Naming your frames" section.)
6. What effect do page property settings have on frames? (See the "Editing frames" section.)
7. How do you set where links in frames will open? (See the "Creating targeted links" section.)

Increasing Productivity

Session Checklist

✔ Changing defaults and preferences

✔ Automating tasks in Dreamweaver

✔ Extending Dreamweaver's capabilities

✔ Working efficiently

**30 Min.
To Go**

You have created pages using nearly all of Dreamweaver's front-end capabilities. I hope you have taken the time to redo any exercises that were confusing for you, because this is a very powerful program that can be learned well only by working with the features. As I mentioned early in this book, the addition of the UltraDev components to Dreamweaver MX simply could not be covered in this book. I do urge you to carry on and learn how to place dynamic content on a page, however. Macromedia is showing great insight to combine these two functions. The future of the Web is dependent on dynamic data.

I have kept you to a pretty basic level of operation as you stepped through the Dreamweaver techniques. In the early chapters, I warned you that I was going to do this because I believe that it is important to learn the basics and then move to the shortcuts. That certainly does not mean that I do not believe in shortcuts. Once you understand the way a program works, it is an excellent idea to look for any shortcut you can find to work faster. Shortcuts and automated tasks also can help to keep your work consistent, which is vitally important when you are working on large sites. There are times with major sites that I do not touch a page for a month once the site has been designed or created from a template. It is much easier to keep total consistency if I can depend on automated features to accomplish the exact task many days or weeks later.

In this final session, you learn how to customize Dreamweaver's settings and create automated actions. You know how to operate Dreamweaver, so let's turn up the speed.

Changing Defaults and Preferences

Many of Dreamweaver's preferences can be set in one comprehensive window. In fact, there are too many to go through one by one here. The manual and online help are good sources for information on all the preference settings. Here is a discussion of the preferences you are most likely to change.

The preferences are all reached through a single menu:

1. Select Edit ➪ Preferences (Mac OSX: Dreamweaver ➪ Preferences) and the Preferences window will open.

2. Click the Category listing to select one of its options, as shown in Figure 30-1.

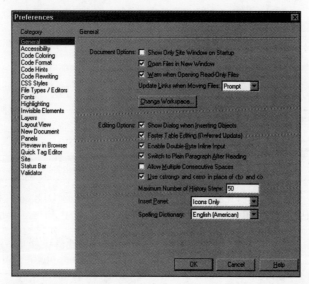

Figure 30-1   *The Preferences window with the General category selected.*

3. Click checkboxes to enable or disable an option. Select options from drop-down lists to activate them.

4. For PC users, one modification I recommend is to change the default value for saving files to an HTML extension from HTM. Be very careful with the following instructions.

   Locate the Configuration/Document types folder in the folder where Dreamweaver MX is installed. Open the MMDocumentTypes.xml document in Dreamweaver and view in Code view. Locate the following code:

```
winfileextension="htm,html,xhtml,shtml,shtm,stm,lasso
```

   Change the first listed file type to html, and the second listed file type to htm. Your code will now read as follows:

```
winfileextension="html,htm,xhtml,shtml,shtm,stm,lasso
```

   Save the file. You must restart Dreamweaver for the change to take effect.

5. You can change options in many categories in the same Preferences session. Simply click another category when you are finished with the first and make your changes. Continue until you have made all changes in the categories you desire and click OK. Changes usually take place immediately, although you will occasionally have to restart the program to see the effect.

Table 30-1 lists commonly adjusted preferences and their functions. It contains only a partial list of the preference settings that can be adjusted in Dreamweaver. You should read through the online help section on preferences. Each Web developer has different needs, and you may find that I have missed a feature that could be very important to you.

Table 30-1 Common Preferences

Category	Feature	Purpose
General	Spelling Dictionary	Changes the spell check to another version.
General	Change Workspace (PC only)	Changes from the default workspace to the Dreamweaver 4 workspace, or changes to a HomeSite-like appearance.
Code Coloring	Default colors for properties and code	Changes the default code colors to match team specifications, or to speed up your work if you often change page properties.
Code Format	Line Breaks	Sets the FTP function to prevent extra lines from appearing in code once it is transferred to the server.
Code Rewriting	Never Rewrite Code	Sets the file types that will never have code rewritten.
File Types/ Editors	External Code Editor	Sets the program that will open when you click Edit ⇨ Edit with External Editor.
Highlighting	Editable Regions, etc.	Changes the color that is used to specify special features in Dreamweaver.
Invisible Elements	All	Toggles on and off for the elements that will show when Invisible Elements are enabled.
New Document	Default Extension	Specifies the default extension that is in place in Dreamweaver and provides a link to the appropriate help file describing how to change the default. See Step 4 in the previous exercise for step-by-step instructions to change the default file extension to HTML from HTM.

Continued

Table 30-1   *Continued*

Category	Feature	Purpose
Panels	Show in Launcher	Sets which features can be accessed through the Launcher Pad at the lower edge of the screen.
Preview in Browser	Browsers	Adds browsers and sets to Primary or Secondary browsers.
Site	FTP Timeout	Increases the value if you have a slow connection and you receive frequent time-outs.
Status Bar	Connection Speed	Sets the speed that determines the download speed shown in the lower portion of the screen for every document.

Repeating Steps

Occasionally, you will find that you are doing repetitive, simple tasks, such as removing the bold command from several words in different locations. For operations such as this, simply highlight the word and remove the bold. You can then repeat the action any number of times by highlighting the next word and selecting Edit ⇨ Repeat *x* (where *x* is the operation you completed). It really pays in saved time only when you use the keyboard shortcut, Ctrl+Y (PC) or ⌘+Y (Mac). However, you can only use this command immediately after performing the task you wish repeated.

Adding Extensions to Dreamweaver

20 Min. To Go

Macromedia is well known for the support it offers through its Web site. You can reach the Dreamweaver Support Center through http://macromedia.com/support/dreamweaver/. Make sure that you visit this site and become familiar with the support system.

One of the most exciting sections of the Macromedia site contains extensions. Extensions are small scripts that are written specifically to enhance Dreamweaver capabilities and which are free to download from the site (www.macromedia.com/exchange/).

It is worthwhile to visit the Macromedia site often, because new extensions are regularly added. If you would like to create your own extensions — and perhaps share them with other Dreamweaver users — all the information you need is in the same place. One that I especially recommend is the Accessibility Testing extension. This little script will check your page for accessibility issues and will help you to be a more inclusive designer.

Working Smart: Production Tips

This is the final section of the book, and I want to leave you with a few tips that I have developed and some that I have gleaned from other designers over the years. If you are expecting a list of keyboard shortcuts, you will be disappointed; those are listed at the back of the Dreamweaver manual. What you will find here are tips that I use every day to speed production and assure quality. Some techniques are translations from the print world, while still others were prompted by questions from students. The source is unimportant. That they are tried and tested, day-to-day working solutions, is what counts.

Organize your work

One word into this topic and I am about to hop onto a soapbox. I cannot stress enough the importance of solid organization for any computer graphics work. Web work is the most susceptible to going out of control with lack of organization.

Make folders

With Dreamweaver, you can easily move files and keep your links intact. If you err, err with too many folders. You can always combine folders later, but file numbers grow very quickly when you are working on a Web site.

See Session 3 to review site structure and folder creation.

Plan ahead

Before you create your site, create a site map. Before you create your pages, know where you are going. Most time-consuming troubleshooting that I have done has been caused by making many changes on a page. I still design in Dreamweaver occasionally, which usually means that I am making lots of serious changes such as redesigning tables. Once my design is established, however, I usually create a file from scratch. This removes any chance that extra code has been left behind.

See Session 17 for a discussion about planning your site. Also, look for my book, *Web Menus with Beauty and Brains* from Hungry Minds, Inc., which is devoted to planning your site for effective navigation.

Use templates

Even if you are going to break every template that you use, it is still worthwhile to start with a template. Once the template is broken, there is no difference between that file and any other, yet you save lots of time and gain consistency if you start with the same template for every page. Spend the time to make your template perfect, and test it well before you create new pages. Your troubleshooting will be held to a bare minimum.

See Session 16 for a discussion of templates.

10 Min.
To Go

Do your design layout in a graphics program

As much as I love Dreamweaver, it was never meant to be an art tool. I create all of my draft sites either in an illustration program such as CorelDraw or Adobe Illustrator, or I use a raster art program that will accomplish slicing like Adobe Photoshop or Jasc Paint Shop Pro. Macromedia Fireworks is an unusual combination of the two program types, and works seamlessly with Dreamweaver. You can slice your graphics in the graphics program, create draft files of the entire page for client approval, or use the image as a pattern for tracing in Dreamweaver. You start this process by creating a full-page mockup of your design. There's a copy of a full-page mockup for the Coffee Times site on the CD-ROM.

Copy the file trace.gif from the Session30 folder on the CD-ROM to the art folder of your Coffee Times site.

Take the following steps to use an image for tracing in Dreamweaver:

1. Create a new document in the Coffee Times site. Save it as **trace.html** in your resources folder.
2. Select Modify ➪ Page Properties to open the Page Properties window. Use the Browse button for the Tracing Image field near the bottom of the window to locate the file trace.gif.
3. Set the Image Transparency to **30%**.
4. Set the Left Margin, Top Margin, Margin Width, and Margin Height settings to **0**. Click OK to return to your document. Figure 30-2 shows the result.

A full-page image is showing in the background. You can use this tracing image to build your page. You might want to use a lower transparency to make the background fade even more and keep it from distracting your view. When you have completed your page, you can remove the trace image.

Work carefully

I participate in a lot of newsgroups, and one of the most common statements I hear is, "Oh, right, I meant to fix that." It is easy to get caught up in the production and leave good code practices behind. I understand this, because it is very much my natural way to work. After all, I am an artist at heart. However, I have learned the hard way that Web work is not forgiving when you are running with the muse. *Do it right the first time* is a perfect motto for Web work.

Learn to read code

At one time, I could hand code HTML pages. Today, I suppose I could, but it would not be easy. I have been spoiled by Dreamweaver's wonderful features. However, I still read code fluently, and this — more than any other skill — has saved me a great deal of time. No, knowing code is not a purist activity. It is purely and simply a timesaver. Learn HTML by taking a course, studying a book (such as Greg Perry's *HTML 4.01 Weekend Crash Course*), or religiously following your code as Dreamweaver creates it. You will save hundreds of hours for every hour you spend learning code.

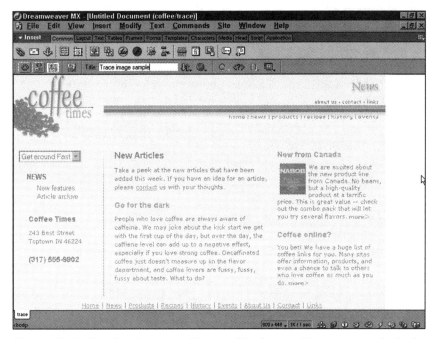

Figure 30-2 *Tracing image applied to a blank page. Your page can be built using the tracing image as a pattern.*

Follow your code

I am surprised that I do not wear out my Code view toggle when I am working with Dreamweaver. I do my design almost completely in Design view, but I am constantly toggling back and forth to Code view. I do not do this because I like code; quite the contrary. I keep a constant eye on my code to make sure that I have not accidentally added extra code (which is easy to do when you change your mind), or that extra spaces have been entered. Dreamweaver does an excellent job with code. Most little extras that get into my pages go there from my own hand, but it is much easier to find them step-by-step than it is when you are having trouble with your page in the testing phase.

Work within the limits of HTML

In Web work, the mark of a professional is often that they have learned to work within HTML limitations. This language was never meant to create the beautiful pages we create today in word processing and page-layout programs. You can do almost anything your artistic heart desires, but the cost is often long download time and unstable pages. At this time, we still must depend on tables for general Web layout. Tables are square. If you find yourself nesting three or four tables just to place an artistic element, stop and think: Is there another way to do this? Does this extra table improve my visitor experience or just make me feel good? Great Web pages are simple pages that download quickly and work in every browser. That does not mean they are ugly pages. Start reading the source code on professionally designed pages and you will see that the best of these use simple layouts and depend on their creativity to make them visually appealing.

Save, save, save

Dreamweaver does not have any type of automatic feature to prevent you from losing your work. Save every time you stop. It is easy to become lost in your work and let an hour go by. I cannot say that Dreamweaver causes me many problems, but I often work with many other active programs and I do occasionally crash my system. My tolerance for losing work is very low, and I am an obsessive saver.

Be a perfectionist

I am usually cautious about tossing the word perfectionist out to an artistic crowd. However, in Web work, perfection is well rewarded. The minute you say, "That's good enough," warning bells should go off. You often are building new features on top of previously created features. The original problem is not always the one that shows. When I first started using CSS, I neglected to check what would work with a linked CSS file — it must be the same as inline CSS, I thought. I spent an entire day trying to figure out why my graphics were flying all over my page in version 3 browsers. The text was fine. I was very lucky to hear from a woman who had had the same problem, which was caused by one command in a linked CSS file. It had NOTHING at all to do with my graphics. I changed that CSS command to an inline style and the problem was fixed; but I could have avoided the problem altogether if I'd done my homework to the level of perfection. That incident taught me a lot. Web design is not fun when you spend an entire day chasing ghosts.

Use Dreamweaver to its fullest

Dreamweaver is a very powerful program. Dreamweaver's designers have done an excellent job in creating a program for both professional and serious amateur Web designers. They have included features that take the tedium and massive organizational tasks of a large Web site and make them child's play. But you have to learn these features well and use them from the beginning of each project to reap the full benefit. Build your pages with templates and library items. Try several ways to accomplish the same task. It seems like too much front-end work at times, but the savings are gigantic at the other end of your project. Trust me on this one.

And there you have it. If you have followed every session and completed each exercise, you have a solid working knowledge of Dreamweaver. Keep your skills active, even if you only use them for personal sites. This field moves too fast to relax even for a few months. Keep surfing for the latest trends and information about how new browsers handle code. This is an exciting field that will never bore you if you make a commitment to stay with it. That — more than any other feature of this career — makes me feel that this is my "real" career.

Done!

REVIEW

In this session, you have covered many small topics, but I would like you to take these special notes with you:

- Defaults and preferences can be changed from the Preferences window. Simply click the category you want to change and make the adjustments.
- You can save time by using the Repeat command to repeat operations.
- Macromedia's Web site provides great support, and you can download extensions for specific tasks.
- Organizing your work is the best production enhancement for any Web work.
- Working carefully as you create your pages is the best way to prevent aggravating and time-consuming troubleshooting.
- Dreamweaver has powerful features. Use them.

QUIZ YOURSELF

1. Where can you find the settings for most Dreamweaver settings? (See the "Changing Defaults and Preferences" section.)
2. The Repeat command can be used only in what circumstance? (See the "Repeating Steps" section.)
3. What are Dreamweaver Extensions? (See the "Adding Extensions to Dreamweaver" section.)
4. Why is a tracing image different from any other image in Dreamweaver? (See the "Do your design layout in a graphics program" section.)
5. Why is it important to learn to work within HTML capabilities? (See the "Work within the limits of HTML" section.)

Sunday Afternoon
Part Review

1. Although layers make creating a page easy, they come with a serious disadvantage. What is it?
2. How is CSS used with layers?
3. Dreamweaver allows you to design with layers but to overcome the problems associated with displaying layer-built pages. How?
4. When working with layers, what is the Prevent Overlaps option designed to do?
5. When you have a nested layer, the nested layer is referred to as the *child* layer. What do the coordinates of this layer refer to?
6. If you are going to use DHTML in pages for the Web, what is an excellent policy to use?
7. What part do Dreamweaver behaviors play in DHTML?
8. What is one way to add animation with DHTML in Dreamweaver?
9. How can you specify when an animation starts in Dreamweaver?
10. When using DHTML for your pages, no matter what you do, one thing is absolutely essential. What is that critical step?
11. What is a frameset?
12. What is the difference between naming a frame and saving a frame?
13. What is a frame?
14. What are the drawbacks of framed documents?
15. When you are adding content to a frame or editing a frame, what should you keep in mind?
16. How can you use a form item to simulate a framed area?
17. Where do you use the Repeat command?
18. What is a Dreamweaver extension?
19. Why is it important for Web developers to learn to work within the limits of HTML?
20. Perfection is always nice. With Web development, it is essential. Why?

Answers to Part Reviews

Friday Evening Review Answers

1. Although you can produce Web pages in Dreamweaver without knowing HTML code, you can customize your work more easily with knowledge of HTML. Troubleshooting a display problem can be very frustrating if you do not understand enough about HTML code to find where a small code error is producing the problem.

2. No standards are accepted by every browser manufacturer, so each browser interprets some code in a different way. Not only do differences exist among brands of browsers, but often the same browser interprets code in a different way on a Mac or a PC.

3. The text that displays on a Web page uses the fonts installed on the viewer's computer. There is no way to guarantee that the viewer has the required fonts installed. To overcome this variation, we design pages with fonts commonly installed on all computers, plus provide a generic choice.

4. A docked panel is locked to the edge of the screen, and the document will only occupy the space that is not filled by the docked panel. A floating panel will sit on top of the document area, and can be moved with the mouse.

5. The Site panel is used to manage all the files in your site. Dreamweaver keeps track of links and can be set to make sure that the local and remote sites are the same at all times.

6. When you use menus rather than keyboard shortcuts, you are exposed to the structure of the entire menu containing the command you choose. If you watch for the keyboard shortcut always listed with the menu item, you also learn the shortcuts for the functions you use most often.

7. A context menu is a pop-up menu that contains only commands for a specific task. For PC users, right-clicking an object opens a context menu. Mac users use ⌘+Click to open a context menu.

8. Dreamweaver panels are the windows that can be opened, providing shortcuts to most commands.

9. To preview a Dreamweaver document in a browser, you must specify the location for the application file for the desired browser. You can specify up to 20 browsers to use for previews.

10. No. You can preview your document without saving it, which is a handy feature. You can check the results of a command and easily undo the command if the results are not satisfactory.

11. Getting a file means copying a file from the remote site to the local site. Putting a file means copying a file from the local site to the remote site.

12. Dreamweaver can use existing files to build a site. When you define your site, simply specify where the existing files are stored, and Dreamweaver will gather the information, and create a site.

13. The root folder is the top folder for all your site files and should contain the entry page for your site.

14. An HTML document cannot be more than one page. There is no limit to the size of the page, but there is no way to specify more than one page. Each HTML page in a site is a separate document.

15. Dreamweaver creates a site map, or graphic illustration of the files in your site, showing the relation of one file to another through links.

16. F10 opens and closes the Code panel.

17. When a page is viewed on the Web, the browser uses font information from the viewer's computer. Dreamweaver only lists the fonts included on almost all computers.

18. Font color and attributes can be adjusted in the Properties panel.

19. Creating hundreds of graphic images when creating a site is not unusual. If the images are not placed in a separate folder, managing your site becomes a nightmare.

20. The most common graphic file types are GIF and JPG. Any browser displays these formats. Many browsers also display PNG format images. You can place files in any of these formats in Dreamweaver, although PNG is best saved for intranet use.

Saturday Morning Review Answers

1. You must use Dreamweaver's FTP function if you wish to use the automated site management features. All file management features are handled through the Site window in Dreamweaver.

2. You must have the host address, the host directory, your login name, and your password.

3. Dragging the root directory on the local site to the remote site transfers the entire site.

4. Nested tables take longer to load and can cause display problems on some browsers if too many levels of nested tables exist.

5. Editing tables can often lead to errors. If you plan your tables well, you are much more likely to achieve what you desire quickly, while maintaining excellent code.

6. Working with your table borders turned on can help to keep the table structure in clear focus. You can turn the borders off as soon as you have your table areas well defined.

7. When you set a table to a fixed size, such as 500 pixels, the table displays at that size as long as the total width of graphics contained is less than the table width. However, if you specify that a table is to be 100%, the table stretches across the screen regardless of monitor resolution. The table may be 600 pixels, 800 pixels, or 1200 pixels wide depending on what the maximum resolution is for the monitor viewing the page containing the table.

8. If you place an invisible graphic, usually a transparent GIF image, that is 200 pixels wide, the image forces the column to a minimum of 200 pixels.

9. When a table is inserted into another table cell (called nesting) and is set to a percentage width, the size for the nested table is calculated from the size of the cell containing it.

10. Yes. You can specify fixed or percentage widths or a combination for columns within the same table.

11. In Dreamweaver, as long as your cursor is in the cell you wish to add a background color to, you simply select the color from the Bg palette on the Properties panel. Dreamweaver automatically adjusts the <td> tag.

12. Select the cell, row, column or table you wish to remove the background from, and delete the entry in the Bg field.

13. When a table has more than one cell, Netscape Navigator starts the pattern over for every cell and leaves any cell-spacing areas blank.

14. Internet Explorer ignores any reference to a background in the <tr> tag. However, it displays a background as part of the <td> tag, so careful planning still allows most effects to be completed.

15. Page backgrounds can be added in the Modify ⇨ Page Properties menu item.

16. Internet Explorer and Netscape Navigator demand their own codes to set page margins. Dreamweaver makes it easy by allowing you to specify left margin, top margin, margin width, and margin height, which covers all the code needed for both browsers.

17. In Dreamweaver, you add a link to a selected image in the Link field of the Properties panel.

18. In Dreamweaver, you have the option to search for code and to replace it with new code. To replace your page margins, enter the current page margin code into the Find field in the Find and Replace window; enter the desired code in the Replace With field, and choose Entire Site from the Find in drop-down box. Click OK, say OK to the alert that appears, and the changes are made.

19. Select the files you wish to move and drag to the location you wish to place the files.

20. If you allow overwriting a local copy of a file with a copy from the remote site, you will lose any changes that you have made to the local copy.

Saturday Afternoon Review Answers

1. The best way to work with code in Dreamweaver is the way that is most comfortable for you. There is no difference in the results when you enter or edit code with the split design/code window, the Code panel, the full code screen, or even the Quick Tag Editor. Most likely, you will find yourself using several different Code view options.

2. There is no difference if you hit your Enter key three times when you are working in Code view. Browsers ignore white space in HTML documents.

3. Simple scripts that you find on the Web can usually be placed by copying a few lines of code and pasting them into your Dreamweaver document, in code view.

4. Script code is usually placed in the Head area of the document and as part of the <body> tag.

5. A link to another site must be given in absolute terms, meaning the full address must be included, such as http://wpeck.com.

6. A named anchor is marked with an Invisible Element marker as long as Dreamweaver has been set to show Invisible Elements.

7. You can update many instances of a link through Dreamweaver's Change Links Sitewide command.

8. Highlight the marker for the JavaScript you wish to edit, and click the Edit button in the Properties panel. The script is presented and can be edited. In order to see the marker, you must have Dreamweaver set to show Invisible items.

9. A simple rollover is one image replacing another when a mouse is passed over the original image.

10. Rollovers must be tested in a browser preview because the action does not occur in Dreamweaver.

11. The Behaviors panel is used to add JavaScript.

12. You use tables to lay out a form for the same reason you use them to lay out your pages. You cannot add format commands to a form or form object with HTML alone, so you must place the form objects in table cells to create an easy-to-follow form.

13. In the Properties panel, when the form is selected, click the Browse for File button for the Action field, and direct Dreamweaver to the CGI script you wish to use to collect and return the data from your form.

14. Radio buttons are used when only one choice is allowed. Checkboxes are used for multiple selections.

15. A hidden field is used to tell the script running a form what information to collect and where to send the results.

16. The Assets panel gathers all the colors you have used in a site and presents them when the Color icon is active in the Assets panel.

17. You can create a Library item from scratch or highlight an existing section of your page and create a Library item from that content.

18. When you delete a Library item from the Assets panel, the link to that Library item is broken for any instances where the item has been placed, but the item is not removed from the pages. To delete the instances of a Library item, you must remove them from every page.

19. You must return to the template file to make changes to a noneditable area of a template page. You can also break the link to the template, which makes the entire page editable.

20. If you delete a template file outside the Assets panel, the Assets panel will assume it is still there and continue to look for the template, indicating an error every time the Assets panel is opened.

Saturday Evening Review Answers

1. The number one thing to understand before you start designing a site is why your visitor visits your site. Without that information, you have a hard time making decisions on the look of the site, how navigation should work, and what type of information should be placed in which location.

2. A site map helps you see how each page is connected or should be connected. It can help you determine the navigation for the site and often leads directly to the perfect route for placing content.

3. Jump menu is the name of a drop-down menu. Jump menus offer many menu choices in a very small space.

4. A Navigation Bar containing many items can be easily created from one menu.

5. The one drawback to a Navigation Bar is that you can only have one per page.

6. The Behaviors panel shows the JavaScript action behind a Navigation Bar, and allows editing.

7. You can edit the Navigation Bar items to show the down version of the rollover graphic when that page is viewed.

8. You can attach design notes to full documents or to individual images.

9. Files that include design notes appear in the Site window with an icon beside the filename, indicating the presence of a note.

10. Select File ⇨ Design Notes to view the design notes screen.

11. The most important task when you are building a template is to identify which areas can remain identical on every page created with the template and which areas must be editable.

12. A transparent graphic is often used to force a table column to display at a minimum size.

13. With two fixed-width columns and a third set to 100%, the third column should always fill whatever space remains. However, in most cases, if only text fills the third column, you still require a transparent GIF file set to a width of at least half of the smallest width the third column will be. If you do not have this graphic in place, the browser may decide to share some of the third column width with the fixed-width columns.

14. It is often best to place plain images for a menu until you have your final position and layout determined. It is a lot easier to move and adjust individual images than images with attached behaviors.

15. It is often faster to turn to your Code view to select an invisible image. Place your cursor in the table cell that contains the graphic, and change to a Code view. The

image should be easy to see in this view because it is the same as any other image when written in code. Make your changes in the Code view, or select the image code, and return to the Design view. The image remains selected.

16. A Library item is an excellent way to add small pieces of content to many pages. Because it is stored in the Assets panel, you can easily drag a Library item into any document.

17. Templates are designed to provide a consistent starting point for many pages.

18. Sure. You can create a Library item for a menu and then detach it from the Library item to make an adjustment to the active page menu item. You still save time, and consistency is still there. However, because the link is broken, you do lose the ability to update the Library item automatically on all the pages containing the item.

19. Once your template is complete, it is an excellent idea to create, and finish, several pages of the site, before you create every page. Small problems can occur once you start creating finished pages, and it is best to ensure that your template works through to finished pages.

20. An editable area in template-based documents can be changed in any way. In a template, editable regions are the only areas you can edit unless you detach the document from the template.

Sunday Morning Review Answers

1. Select the jump menu, and click List Values in the Properties panel. You can add, remove, or edit menu entries.

2. So many of Dreamweaver's commands can be accomplished through the Properties panel. Just by always watching this little window, you can see where operations are completed even when you do not need that feature today.

3. You can change the way the Insert toolbar displays options in the Preferences window.

4. If you click on a column header in an Assets panel listing, your assets will be sorted using the column property you have chosen.

5. JPG images are best for images containing graduated color changes, such as photographs.

6. GIF images are best for images with large areas of solid color.

7. Optimizing images means reducing file size as much as possible without compromising quality.

8. When you use CSS in a separate file to control your text, you can make changes to text formatting across your site by simply editing the CSS file.

9. When you use the Attach Style Sheet command, Dreamweaver creates a separate document to hold your CSS styles and attaches a snippet of code in your document to look for the text styles in that location.

10. Select Text ➪ CSS Styles ➪ Edit Style Sheet to make changes to an existing style sheet.

11. A custom class style is defined and applied to a menu when you wish to assign different attributes to the text in that menu.

12. When you are naming a series of graphics, like in a menu, make sure you start the filename for each image with the same word or set of characters, like menuhome.gif, menucontact.gif. This is much more convenient when locating files than using names such as homemenu.gif, contactmenu.gif.

13. An active state graphic is the way you let your visitor know that he or she is on the page represented by the corresponding menu item. It can have any effect as long as it is not the same as the original graphic.

14. An Alt tag is the text that appears when the mouse is held over a graphic. You enter an Alt tag in the Alt field of the Properties panel.

15. Adding an alignment command to an image in the Properties panel allows text to wrap around that image.

16. Adding to Personal when checking spelling adds the active word to your personal dictionary. That word is no longer considered a spelling error, so be careful when you are using this command.

17. You can use Clean Up HTML to remove redundant or empty tags.

18. Create a personal page to satisfy your desire to experiment and to learn new techniques.

19. Visitors should always have the option to stop sound or, better yet, be invited to start sound.

20. An image map uses no JavaScript, so it will display in any browser, no matter how old. Also, if the visitor surfs with JavaScript turned off, the image map will still work.

Sunday Afternoon Review Answers

1. Layers are not fully supported by all browsers and can cause some serious problems when viewed on the Web.

2. CSS is used to position layers.

3. Dreamweaver allows you to convert well-designed layers to tables, which display properly in almost every browser in use today.

4. The Prevent Overlaps command should be used when you intend to covert layers to tables at any point. This prevents layers from overlapping, which would prevent tables from being created.

5. The coordinates on a child layer are stated in reference to the parent layer.

6. It is a good idea to not use DHTML for features on your site that render it useless if the visitor's browser does not support DHTML.

7. Behaviors provide the JavaScript that allows layers to move in DHTML.

8. The Dreamweaver Timeline function provides a method to animate layers.

9. You use the Dreamweaver Behaviors panel to add the JavaScript to a link that starts an animation.

10. It is absolutely essential that you test, test, and test again when you are creating pages with DHTML. More skill is required to troubleshoot DHTML than to build pages with it.

11. A frameset is a document that collects HTML pages into a specified arrangement on a page.

12. Naming a frame assigns a name to the frame in the same way you assign a name to an image. This is done in the Properties panel. Saving a frame creates an HTML document that the frameset calls to create a page.

13. A frame is actually a separate HTML document that can be created separately and just called into a frameset. You can also create a frame from within the frameset page. No matter how you create it, a frame remains a separate document.

14. Framed documents are a designer's dream, but they can cause problems. Framed documents are hard to bookmark and print for visitors who are not Web savvy. Search engines have a harder time finding information on framed documents, and people with low-resolution monitors often dislike frames because frames can create a cramped document.

15. Frames are easy to understand if you always remember that each frame is an individual document. If you wish to change the background color, you can use Page Properties to set the color. To change the margins, you also use Page Properties.

16. If you insert a multiline text area in a document, you can enter text and have that text scrollable without using frames.

17. The Repeat command is used to repeat the exact action many times, as in changing background colors in noncontiguous cells in a table.

18. Dreamweaver Extensions are small bits of codes, or tiny programs that have been created by other Dreamweaver users. You can download many of these files for no charge at the Macromedia Web site.

19. Effort spent to find creative ways to produce interesting, effective work within the limitations of HTML is better than trying to push the limits of HTML to the point where you are creating pages that contain tags that are not well supported. Learning HTML is one of the best things you can do to help you make the most of the language. An excellent understanding of HTML, and accepting what it can and can't do, allows you to spend your time designing rather than troubleshooting and testing.

20. Although HTML is not officially a programming language, it is still fussy. Browsers are not standardized. Monitors are far from standard. People reach Web pages by using everything from very slow modems to screaming fast, cutting edge, direct connections. Plus, they may be using a Mac or a PC — no way to tell ahead of time. Given the variables in the Web world, it is a wonder that any pages display properly. Every error you make with code, or extra demands you make with things such as several nested tables, can set a chain reaction in motion. In Web development, perfection is not just a nice thing to have; it is the key to creating successful pages.

APPENDIX

What's on the CD-ROM?

This appendix provides you with information on the contents of the CD that accompanies this book. For the latest and greatest information, please refer to the ReadMe file located at the root of the CD. Here is what you will find:

- System Requirements
- Using the CD with Windows and Macintosh
- What's on the CD
- Troubleshooting

System Requirements

Make sure that your computer meets the minimum system requirements listed in this section. If your computer doesn't match up to most of these requirements, you may have a problem using the contents of the CD.

For Windows 9x, Windows 2000, Windows NT4 (with SP 4 or later), Windows Me, or Windows XP:

- PC with a Pentium processor running at 120 MHz or faster
- At least 32MB of total RAM installed on your computer; for best performance, we recommend at least 64MB
- Ethernet network interface card (NIC) or modem with a speed of at least 28,800 bps
- A CD-ROM drive

For Macintosh:

- Mac OS computer with a 68040 or faster processor running OS 7.6 or later
- At least 32MB of total RAM installed on your computer; for best performance, we recommend at least 64MB

Using the CD with Windows

To install the items from the CD to your hard drive, follow these steps:

1. Insert the CD into your computer's CD-ROM drive.
2. A window will appear with the following options: Install, Browse, eBook, Links, and Exit.

   Install: Gives you the option to install the supplied software and/or the author-created samples on the CD-ROM.

   Browse: Allows you to view the contents of the CD-ROM in its directory structure.

   eBook: Allows you to view an electronic version of the book.

   Links: Opens a hyperlinked page of web sites.

   Exit: Closes the autorun window.

   If you do not have autorun enabled or if the autorun window does not appear, follow the steps below to access the CD.

1. Click Start ➪ Run.
2. In the dialog box that appears, type ***d:\setup.exe***, where *d* is the letter of your CD-ROM drive. This will bring up the autorun window described above.
3. Choose the Install, Browse, eBook, Links, or Exit option from the menu. (See Step 2 in the preceding list for a description of these options.)

Using the CD with the Mac OS

To install the items from the CD to your hard drive, follow these steps:

1. Insert the CD into your CD-ROM drive.
2. Double-click the icon for the CD after it appears on the desktop.
3. Most programs come with installers; for those, simply open the program's folder on the CD and double-click the Install or Installer icon. Note: To install some programs, just drag the program's folder from the CD window and drop it on your hard drive icon.

What's on the CD

The CD-ROM included with this book contains all the images, scripts, and sample files you need to complete the exercises. You'll also find resources for Web development and trial versions of software programs often used with Dreamweaver. (See Appendix C to learn more about these programs.) There's also a self-assessment test to help you determine your current level of expertise and to track your progress.

Files Required for Exercises

To complete most of the exercises in this book, you require image files or text files. Watch for CD-ROM notes that tell you which files you require and where to place these files on your computer. The files on the CD-ROM are in folders that correspond to session numbers. Some sessions do not have folders.

Resource Files

In addition to files you need to complete exercises, the CD-ROM also contains several resource files that help you locate important Web sites. Watch for CD-ROM notes throughout the book that refer you to the resource file that corresponds to the session topic. The resource files are HTML pages, and you can view them by using your standard browser; you can click the links when you are connected to the Web for easy access.

Software Programs

Shareware programs are fully functional, trial versions of copyrighted programs. If you like particular programs, register with their authors for a nominal fee and receive licenses, enhanced versions, and technical support. *Freeware programs* are copyrighted games, applications, and utilities that are free for personal use. Unlike shareware, these programs do not require a fee or provide technical support. *GNU software* is governed by its own license, which is included inside the folder of the GNU product. See the GNU license for more details.

Trial, demo, or evaluation versions are usually limited either by time or functionality (such as being unable to save projects). Some trial versions are very sensitive to system date changes. If you alter your computer's date, the programs will "time out" and will no longer be functional.

You will find a trial copy of Dreamweaver MX on the CD, but this program does not work alone. You must create the images you require in graphics programs like the ones included on the CD-ROM, and you also require Internet Explorer and Netscape Navigator for testing your pages.

You will require Internet Explorer 6.x, and Netscape 6.x to complete the exercises in this book. You can download Internet Explorer from the Microsoft site (www.microsoft.com), in the Products Downloads section. You can download Netscape 6.x at the Netscape site (www.netscape.com), in the New Download section.

Acrobat Reader

Freeware version. Adobe Acrobat Reader is required to read any PDF document (such as the eBook version of this book). The program is included with most current browsers, or you can install it directly from the CD-ROM.

Macromedia Dreamweaver MX

Trial version. You can follow the instructions in the book with the trial version of Dreamweaver MX, included on the CD.

Image Optimizer

Shareware version. Most commercial graphics programs designed to create images for the Web have optimization features built into them, but not all do the job well. Image Optimizer is a program devoted to optimizing images, and will take any JPG, GIF, or PNG image and reduce the file size while the results display. If you are not happy with the quality or method of optimization in any graphics program, try Image Optimizer. More information is available from the Xat Website (www.xat.com).

Macromedia Fireworks MX

Trial version. Macromedia Fireworks is a 30-day, fully functional trial version of Macromedia's specialized Web graphic creation program. This program integrates seamlessly with Dreamweaver and is powerful and easy to learn. Check out Macromedia's Web Site (www.macromedia.com) for more information.

Macromedia Flash MX

Trial version. Macromedia Flash is another Macromedia product designed for Web development. Try your hand at creating movies for the Web with this full-featured, 30-day trial. Check out Macromedia's Web Site (www.macromedia.com) for more information.

Freehand 10

Trial version. Macromedia Freehand is a popular vector illustration program and has some features designed to integrate seamlessly with Dreamweaver. If you have never used a vector program, and are using Dreamweaver, Freehand is a natural starting point. Macromedia's Web Site (www.macromedia.com) can provide more information.

Paint Shop Pro

Evaluation version. Enjoy a 30-day evaluation version of Jasc Paint Shop Pro, a powerful yet easy-to-learn program. Its affordable price makes it a popular choice for many designers, including professional Web developers. For more information, check out Jasc's Web site (www.jasc.com).

Photoshop Elements

Thirty-day trial version. Adobe Photoshop Elements is a 30-day trial version of the most popular graphics editor among professional designers. This powerful program offers image editing and special effects and includes ImageReady, a program dedicated to producing images for the Web. For more information, check out Adobe's Web site (www.adobe.com).

TopStyle Pro

Trial version. TopStyle is a popular CSS editor, in a class of its own. Use the trial version to create a few style sheets, and experience the time savings it offers. Files created with TopStyle can be used as any other CSS file.

eBook version of Dreamweaver® MX Weekend Crash Course™

The complete text of this book is on the CD in Adobe's Portable Document Format (PDF). You can read and search through the file with the Adobe Acrobat Reader (also included on the CD). Although a Table of Contents and Index can help you when you are looking for information, nothing can beat an electronic search for returning results.

As you work through the exercises, you may find it is more convenient to have the eBook version of the book open as a window on your screen. You can toggle between your work and the screen version of the exercises.

Self-assessment Test

The self-assessment test software helps you evaluate how much you've learned from this Weekend Crash Course. It will also help you identify which sessions you've perfected, and which you may need to revisit.

Troubleshooting

If you have difficulty installing or using any of the materials on the companion CD, try the following solutions:

- **Turn off any anti-virus software that you may have running.** Installers sometimes mimic virus activity and can make your computer incorrectly believe that it is being infected by a virus. (Be sure to turn the anti-virus software back on later.)
- **Close all running programs.** The more programs you're running, the less memory is available to other programs. Installers also typically update files and programs; if you keep other programs running, installation may not work properly.
- **Accept the default installation settings whenever possible.** Graphics programs often have complex relations to other programs or functions on a computer. Installing to a different directory or drive than the default can cause confusion at a later date.
- **Reference the ReadMe:** Please refer to the ReadMe file located at the root of the CD-ROM for the latest product information at the time of publication.

If you still have trouble with the CD, please call the Customer Care phone number: (800) 762-2974. Outside the United States, call 1 (317) 572-3994. You can also contact Customer Service by e-mail at techsupdumwiley.com. Wiley Publishing, Inc. will provide technical support only for installation and other general quality control items; for technical support on the applications themselves, consult the program's vendor or author.

Working with Other Software

Dreamweaver is a powerful program, but it cannot work alone. In fact, Dreamweaver is nothing more than a gathering tool for Web-bound content. To complete Web sites, you need at least one graphics program. Choosing can be a daunting task. To help clear the initial fog, I have compiled a short description of the most popular graphics programs Web designers use.

See Session 22 for more about raster and vector graphics formats.

Adobe Photoshop/ImageReady

Photoshop is probably the most popular graphics program in the world, and it is an excellent tool for Web design. It is primarily a raster program, with limited vector capability. Photoshop comes bundled with ImageReady, a full-featured, Web graphics preparation program. Photoshop is often used for creating the initial design, with ImageReady preparing sliced images, HTML for Web pages, and animated GIF images. Photoshop can handle any image-preparation task, and ImageReady is one of the best pre-Web preparation programs. However, this package comes with a high price tag, and because of the power it contains, it does have a steep learning curve. Photoshop is available for both Mac and PC platforms, with an abundance of tutorials available on the Web. (A Photoshop demo version is included on this book's CD-ROM.)

Jasc Paint Shop Pro

Paint Shop Pro (PSP) is a fine graphics-preparation program and is perfect for Web design, although it is available only for the PC platform. It is primarily a raster program, with limited vector capability. Don't dismiss this program because of its low price tag. Many professional Web designers use PSP exclusively. You can use PSP for initial design, image preparation, slicing images, and creating animated GIF files. (Jasc Animation Shop is included with PSP.) Many people find that PSP is one of the easiest graphics programs to learn, and it is well supported with Web-based tutorials. (A Paint Shop Pro demo version is included on this book's CD-ROM.)

Macromedia Fireworks

Fireworks is an interesting hybrid program, combining powerful raster editing features with strong vector creation tools. Fireworks has led the industry in image slicing capability and has the advantage of working seamlessly with Dreamweaver, which can be important if you are using your graphics program to create HTML for sliced images. You should try Fireworks if you are working with Dreamweaver. (A Fireworks demo version is included on this book's CD-ROM.) Animations created in Fireworks can be exported as animated GIF files or as a Flash SWF file. (See Flash later in this appendix.)

Vector Programs

Vector programs such as CorelDraw (www.corel.com), Adobe Illustrator (www.adobe.com), and Macromedia Freehand (www.macromedia.com) can also be used to create Web graphics. Many designers, especially those who have a print background or those who supply print graphics, in addition to Web content, to clients still do much of their design in vector programs. I do. Vector programs are object based, which means there is no need to work in layers to keep objects separate. However, this class of programs is secondary for Web design. Many designers are working without a vector-based graphics program, but few are working without a raster-based graphics program.

Macromedia Flash/Adobe Live Motion/Corel R.A.V.E.

Flash is well known for creating movies for the Web. LiveMotion and R.A.V.E. are Adobe and Corel's competing programs. Flash is still the leader, especially for scripting, and provides the ability to use programming to control how the movie behaves. Some designers are completing entire sites, including the site navigation, in Flash. LiveMotion and R.A.V.E. claim to be easier to use — easier for designers than programmers. Luckily, demo versions are available for all three programs. (A Flash demo version is included on this book's CD-ROM.) Although beginning Web designers do not need to know how to make a movie, it is a good idea to learn to create a basic movie as you build your skills.

Choose Your Graphics Program Based on Your Needs

There is no right or wrong program for creating Web graphics. As long as you can create well-optimized, quality graphics, you are using the right program. Web developers tend to become very attached to their programs and often speak strongly for or against specific programs. Listen to any valid points they may have for choosing or avoiding a software program, but always remember that each designer works in a different way. Use trial versions whenever you can to see whether a place in your workflow exists for a specific program. Trust you own instincts in the end.

Index

Continued

Continued